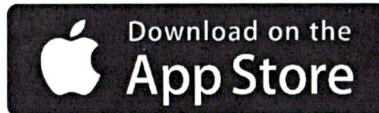

ISBN 978-1-330-21208-0
PIBN 10053940

Similar Books Are Available from
www.forgottenbooks.com

Researches in Biblical Archaeology

ISSUED UNDER THE AUSPICES OF THE ORIENTAL SOCIETY OF
THE WESTERN THEOLOGICAL SEMINARY

EDITED BY

OLAF A. TOFFTEEN, Ph.D.

THE HISTORIC EXODUS

Books by the Same Author

Ancient Chronology, Part I

(Researches in Biblical Archaeology, Vol. I)

Price: $2.50

Postage extra, 20 cents

Researches in Assyrian and Babylonian
Geography, Part I

Price: $1.00

Postage extra, 4 cents

The Historic Exodus

BY

OLAF A. TOFFTEEN, Ph.D.

PROFESSOR OF SEMITIC LANGUAGES AND OLD TESTAMENT LITERATURE
WESTERN THEOLOGICAL SEMINARY

1863-1929

PUBLISHED FOR THE
ORIENTAL SOCIETY OF THE WESTERN THEOLOGICAL SEMINARY

CHICAGO
THE UNIVERSITY OF CHICAGO PRESS
1909

Composed and Printed By
The University of Chicago Press
Chicago, Illinois, U. S. A.

TO

THE REV. WILLIAM OTIS WATERS, S.T.D.

Президент of the Oriental Society

of the

Western Theological Seminary

PREFACE

Scarcely two years have passed since I published, in this series, my *Ancient Chronology*, Part I. In that volume I treated biblical chronology solely on the basis of dates furnished by the Bible, taking them at their face value, and without any inquiry either into the age of the documents in which they occurred, or into their historicity. I promised then that these questions would be taken up in a future volume, to be called *Side-Lights on Biblical Chronology*. This is that volume. It has been found advisable to confine it more closely to the Exodus than was originally purposed, and consequently the title has been changed, the more closely to fit the contents.

The reception of my former book has been most gratifying to me. In a work of so broad a scope, and in a field so uncertain and unexplored, it was not to be expected that all my conclusions should meet with unanimous approval. What I did hope for was that critics might recognize the earnestness of purpose which I had in presenting it, and the great care which I had taken to be accurate and scholarly in both my views and my methods. It is with the greatest pleasure that I record that, with two exceptions, the book was received in that spirit. Perhaps the most gratifying thing that has ever been said of my work was the criticism of Professor Lieblein of the University of Christiania, who, although he disagreed with me on some points, which was, as I have said, to be expected, nevertheless was kind enough to say of my book, "The author is a serious and conscientious scholar, who, without having become partisan in favor of any one more or less erroneous school, seeks the truth in sincerity."[1] And, indeed, on the Continent my book has everywhere met with the kindest appreciation.

I wish to record my thanks and appreciation of the letters which I have received from many of the most distinguished scholars in regard to my former book. Among these have been: Professor C. H. W. Johns of Cambridge, Professors D. S. Margoliouth and S. R. Driver of Oxford, Dr. E. A. Wallis Budge of the British Museum, Professor Ad. Erman of Berlin, Professor Fritz Hommel of Munich, Professor P. Rost of Königsberg (Pr.), Professor J. A. Knudtzon of Christiania, Professor Ernst Andersson of Upsala, Professor Knut Tallqvist of Helsingfors, Professor Le P. Ronzevalle of Beyrouth, M. F. Thureau-Dangin, of Paris, and Professor C. Fossey of the Collège de France. I am especially grateful to those of this number who have offered me their suggestions.

Many of my conclusions, which seemed astonishing at the time of publication, have now been generally accepted by the scholarly world. I do not mean to imply that it was entirely because of my book that these conclusions have been reached. I only state that scholars have reached the same results. It is some gratification to feel, however, that I was first in the field. For example, the date for Sargon of Akkad, which I placed *ca.* 2550 B. C., has since been placed by Eduard Meyer at the same date. The eminent Assyriologist, M. Thureau-Dangin, has not only given the same date for the Hammurabi Dynasty as I did, but has also shown that there was a lacuna between this and the Kassite Dynasty, and that

[1] *Sphinx*, Vol. XII, p. 249.

the Second Dynasty was partly contemporary with both
of them, both of which conclusions I reached first. Pro
fessor Bennett has likewise accepted my date of Ham
murabi.[1]

As for Egyptian chronology, Professor Lieblein has
shown that Dynasties VIII and IX were contemporary,
just as I asserted. Eduard Meyer and Breasted have both
corrected themselves in their interpretation of the Turin
papyrus, regarding the succession and number of kings
in Dynasty XI, coming to practically the same conclusions
as I. Mr. Griffith has shown that the reign of Amen
hotep II was very short, say three to five years. I suggested three for his independent reign.

These examples may suffice to show that, although I
was working on independent lines, I was still, in my former
book, well within the bounds of legitimate research.

I stated in my book that many of the dates could
only be approximated. Later discoveries have caused
me to modify my opinions in regard to some of them.
These instances will be treated in an appendix to this
volume.

In this present volume I have refrained from cumber-
ing my text with multitudinous notes referring to individual
scholars. But this must not be taken as evidence that I
am not acquainted with the literature that has appeared
on this subject. The appended bibliography represents
merely those books which have constantly been at my
hand in the preparation of this volume. The "Hibbard
Egyptian Library," which has been placed at my disposal,
has given me a splendid opportunity to consult all the best
works in all branches of this science. I claim to be

[1] *Exodus* ("The New Century Bible"), p. 289.

thoroughly cognizant of the views of all the more prominent writers bearing upon this work.

But sometimes *nomina sunt odiosa.* By bringing in a number of names of scholars whom I highly respect and by whose labors I have greatly profited, but with whom I feel constrained to disagree, some readers might be led to suppose that I was criticizing individuals. Nothing could be more foreign to my purpose. Like them I am searching for truth, and this present work is merely an honest and sincere endeavor to add something to our knowledge of a very important subject. If it be found that I have utterly failed, I shall feel, nevertheless, that I have rendered service to the cause of truth by showing what can *not* be accepted. If, on the other hand, this book contain anything of value, anything worth considering, I trust that the minds of scholars will not be so prejudiced as to refuse it their consideration, even if this imply, as the acceptance of my theories certainly will imply, a total reconstruction of the Evolutionary Hypothesis of modern higher criticism. It is my wish that all might be ready and willing to look questions such as are raised in this book ¦squarely in the face. Our purpose should ever be, not the support of any theory, but solely the search for truth. Truth will, in any case, prevail.

It may be surprising to some of my readers that the Exodus and not the patriarchal period is treated first in this series. The reason for this is the fact that the dating of the patriarchs depends quite definitely upon the dating of the Exodus, which, therefore, I have had to treat first. The patriarchal period will be the subject of a future volume.

In treating of the Exodus, I have totally ignored the

theory, held by some radical critics, that there never was a Hebrew exodus out of Egypt. Although I certainly admit that there was a land *Muzur* in Philistia or southern Palestine, which is a great question by itself, still there has never been advanced a single scrap of competent evidence in favor of the theory which connects the Exodus with that land. The whole hypothesis is a pure assumption, lacking both scientific basis and common-sense. The "Jerakhmeel" theory, which is an outgrowth of this *Muzur* hopothesis, and acording to which about two-thirds of the biblical names of this period are wholesale coruptions of the one word "Jerakhmeel," deserves no notice. The corruptions are not in the Bible, but rather in the mind of the scientist who originated the theory. The "pan-Babylonistic" view, which sees in all these names and events merely sun, moon, and zodiacal motives, has also been deemed unworthy of consideration. The present work seeks to establish the historicity of the Exodus out of Egypt. If that be established all the other theories disappear.

In discussing the dates of the documents I have paid no attention to the hypothesis advanced by Dillmann, Schrader, and others of that school, namely that the P(riestly) document was written in the period of the Davidic or Solomonic monarchy. Although this comes surprisingly near the date which I have myself suggested, I have been loath to use the conclusions of these scholars, because they assume that this document is the oldest. With the Wellhausen school I still feel constrained to regard P as the latest of the Hexateuchal documents.

Several scholars have lately revolted against many tenets of the higher criticism. Much of their feeling and argument I accept, of course, but in no case have I been able to accept them *in toto*. With Baentsch I agree that Moses must have been a historic personality. In chaps. ii and iii the reader will find that my views often coincide with those of Eerdmanns, although in his reconstruction I find myself as far apart from him as from the Wellhausen school. Orr has certainly rendered great service to the cause of biblical criticism, but I cannot help feeling that he has underestimated, in several important particulars, the critical arguments in regard to contradictions between P and J, E, and D. And as Orr seems unwilling to admit even the existence of independent documents in the Hexateuch, of course I could not make any extensive use of his arguments. Consequently, agreement between myself and Orr or Eerdmanns is limited to some of the negative arguments. In my reconstruction I dare claim an entirely independent line of thought, both in regard to the documents and in regard to the history of the period treated.

Professor Burney of Oxford has lately argued in favor of the Mosaic origin of the Decalogue. His reconstruction of religious conditions in the period of the Judges had in substance been presented by myself a year earlier, and the present volume is only an enlargement of what I then presented.

Perhaps, too, some of my readers may be surprised to find that in the great majority of cases I adopt the reading of the Greek texts in preference to that of the Massoretic Hebrew, which is the basis of our English text. I do this because I have become convinced, after minute study of the Greek codices, that they are not only translations of an archetype much older and more accurate than that from which our text has been derived, but also that, representing, as they do, manuscripts over five hundred years older than any we have in Hebrew, they have escaped centuries of Massoretic tinkering.

What is here presented is the fruit of many years of thought and labor. I have taken care not to present anything which has not a bearing on the question of the Exodus. The chapters dealing with the documents are necessary, as I think will be clear, for a basis on which to study the Exodus in the later chapters.

Before closing this preface, I wish to thank most sincerely Rev. H. L. Cawthorne of Chicago, through whose earnest efforts and interest in this work I was enabled to obtain the services of a secretary in the preparation of this volume.

I wish also to thank two of my pupils for their help. One of these, my secretary, Mr. Bernard Iddings Bell, has had a large share in the preparation of this volume, not only in his careful work in taking my dictation and preparing the volume for the press, but also in many valuable suggestions and helpful criticism which he has offered on questions presented in the book.

Mr. Walter Blake Williamson, the other of these pupils, has prepared the map, under my direction, with a care which I very much appreciate. In studying this book, my readers will, I believe, find this map useful.

Again I take pleasure in recording my deep appreciation of the generosity and the interest which a member of our Oriental Society has shown by guaranteeing a large part of the cost of publishing this volume.

OLAF A. TOFFTEEN

WESTERN THEOLOGICAL SEMINARY
September 1, 1909

CONTENTS

xvii

BIBLIOGRAPHY

I. Abbreviations

ARE=Ancient Records of Egypt, Vols. I–V, by J. H. Breasted.

A. V.=Authorized Version.

BA.=Beiträge zur Assyriologie.

BC.=Biblischer Commentar.

BE.=Babylonian Expedition of the University of Pennsylvania.

CBSC.=Cambridge Bible for Schools and Colleges.

HAT.=Handkommentar zum Alten Testament.

HCC.=Historical and Critical Commentary.

ICC.=The International Critical Commentary.

JA.=Journal asiatique.

JBL.=Journal of Biblical Literature.

JHS.=Journal of Hellenic Studies.

JQR.=Jewish Quarterly Review.

KEH.=Kurzgefasstes exegetisches Handbuch.

KHC.=Kurzer Hand-Commentar zum Alten Testament.

KK.=Kurzgefasster Kommentar.

LOT.=An Introduction to the Literature of the Old Testament, by S. R. Driver.

LXX=Septuagint, The Greek Version of the Old Testament.

MAFC.=Memoires publiés par les membres de la Mission Archéologique Française au Caire.

MDOG.=Mittheilungen der Deutschen Orient-Gesellschaft.

MOS.=Mittheilungen aus den orientalischen Sammlungen der Königl Museen zu Berlin.

MSI.=Monumenta Sacra Inedita, by C. Tischendorf.

MSP.=Monumenta Sacra et Profana, by A. M. Ceriani.

MVG.=Mittheilungen der vorderasiatischen Gesellschaft.

NCB.=The New-Century Bible.

OLZ.=Orientalistische Literatur-Zeitung.

PEFQS.=Palestine Exploration Fund, Quarterly Statement.

PSBA.=Proceedings of the Society of Biblical Archaeology.

RAO. = *Recueil d'archéologie orientale.*

RB. = *Revue biblique.*

RE. = *Revue égyptologique.*

RT. = *Recueil de travaux relatifs à la philologie et à l'archéologie égyptiennes et assyriennes.*

R. V. = *Revised Version.*

SBOT. = *Sacred Books of the Old Testament.*

VAB. = *Vorderasiatische Bibliothek.*

WZKM. = *Wiener Zeitschrift für Kunde des Morgenlandes.*

ZA. = *Zeitschrift für Assyriologie.*

ZA. = *Zeitschrift für Ägyptische Sprache.*

II. Books

C. A. Briggs. *General Introduction to the Study of Holy Scriptures.* New York, 1900.

C. Cornill. *Introduction to the Canonical Books of the Old Testament.* Eng. transl. by G. H. Box. London, 1907.

S. R. Driver. *An Introduction to the Literature of the Old Testament.* 12th ed. New York, 1906.

J. G. Eichhorn. *Einleitung in das Alte Testament.* Vols. I–V. Göttingen, 1823–24.

E. E. Gigot. *General Introduction to the Study of the Holy Scriptures.* New York, 1905.

H. A. C. Hävernick. *General Historico-Critical Introduction to the Old Testament;* Eng. transl. by W. E. Alexander. Edinburgh, 1852.

E. König. *Einleitung in das Alte Testament.* Bonn, 1893.

W. M. L. de Wette. *Lehrbuch der historisch-kritischen Einleitung in die kanonischen und apokryphischen Bücher des Alten Testaments;* neu bearbeitet von E. Schrader. Berlin, 1869.

C. H. H. Wright. *An Introduction to the Old Testament.* New York, 1905.

E. Buhl. *Kanon und Text des Alten Testaments.* Leipzig, 1891.

M. Dods. *The Bible, Its Origin and Nature.* New York, 1907.

A. K. Fiske. *The Jewish Scriptures.* New York, 1896.

W. H. Green. *General Introduction to the Old Testament; the Canon.* New York, 1905.
H. E. Ryle. *The Canon of the Old Testament.* London, 1904.

E. Watson. *Inspiration.* London, 1906.

W. E. Addis. *The Documents of the Hexateuch.* Vols. I, II. London, 1892-98.
C. A. Briggs. *The Higher Criticism of the Hexateuch.* New York, 1897.
J. E. Carpenter. *The Composition of the Hexateuch.* London, 1902.
C. F. Kent. *Narratives of the Beginnings of Hebrew History.* New York, 1905.
J. J. Lias. *Principles of Biblical Criticism.* London, 1893.
O. Procksch. *Das nordhebräische Sagenbuch, die Elohimquelle.* Leipzig, 1906.
H. Winckler. *Alttestamentliche Untersuchungen.* Leipzig, 1892.
Wellhausen, *Prologomena to the History of Israel.* Eng. transl., 1885.
————. *Composition des Hexateuchs,* 1899.

W. Bacher. *Die exegetische Terminologie der judischen Traditions-literatur.* Leipzig, 1905.
Bacon. *The Triple Tradition of Exodus.*
L. W. Batten. *The Old Testament from the Modern Point of View.* New York, 1901.
C. A. Briggs. *The Papal Commission and the Pentateuch.* London, 1906.
T. K. Cheyne. *Bible Problems.* London, 1904.
————. *Traditions and Beliefs of Ancient Israel.* London, 1907.
J. D. Davis. *Genesis and Semitic Tradition.* London, 1894.
R. B. Girdlestone. *Deuterographs.* Oxford, 1894.
A. R. Gordon. *The Early Traditions of Genesis.* Edinburgh, 1907.
H. Gunkel. *The Legends of Genesis.* Eng. transl. by W. H. Carruth. Chicago, 1907.
————. *Schöpfung und Chaos in Urzeit und Endzeit.* Göttingen, 1895.

R. H. Kennett. *In Our Tongues.* London, 1907.

A. F. Kirkpatrick. *The Divine Library of the Old Testament.* London, 1906.

P. Koch. *Die Mythen und Sagen der Bibel.* Berlin, 1907.

J. E. McFadyen. *Old Testament Criticism and the Christian Church.* New York, 1906.

H. McIntosh. *Is Christ Infallible and the Bible True?* Edinburgh, 1902.

J. B. Mozley. *Ruling Ideas in Early Ages.* London, 1900.

R. L. Ottley. *Aspects of the Old Testament.* London, 1904.

H. E. Ryle. *The Early Narratives of Genesis.* London, 1904.

G. A. Smith. *Modern Criticism and the Preaching of the Old Testament.* New York, 1902.

W. R. Smith. *The Old Testament in the Jewish Church.* London, 1902.

Studia Biblica. Vols. I–IV. Oxford, 1885–96.

A. W. Vernon. *The Religious Value of the Old Testament.* New York, 1907.

———————

W. L. Baxter. *Sanctuary and Sacrifice:* a Reply to Wellhausen. London, 1896.

E. C. Bissell. *The Pentateuch, Its Origin and Structure.* New York, 1906.

B. D. Eerdmans. *Alttestamentliche Studien,* Parts I, II. Giessen, 1908.

W. E. Gladstone. *The Impregnable Rock of Holy Scripture.* Philadelphia, 1896.

W. H. Green. *The Higher Criticism of the Pentateuch.* New York, 1903.

———. *The Unity of the Book of Genesis.* New York, 1901.

D. S. Margoliouth. *Lines of Defense of the Biblical Revelation.* London, 1903.

J. M. McMullen. *The Supremacy of the Bible.* Toronto, 1905.

J. Orr. *The Bible under Trial.* New York, 1907.

———. *The Problem of the Old Testament.* New York, 1906.

G. H. Rouse. *Old Testament Criticism in New Testament Light.* Philadelphia, 1905.

———————

T. K. Abbott. *Essays on the Original Texts of the Old and New Testaments.* London, 1891.

E. G. Kenyon. *Our Bible and the Ancient Manuscripts.* London, 1898.

P. de Lagarde. *Mittheilungen,* Vols. I–IV. Göttingen, 1884–91.

E. Nestle. *Urtext und Übersetzungen der Bibel.* Leipzig, 1897.

B. Baentsch. *Exodus-Leviticus-Numeri (HAT).* Göttingen, 1903.

W. E. Barnes. *Chronicles (CBSC).* Cambridge, 1899.

W. H. Bennett. *Genesis (NCB).*

———. *Exodus (NCB).*

———. *The Book of Joshua (SBOT).* New York, 1899.

F. Delitzsch. *Neuer Commentar über die Genesis.* Leipzig, 1887.

A. Dillmann. *Die Genesis (KEH).* Leipzig, 1892.

S. R. Driver. *The Book of Genesis (WC).*

———. *The Book of Leviticus (SBOT).* New York, 1898.

———. *Deuteronomy (ICC).* New York, 1906.

J. R. Dummelow. *The One-Volume Bible Commentary.* New York, 1909.

G. B. Gray. *Numbers (ICC).* New York, 1903.

H. Gunkel. *Genesis (HAT).* Göttingen, 1902.

W. R. Harvey-Jellie. *Chronicles (NCB).*

H. Holzinger. *Genesis (KHC).* Leipzig, 1898.

M. M. Kalisch. *Genesis (HCC).* London, 1858.

E. Keil. *Genesis und Exodus (BC).* Leipzig, 1878.

A. R. S. Kennedy. *Samuel (NCB).*

A. F. Kirkpatrick. *Samuel, I, II (CBSC).* Cambridge, 1905.

R. Kittel. *Die Bücher der Könige (HAT).* Göttingen, 1900.

———. *Die Bücher der Chronik (HAT).* Göttingen, 1902.

A. Klostermann. *Die Bücher Samuelis und der Könige (KK).* Nördlingen, 1887.

J. J. Lias. *Judges (CBSC).* Cambridge, 1902.

J. R. Lumby. *Kings (CBSC).* Cambridge, 1903.

G. F. Maclear. *The Book of Joshua (CBSC).* Cambridge, 1904.

A. H. McNeile. *The Book of Exodus (WC).*

G. F. Moore. *Judges (ICC).* New York, 1903.

———. *The Book of Judges (SBOT).* New York, 1898.

W. Nowack. *Richter, Ruth und Bücher Samuelis* (*HAT*). Göttingen, 1902.

S. Oettli. *Das Deuteronomium, die Bücher Joshua und Richter* (*KK*). München, 1893.

H. W. Robinson. *Deuteronomy and Joshua* (*NCB*).

Skinner. *Kings* (*NCB*).

H. P. Smith. *The Books of Samuel* (*ICC*).   New York, 1904.

H. L. Strack. *Die Genesis* (*KK*).   München, 1905.

C. Steuernagel. *Deuteronomium und Joshua* (*HAT*).   Göttingen, 1900.

G. W. Thatcher. *Judges and Ruth* (*NCB*).

E. Tuch. *Commentar über die Genesis*.   Halle, 1871.

G. W. Wade. *The Book of Genesis*.   London, 1896.

———

H. J. D. Astley. *Prehistoric Archaeology and the Old Testament*. Edinburgh, 1908.

L. Benziger. *Hebräische Archaeologie*.   Tübingen, 1907.

H. Brugsch. *Die biblischen Sieben Jahre der Hungersnoth*.   Leipzig, 1891.

———. *L'éxode et les monuments égyptiens*.   Leipzig, 1875.

W. St. G. Boscawen. *The Bible and the Monuments*.   London, 1896.

A. T. Clay. *Light on the Old Testament from Babel*.   Philadelphia, 1907.

F. Delitzsch. *Babel and Bibel*.   Eng. transl.   by C. H. W. Johns. London, 1903.

J. G. Duncan. *The Exploration of Egypt and the Old Testament*. New York, 1908.

G. Ebers. *Aegypten und die Bücher Moses*.   Leipzig, 1868.

E. W. Hengstenberg. *Egypt and the Books of Moses*.   Eng. transl. by R. D. C. Robbins.   Edinburgh, 1845.

D. G. Hogarth. *Authority and Archaeology*.   London, 1899.

E. Hommel. *The Ancient Hebrew Tradition*.   London, 1897.

A. Jeremias. *Das Alte Testament im Lichte des alten Orients*. Leipzig, 1906.

R. A. S. Macalister. *Bible Side-Lights from the Mound of Gezer*. New York, 1906.

J. F. McCurdy. *History, Prophecy, and the Monuments.* Vols. I III. New York 1898–1906.

A. Michaelis. *A Century of Archaeological Discoveries.* Eng. transl. by Bettina. New York, 1908.

W. Nowack. *Lehrbuch der Hebräischen Archäologie.* Leipzig, 1894.

Th. G. Pinches. *The Old Testament in the Light of the Historical Records and Legends of Assyria and Babylonia.* London, 1903.

A. H. Sayce. *The Higher Criticism and the Verdict of the Monuments.* London, 1901.

———. *Fresh Light from the Ancient Monuments.* London, 1885.

E. Schrader. *Die Keilinschriften und das Alte Testament.* 3te Auflage von H. Zimmern und H. Winckler. Berlin, 1903.

E. Stähelin. *Israel in Aegypten.* Basel, 1908.

G. St. Clair. *Buried Cities and Bible Countries.* London, 1892.

Olaf A. Toffteen. *Ancient Chronology,* Part I. Chicago, 1907.

———. *Researches in Assyrian and Babylonian Geography,* Part I. Chicago, 1908.

D. Volter. *Aegypten und die Bibel.* Leiden, 1907.

W. M. L. de Wette. *Lehrbuch der Hebräisch-judischen Archäologie.* Leipzig, 1814.

Introduction

To Professor We...... hawen ... bdgs the distinction o having pointed out that the ... Hich is made up of *four great documents*, and subsequent scholars have developed this hypothesis and ... have endeavored to distinguish these documents more cert...ainly in the ... Th...e is now a ... geal agreement among critical scholars as to the extent of ... dnts, although there still remain ... ige ... sope and vari...ty of different opinions in r...gard to minor details, such as in assigning certain ...tons to one ... dment or to ...

Documents of the Hexateuch

Criti...al scholarship has agreed to designate these ... dats by the ... dets J (Jahvistic), E (Elohistic), D (Deuteronomic), and P (Priestly).

The division of the text into ... hets is the ... sult of the following ...:

a) Differences in vocabulary and style;
b) Doublets and ... pats of texts,
c) Several divergent or sometimes paralle ... les;
d) Diff...r...nt historical and geographical ... dnts,
e) Differences in ... drine names and conceptions of ... lign, ... ods, and ... omies

The careful student of the Old ... cannot help acknowledging that the principles on whi...h the...his Documentary Hypothesis is built are reasonable, and are not to be disregarded by anyone who desires to understand

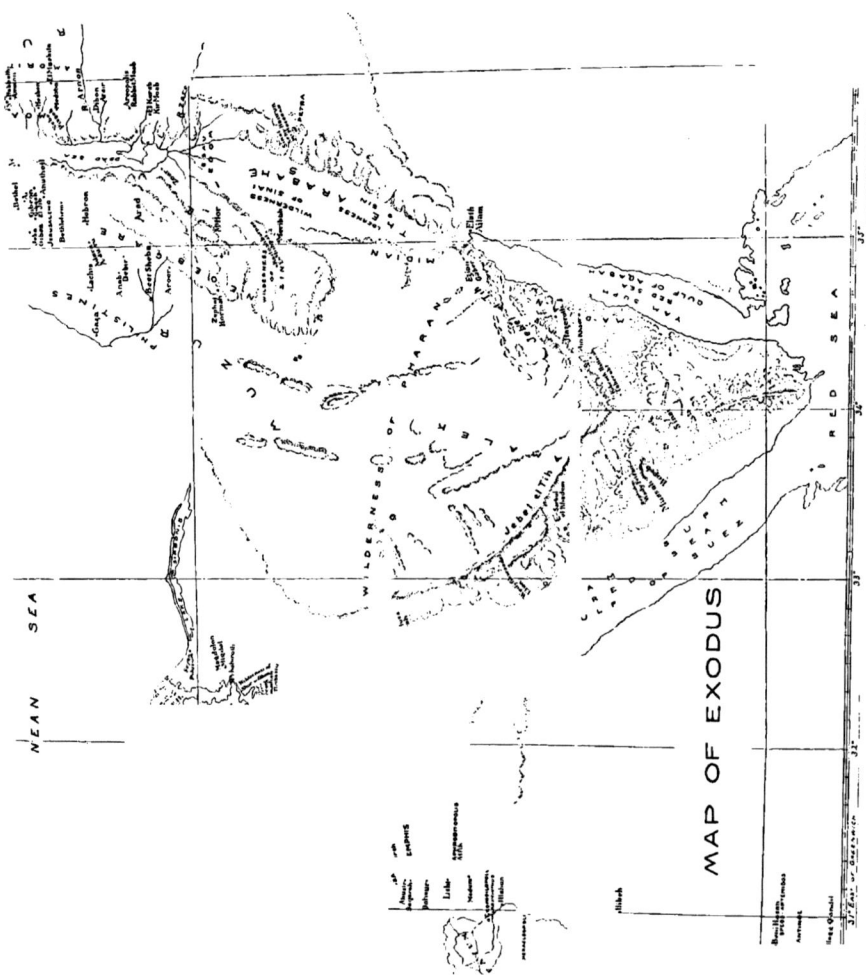

MAP OF EXODUS

CHAPTER I

Introduction

To Professor Wellhausen belongs the distinction of having pointed out that the Hexateuch is made up of *four great documents*, and subsequent scholars have developed this hypothesis and have endeavored to distinguish these documents more certainly in the text. There is now a general agreement among critical scholars as to the extent of these documents, although there still remain large scope and variety of different opinions in regard to minor details, such as in assigning certain sections to one document or to another.

Documents of the Hexateuch

Critical scholarship has agreed to designate these documents by the letters J (Jahvistic), E (Elohistic), D (Deuteronomic), and P (Priestly).

The division of the text into these documents is the result of the following considerations:

a) Differences in vocabulary and style;

b) Doublets and triplets of texts;

c) Several divergent or sometimes parallel law-codes;

d) Different historical and geographical statements;

e) Differences in divine names and conceptions of religion, morals, and ceremonies.

The careful student of the Old Testament cannot help acknowledging that the principles on which this Documentary Hypothesis is built are reasonable, and are not to be disregarded by anyone who desires to understand the sources of the text. The process by which modern criticism has reached these results has been tedious. Modifications have been constantly admitted. And they are still to be expected. The time has not yet come for us to put such a comparatively new and important theory into a stereotyped form. But although scholars have differed and still do differ on certain details, it must at least be admitted that in the Hexateuch we have several documents. That this number should be confined to four is at present the accepted creed of critics. The correctness of this limitation is, however, open to grave suspicion. But even though we may have to admit a larger number of documents as sources of our text, still the text itself bears witness that it is a compilation, made from several sources.

The Evolutionary Hypothesis

But modern criticism has not been satisfied with merely pointing out the existence of four great documents in the Hexateuch. It has also undertaken to assert when these documents themselves were written. The basis for this determination has been sought for in the history of Israel, and each document has been fitted into a period when history might seem to warrant its appearance. A document representing simpler or more naïve forms of religion and society is placed earlier, and one which presents more complex forms later. The older Documentary Hypothesis has thus been modified into an Evolutionary Hypothesis, according to which the J document should represent the religious and social condition of Israel *ca.* 850–800 B. C , the E document a somewhat later development, say *ca.* 800–750 B. C., the D document the conditions surrounding the reforms of Josiah, 621 B. C., and the P document those conditions which prevailed under Ezra and Nehemiah and their promulgation of the "book of the law" in 444 B. C. In regard to this last, however, scholars differ considerably, some of them assuming that at least the earlier sections of the P document, and others that the whole of it, date from the time of Ezekiel, *ca.* 585 B. C., and that Ezra's law-book represents our whole Pentateuch. But even according to these men, the whole Pentateuch is not thought to have reached its present form before *ca.* 400 B. C. A few of the radical critics have not hesitated to assign some sections of Exodus to even as late as the Maccabean period.[1] But these forget that the sections they so date were translated, with the rest of the Pentateuch, into the Greek Septuagint, about one hundred years before the Maccabean period, and that they are also to be found in the Samaritan Pentateuch, which can hardly be of a later date than 432 B. C.

Whatever we may think about the dates assigned to these documents we are bound to recognize as valid the principle underlying modern critical research that the Hexateuch is composed of several documents. This principle seems so evidently correct and so necessary for gaining an understanding of this portion of the Scriptures that we are constrained to accept it.

Critical Results

But the conclusions which modern criticism has reached by working on this principle may not be so certain. They

[1] See the earnest protest by Eb. Nestle against this kind of reckless criticism, *OLZ,* 1908, pp. 240–42.

are summed up, broadly speaking, in the two following statements:

1. The Hexateuch consists of four great documents, and four only, which documents are to be found *complete*, if only scholarship is keen enough to detect traces of them, and to assign them to their respective places. The use of the word "document" presupposes that we deal here with a complete document, and not with mere fragments. The Documentary Hypothesis stands in contrary position to the Fragmentary Hypothesis, according to which the Pentateuch is composed of a number of fragments.

2. These documents were compiled at or about the times given above. This presupposes that the institutions mentioned in these documents and codes were codified—perhaps in most cases came into existence—first at the time when the particular document containing them was written. The peculiarities of language in the documents are supposed to reflect the language of the various times in which they are alleged to have been written.

By means of these documents and their alleged dates the critical hypothesis ordinarily undertakes to explain the apparent difficulties, inconsistencies, contradictions, and peculiarities which are supposed to exist in the Hexateuch. There were different traditions, say the critics as a rule, lying back of and leading up to the peculiar statements found in each document. When a tradition, institution, or law, promulgated in a later document, is unknown to an earlier document, we must assume, say the critics, that such a particular tradition, institution, or law has arisen after the earlier document was compiled. In regard to religious, civil, and social institutions, we must also assume, so they say, that those mentioned only in a later document and not in previous documents, perhaps even contrary to those mentioned before, must have been instituted after the preceding documents were composed.

The Documentary Hypothesis places thus vividly before us the apparent discrepancies in the different documents and gives some explanation thereof, however unsatisfactory such explanation may prove to be; but it does not *remove* the difficulties, contradictions, or inconsistencies which seemingly do exist. It is therefore no wonder that many devout persons who wish to retain a belief in the inspiration and the integrity of Holy Scripture are slow to accept the results of modern criticism. For its main feature seems to be a focusing of attention upon inconsistencies already quite prominent enough to the adherent of the older method, who looks on the Hexateuch, or at least the Pentateuch, as one continuous document.

Inspiration of Holy Scriptures

Now, it is to be admitted that, even though inconsistencies and contradictions may exist in Holy Writ, that fact does not nullify its inspiration. For inspiration is the self-revelation of God through the Holy Ghost to man, and Holy Writ is the record of that self-revelation. The fact of that self-revelation in itself, even though errors in detail may have crept into the record thereof, is evident in the Hexateuch, even as modern scholars conceive it, and this fact alone is amply sufficient to establish the truth of its inspiration. Supposed errors in the Hexateuch are not necessarily to be attributed to an erroneous revelation, but should be attributed, rather, to other causes. The man or agent to whom a revelation was originally made may, we have every right to believe, have received and recorded it correctly. But a revelation may have been made to two or more individuals, and the resulting accounts may have been colored by their respective viewpoints and various modes of expression. It is not contrary to any orthodox belief in the doctrine of Plenary Inspiration to admit the human factor in the composition of Holy Writ. In later periods, too, when the various documents of an earlier age came to be incorporated into one, it is but natural that the lapse of centuries should have caused more or less confusion. Records of different events which were similar may easily have been regarded as but different accounts of the same event. Conversely, different accounts of a single event may have become so separated as to have been regarded as records of distinct events. All this is natural, indeed inevitable, if the books of the Old Testament were compiled, under the inspiration of God the Holy Ghost, solely for the purpose of recording God's revelation of himself.

Purpose of the Hexateuch

Now, the Hexateuch in its present form bears on its face the evidences of having been compiled for the sole purpose of recording God's dealings with man. It does not assume to be a treatise on history, geography, biography, or any other science. We cannot, therefore, expect to find in it exact scientific terminology and method. A historical and geographical misunderstanding in our Hexateuch may thus be admitted, where the avowed purpose is solely to record the transactions which have happened between God and man.[1]

[1] *Torah*, the Hebrew term for the Pentateuch, means originally "teaching," that is, *par excellence*, the teaching of God's self-revelation to man, as recorded in that book.

Still, however, after having admitted these necessary definitions of the scope and purpose of the Hexateuch, readers of the Bible will wonder why, in a self-revelation of God and of his transactions with man, there should have been so little of historical and geographical correctness as modern critics apparently would have us believe. Conservative readers are beginning to wonder if there may not be some scientific and historical hypothesis by which more of historic fact may be admitted in the Bible than most modern students assume.

Reconsideration of the Critical Hypothesis

There is the possibility that the results reached by modern criticism on the general principle of the evolutionary theory are not legitimate. And surely the time has not yet come when that theory and its alleged results are so certain that they can be put into stereotyped form. That they can be so put is a delusion into which many of the most distinguished of modern scholars seem to have fallen. The theory is of comparatively recent date; and the divergent opinions of almost all the critical scholars on a very large number of points are not especially reas suring to us, and do not give us perfect confidence that all questions in regard to the Hexateuch have been forever settled. It may be claimed, and with much truth, that these differences are now confined to only the minor details, but some of the details on which differences of opinion still exist are so important that the whole fabric of the modern critical structure is affected thereby.

This assumption of perfect certainty on the part of some critics is especially to be deplored when we consider the fact that our present knowledge of the Hebrew and kindred languages, in which the Old Testament was originally written, is as yet very imperfect, and is growing, in fact, with each passing day, and when we remember further that all of our lower or textual criticism has not as yet enabled us to determine what really was the original text of these Hebrew scriptures.

At any rate, the time is not yet past for further inquiry into the alleged results of the Evolutionary Hypothesis. *Are there only four documents in the Hexateuch? Can these documents have been written at the times which modern criticism generally postulates for them? Is there no hypothesis which will enable us to believe that the documents are themselves historical, and that they were written at the time they themselves seem to imply?* In attempting to answer these questions, let us begin with the P document and code.

CHAPTER II

The Date of the P Document

Although some critics are willing to date the P document as far back as 585 B. C., most of them are inclined to date it 444 B. C. They do this because, so they say, the institutions and the religious ideas therein set forth are not to be found in the history of the children of Israel up to that time. If this be so, we must expect that the geography set forth in P will be the geography known at that time. If history or chronology is dealt with, it must be the history or chronology known at that time. If there are intimations of the character of God, or of religion, or of religious institutions, these must all be such as would be natural to those living at that time. Let us examine the biblical records, and test the P document and code from these standpoints, to see whether or not the facts substantiate the theory.

This evidence we will divide for convenience into two sorts: internal evidence, and external evidence.

A. INTERNAL EVIDENCE

I. Geographical Considerations

a) It seems quite impossible that a man in the time of Ezra (444 B. C.), or more especially Ezra himself, if he were the author of the P document, could have written a table of nations,[1] particularly one of the Aryan nations,[2] without mentioning the Persians, who were in his day rulers of Asia. It is to be remembered that Ezra himself stood

[1] Gen., chap. 10.   [2] Gen. 10: 2–5.

in special favor with the Persian king, that Nehemiah, his associate, was a special ambassador from the Persian court, and that they had the support of that court in the reforms which they carried out. The document mentions Media and Ionia,[1] which were at this time merely subject nations to the Persians. Now the Persians appear on the Assyrian inscriptions as early as 837 B. C.,[2] and it seems improbable, therefore, that this document should have been of a much later date. For if the author knew of Media, which was farther away, why should he not have mentioned Persia, which lay near his own land?

b) In Gen. 10:22 Elam is described as a son of Shem. But in the time of Ezra every Jew living in Babylonia knew that the Elamites were not related to the Semites, either ethnically, geographically, or politically. The latest discoveries in Susa have shown, however, that prior to the Hammurabi Dynasty a Semitic people lived in Elam and Semitic governors ruled in Susa, the capital of Elam. We must then have here a document, or a fragment embodied in the P document, which goes back to a time when the relations between the Semites and the Semitic inhabitants of Elam were real, or at least well known.

c) In Gen. 10:2–5 one of the sons of Japheth is called Tirash. He is undoubtedly identical with a people called *Teresh*, who appear on the Egyptian monuments in company with the Philistines when they invaded Palestine *ca.* 1180 B. C. Shortly after this the name disappears from these monuments. We are inclined to identify this Teresh,

[1] Javan.

[2] *mât Par-su-a*, Shalmaneser II, *Annals*, ll. 120 *bis.* 172, 173 *bis*, 185. This people had at this time a large number of fortified cities, and twenty-seven city-kings of theirs are mentioned. This presupposes that at that time the northern Persia had already been settled for a long period.

not only with the biblical Tirash, but also with the Etruscan people of Italy. Now, the Etruscan migration into
Italy can hardly be placed later than 1100 B. C. This
accounts for its total disappearance, both from the monuments of Egypt and from the narratives of the Bible.
After 1100 B. C. the Hebrew people did not come into
contact with this nation, and consequently could not have
known of it. At least this portion of the P document
must depend upon a written document which is not later
in origin, or at least not very much later, than this date.

d) In Gen. 10:2 we find a mention of Gomer, which of
course is a name for what are generally known as the
Cimerian people. The Assyrian for them is *Gimirrai*.
Now these people appear first on the Assyrian monuments
in the Sargon period, i.e., *ca.* 720 B. C. Assyriologists
have assumed, since they have their first Assyrian mention
at this date, that therefore the P document with its mention of them cannot possibly have been written before
this time. Modern critics have seemed inclined to agree
with them in this. This custom of dating a biblical document by the mere mention of a geographical name on an
Assyrian monument is very precarious. This is especially
true in this case, for the political horizon of the Assyrians
up to the time of Sargon was very narrow indeed, and
there was no occasion for them to mention the Gimirrai
before his time. That the people were known before his
time is seen from Homer's *Odyssey*, where we are told that
Odysseus, fleeing from Troy, visited the Cimerians. It
does not matter much when the *Odyssey* was actually
composed. The tradition embodied in it affirms the
existence of the Cimerians on the horizon of the Greek
peoples as early as the Fall of Troy, 1183 B. C. Thus

Gomer was known in Palestine at the same time that Tirash, mentioned above, was known there. And this is the very time when the entrance of the Aryan race into Asiatic politics commenced to cause immense upheavals there.[1]

II.   Chronological Considerations

a) In Gen. 7:24; 8:3, 4 are references to the solar year (150 days, equal to five months of thirty days each). In the exilic and post-exilic periods the Jews used Babylonian chronology, based on the lunar year. The use of the solar year must have ended before the Exile. The date of the P document must then be earlier than 587 B. C., when the Exile and the change in the chronological system commenced.

b) If the P document and code were composed in the exilic or post-exilic period we should expect that it would use the names of months that then were usual, namely the Babylonian month names, such as Nisan, Ijjar, Sivan, etc. But the P document does not give us one instance of the use of these Babylonian names. It has a system of its own. It refers to the months as the first, the second, the third, etc. Now, we find that this same system was in vogue as early as the establishment of the monarchy. It is utterly inconceivable, if its origin was exilic or post exilic, that P should show no trace of the use of the Babylonian system.

c) And further, it is assumed, or claimed at least, that the author of P had accepted and reckoned by the Babylonian custom of beginning the civic year in the spring instead of in the autumn and that this custom was introduced among the Jews in the exilic period. But if this be true

---

[1] Toffteen, *Ancient Chronology*, Part I, p. 209.

the utter absence of Babylonian month names in P becomes still more difficult to explain. Further, the Holiness Code,[1] which is a part of P, contains the law on the Feast of Trumpets, which was celebrated, as we know, at the autumnal equinox. We know also that it was a celebration of a Hebrew new year. It seems, therefore, very singular that we should here have a law promulgated under the Exile or afterward, establishing a new-year festival in the autumn, when in fact everyone, including the promulgators, began the year in the spring—and this without a single reference to the Babylonian calendar, then universally observed among the Jews. In view of these facts, the unprejudiced mind can hardly help assuming that this law, at least, was written and promulgated at a time when the Hebrew year began in the autumn, i. e., long before the Exile.[2]

[1] Lev. 23:24, 25; cf. Num. 29:1–6 (P).

[2] The Old Testament knows of and uses four calendar systems:

a) The *Canaanitic* calendar, in which the word for month is *yerakh* (=29½ days), and has a *lunar* year of 354 days. Only three of the month names are known in the Bible, *Ziv, Ethanim,* and *Bul;* but the Phoenician inscriptions have added seven other names of months. This system was adopted by the early Hebrew settlers in Canaan, and was still the official calendar in the time of Solomon (I Kings, chaps. 6–8.)

In the Deluge story is a trace of this system. Thus, if we compare Gen. 7:11 with 8:4 Noah stayed in the ark one year and ten days, according to the Hebrew text, but an even year according to the Greek text. These ten days mark the difference between the Canaanitic and the Egyptian years. The two texts do, therefore, really agree, indicating that Noah stayed in the ark a full year of 365 days.

b) The *Egyptian* calendar, in which the word for month is *khodesh,* (=30 days). It was a *solar* year, consisting of 5 intercalary days and 12 months, each of 30 days, making a year of even 365 days. The months are therefore moveable. Only one month name is known in the Old Testament—*Abib,* corresponding to the Egyptian *Epiphi.* This system underlies the J E D codes (Exod. 23:16 [E]; 34:22 [J]; Deut. 16:13–16 [D]). The word, "end of year" (Exod. 23:16 [E]; "revolution of year," Exod. 34:22 [J]) should be translated, "beginning of year," because the word *yazah,* "to go out," is the

III. The Nature and the Names of God

a) In 444 B. C. no pious Jew could have written Gen.
1:26, which is plainly polytheistic. "Let us make man
in our image" certainly implies a recognition of more than
one God.

b) A strict monotheistic Jew, such as that of the time
of Ezra, could not have written Gen. 5:22, 24 and 6:9,
where Enoch and Noah "walked with Elohim," i. e.,
"had dealings with Elohim," because the language here
used is as anthropomorphic as in any J story in the
Pentateuch.

Even though we admit that the compiler of P depended
on earlier traditions which made use of such expressions
as these, we cannot admit that he would consent to pro-
mulgate views so radically different from his own.   A man

technical term for the beginning of some definite period of time. It was originally applied to the sun-god going out from his bridal chamber in the morning,
i. e., of the dawn (Ps. 19:4–6). It is therefore a calendaric term, and should
be understood here in this technical sense. When the Hebrews adopted this
system, the civil new year was celebrated in the fall. The "feast of ingather-
ing" (later "feast of tabernacles") was therefore, originally, a new-year festival.

c) The *Hebrew* calendar, in which the word for month is *khodesh* (30 or
31 days). It was a *solar* year of 365 days, beginning with the vernal equinox,
and distinguished the months by numbering them. This system is used
in P. When this system was introduced (Num., chaps. 28, 29; Lev., chap. 23),
the autumnal equinox came 15 days before the New-years' Day of the *Egyptian*
calendar then used; and a new feast—that of trumpets—was introduced to
mark the beginning of the civil year, while the Feast of Tabernacles ("ingather-
ing") was kept as a survival of the old Egyptian New-year's festival. The
New-year's Day of the Hebrew or P system was celebrated at the vernal equinox
and came to mark the beginning of the ecclesiastical year.

d) The *Babylonian* calendar. It had a lunar year of 12 months, and an
intercalary month. Each month had a separate name, like Nisan, Sivan,
Elul, etc. The year began at the vernal equinox, and was introduced among
the Hebrews in the exilic and post-exilic periods. This system is known,
therefore, in Zechariah, Nehemiah, Ezra, Esther, and the Apocrypha. Not
a trace of this system is found in P, or in any other document of the
Hexateuch.

who wrote the history of God's dealings with man after the prophecies of Isaiah, Jeremiah, and Ezekiel had been proclaimed, would certainly have adapted his traditional material to suit the religious beliefs of his time.

It is assumed that the author of P is a strict monotheist, to whom God is the exalted, supra-mundane being, of whom all anthropomorphic expressions are unworthy. We have already called attention to the fact that Gen. 1:26 uses Elohim in a polytheistic sense. We are willing to admit that possibly some Trinity-idea[1] may lie behind it, but even this idea is utterly foreign to the time of Ezra. The same use of Elohim in a plural sense occurs, either explicitly or implicitly, in Gen. 6:13 and 9:16. And with these we should compare the Jahvistic sections of Gen. 3:22 and 11:7. We cannot be very much mistaken if we say that in the earlier sections of Genesis the biblical *Elohim* often approaches the Babylonian expression, *Ilâni-Rabûti*, "the great gods." This becomes still more apparent when we refer to the expression *Yahweh Elohim* in Gen., chaps. 2 and 3, which can hardly mean anything else than "Yahweh of the Gods," or "Lord of the Gods." And this expression occurs again and again throughout Genesis, in both J and P sections, at least if we may rely upon the evidence furnished by the Septuagint.

We have also called attention to Gen. 5:22, 24, and 6:9, where Enoch and Noah are said to have transacted business with Elohim. The anthropomorphism of these expressions is so evident that it is hard to see any difference between P and J, the document which critics claim is the most anthropomorphic of all. Similar ideas meet

[1] Like the Babylonian Anu, Bel, and Ae; or the Greek Zeus, Poseidon, and Hades; Vedic Brahma, Vishnu, and Shiva; Icelandic Odin, Vilir, and Vei.

us once more in P expressions, when God is said to "arise" from Abraham and Jacob.[1]

c) Still more significant are the references to the cave of Machpelah, which contained the tombs of the patriarchs.[2] The patriarchs are said to be "gathered to their fathers" when they die, and this presupposes some survival of ancestor-worship.

But waiving for the present the question of the date of the composition of P, we must at least admit that P constantly uses material dating from a time when the strict monotheism of the exilic and post-exilic periods was unknown.

d) In view of the religious beliefs prevailing in the time of Ezekiel and from then on down to that of Ezra, it does not seem probable, in fact it seems quite impossible, that a document should be put forth by men, both priests and prophets, very zealous in their worship, which promulgates the worship of El-Shaddai. It is also almost incredible that it should have been received by a people which had been so severely chastened in the Exile. We cannot deny that this name was an epithet for Yahweh; but the true God is here presented to the people in a local aspect.[3] In referring to God as El-Shaddai the author of P has identified him with a local divinity. This is impossible for Ezra's time, for the henotheistic conception certainly did

---

[1] Gen. 17:22; 35:13.

[2] Gen. 25:8, 9; 49:29–32; 50:12–13.

[3] The name came from northern Syria. The same god was introduced into the Egyptian pantheon under the name of *Set* or *Sed*, which should probably be pronounced *Saddai*. The center of this worship was in Tanis and Avaris, and the god's totem was the ass, which connects him with the worship of Hadad of the *Amurru* or Amorite people of Syria, the Amorite name itself being the older Canaanite name of *Chamor* or "he-ass."

not last longer than to the great prophets of the eighth century.

e) There is another similar name used in P, in Gen., chap. 14, where Melchizedek is said to worship El-Elyon, who is the local God of Salem,[1] and the religion is certainly sanctioned and considered perfectly proper, for Abraham receives a blessing from him.

Thus in certain sections of P we find the religious views entirely dissonant with the theology of Ezra or Ezekiel. Sometimes God is looked at in a polytheistic or at least, possibly, a trinitarian way. In other cases he is worshiped as a henotheistic or local god, under special and local names. In still other cases, the document acquiesces in ancestor-worship, and in other peculiar forms of worship, as, for instance, when it introduces the rite of circumcision. These sections of the document must antedate the period of the great prophets.

IV. Religious Institutions

a) It is assumed by modern critics that the D document is the one which introduces the central sanctuary, and that, although the P document and code do not mention such a sanctuary, they do presuppose it. Ergo, say the critics, the P document is later than D. It is to be deplored that critical research undertakes to read so much into the Bible that never was there. If the P document or code does not mention a single central sanctuary, we should not attribute to it any such institution unless we have further evidence. If the document does not mention it, it may be supposed that quite possibly it neither knew of it nor intended to refer to it.

[1] Gen. 14:18.

On closer examination of the P code, though, we find
that it both knows of and acquiesces in more than one
sanctuary.[1] Now, the P code was written in the wilderness of Sinai, if we may believe its own statements, and
there, of course, the people had only one sanctuary, the
Tent of Meeting. In it, therefore, we could hardly
expect references to more than one sanctuary. But the
passage just alluded to implies that in the future more than
one sanctuary was to be expected. But such a thought
as this would be entirely impossible in the time of Ezra,
or even in the time of Ezekiel.

In Ps. 43:3; 46:4, and 84:1[2] are references to several
"dwelling-places of Yahweh." The word for "dwelling-
place" is purely a P expression. But the tone of the
references makes it necessary to believe that in the time
they were written more than one sanctuary was not only
permitted but extolled. Incidentally, too, it may be
remarked that none of these psalms can possibly be
assigned, on this account, to a post-exilic date.

b) In assigning the P document and code modern
criticism has given as its reasons the statement that the
characteristic institutions of this code are not known to
the history of Israel until the time of Ezra. References
to such institutions in the poetical books are explained
by the assumption that such books belong to the *exilic
or post-exilic periods*. The chief trouble with this hypothesis is the fact that after the time of Ezra Hebrew history
becomes a blank. We know almost nothing about it.
Consequently it can quite easily be claimed, though even
more easily denied, that several of these P institutions
were never put into effect, and that they represent merely

[1] Lev. 26:31; cf. Ps. 68:35.　　　[2] Cf. Ps. 132:5.

the pious hopes of the poverty-stricken priests of Jerusalem, hopes which were never to be realized.

The case is, however, not so clear as, on a first glance, it might appear to be. The preceding history of Israel is not, as is claimed, entirely free from reference to these P institutions. On the other hand, we could hardly expect that some of them should be so mentioned. Much weight is attached to the fact that the institutions, so prominent in P, of the sin-offering, the meal- and peace-offerings, and the thank-offerings, although so prominently featured in Leviticus,[1] are not referred to in the historical books. It is claimed that these sacrifices could not have been in existence in the time of these books. But it must be observed in this connection that the laws on these sacrifices in P were made for *private cases*. They are all private sacrifices. Even the law in Leviticus on the holocaust,[2] refers to a private sacrifice. They provide for an individual making a sacrifice, not for a people. And therefore we ought not to expect that these sacrifices should be mentioned in the historical books. There were other sacrifices of a public nature, and the law for them is to be found in Num., chap. 28. In this place the P code confines itself to the holocaust, with regulations as to offering it on every week-day, on the Sabbath, and on the new-moons. The offering of *public* holocausts is, however, not unknown to the earlier history of Israel, which refers frequently both to public holocausts and to public peace-offerings. Deuteronomy also legislates about these two sacrifices. Isaiah knows not only of the great feasts,[3] but also of oblations, incense, new-moons, solemn convocations, and calling of assemblies,[4] all of them P

---

[1] Lev., chaps. 2–5.   [2] Lev., chap. 1.   [3] Isa. 29:1.   [4] Isa. 1:13.

institutions, which, on the assumption of the critics, should be unknown to his time. But his references to them indicate a regular observance, and presume a codified law.

But these institutions, of which we have seen traces in the time of Isaiah, are visible through all of Hebrew history.

The *meal-offering*, for instance, is mentioned at least in Judg. 13:19, 23; I Kings 8:64 (the time of Solomon); II Kings 3:20; 16:13, 15; Amos. 5:22, 25; Zeph. 3:10. Of course no one can dispute the authority of Amos, at least. The *peace-offering* is not only known to E and D, but is mentioned in all the historical books, and in Amos,[1] who speaks of it as a regular sacrifice. The *thank-offering* is also well known to Amos.[2] The trespass-offering is mentioned in I Sam.[3] *Incense* was a part of Eli's worship. Solomon offered it also. And it was regularly used in the times of Isaiah and Jeremiah. Calling of assemblies is testified to by Isaiah.[4] The *new-moon festivals* were celebrated *regularly* in the time of Elisha, Hosea, Amos, Isaiah, and Ezekiel.[5]

Many critics are willing to admit that these customs may perhaps have existed, but they qualify their admission by saying that there were no codified laws regulating them. But anyone who recognizes the truth that in all other lands the temple rituals were carefully regulated by ceremonial codes finds it hard to believe that the Hebrew temple ritual was any exception to the rule. But, after all, we are not dealing with the question of codes just here. We are merely controverting that argument which says that the absence of these institutions before the Exile and their

---

[1] Amos. 5:22.   [3] I Sam. 6:3, 4, 8, 17.   [5] Ezek. 45:17; 46:1, 3, 6.

[2] Amos. 4:5.   [4] Isa. 1:13; 4:5.

presence in P is good reason for dating the latter during or after the Exile. We have felt constrained to decline the conclusion. The first premise is a mere assumption, and one contrary to the evidence which the Bible itself furnishes.

c) Much stress has been laid upon the different ways in which the D and P codes regard the priests and Levites. It is undoubtedly true that the D document represents all Levites as priests, while the P document and code recognize as priests only the sons of Aaron, and regard the Levites generally as belonging to an inferior order. Modern criticism seeks to explain the discrepancy by assuming that a degradation of idolatrous priests into Levites took place after D was published in 621. Critics seek to base this degradation on the code of Ezekiel,[1] where Ezekiel suggests that only priests coming from Zadok ("sons of Zadok") should be permitted to offer sacrifices in the temple, and that all the other Levites should perform the menial offices in the temple.

The theory seems plausible, but is so only on the surface. For one thing, the P code and document do not know of "sons of Zadok;" they speak of "sons of Aaron." And these terms cannot be made equal. Further, if the degradation of the Levites was based on Ezek. 44:4 ff., its first promulgation was, of course, made at the great Feast of Tabernacles in 444 B. C., when Ezra read his law-book to the people. Is it not somewhat remarkable that all the people, including the Levites themselves, accepted these new laws with shouts of joy, and that not one single murmur of objection was made by those who now heard that they were degraded from priests into mere

[1] Ezek. 44:4 ff.

temple menials? Up to the arrival of Nehemiah, Ezra had not been much in the favor of the people, but he had done nothing toward degrading the priests. He had not even mentioned anything of the kind. And are we to believe that now, when he puts forth a law-book in which a very large proportion of his own Levitical tribesmen are degraded, this act establishes him firmly in their good graces? And would we not expect that this stupendous change in priestly arrangements might have some effect upon the people, who now hear of it for the first time? Still, they display not a trace of surprise. They take it quite as a matter of course. They are highly and unanimously satisfied. That this degradation took place in Ezra's time is to the highest degree improbable. Ezekiel's suggestion that the high-priesthood be confined to the sons of Zadok may have been carried out by Ezra, but this much is certain, that the P code knows not one thing about it. In the later chapter on the priesthoods we shall consider this more fully.

V. Historical Determinants of the Date

a) It is admitted by a large number of conservative critics that Ezekiel was acquainted with the Holiness Code[1] in the form that we now have it. This means, then, that in 585 B. C. at least the following institutions were known and in operation: the Aaronic priesthood,[2] the high priest,[3] the sin- and trespass-offerings,[4] the Day of Atonement,[5] the three great festivals,[6] the Feast of Trumpets,[7] the oil for the lamps,[8] the shewbreads,[9] the sabbatical

---

[1] Lev., chaps. 17–26.

[2] Lev. 17:2; 21:1, 17, 21.

[3] Lev. 21:10–15.

[4] Lev. 19:21, 22; 23:19.

[5] Lev. 23:27–32; 25:9.

[6] Lev. 23:1–44.

[7] Lev. 23:23–25.

[8] Lev. 24:1–4.

[9] Lev. 24:5–9.

year,[1] the year of Jubilee,[2] and Levitical cities.[3] And further, this means that these laws must have been in operation before the Exile began.

b) Leviticus contains a law on clean and unclean animals.[4] The same law is found in Deuteronomy.[5] The verbal agreement and the order of enumeration of the animals is so closely parallel that the two codes must have known of one another, in this point at least, and the one must have borrowed from the other. It might perhaps be assumed that both had borrowed from a common source. But the language is not Deuteronomic but priestly. Most critics admit that, in this case, D must have borrowed from P. This means, then, that a part of P existed in its present form before Deuteronomy was published, or at least in the same time; and as the promulgation of Deuteronomy cannot be placed later than 621 B. C., at least this chapter of the P code must be earlier than that date. And as this law belongs, not to the Holiness Code, but to those general laws of P which are assumed to be the later strata of that code, we conclude that not only the Holiness Code, but the whole P code probably—most probably—existed before 621 B. C.

The connection between the D and P codes is further emphasized by a number of institutions similar in both codes: the year of release[6] and the sabbatical year,[7] uncleanness[8] and ceremonial impurity,[9] the laws on leprosy,[10] the laws on incest,[11] and the laws in regard to the Levites.[12]

[1] Lev. 25:1–7.
[2] Lev. 25:8–13.
[3] Lev. 25:32, 33.
[4] Lev. 11:2–19.
[5] Deut. 14:4–20.
[6] Deut. 15:1 ff.
[7] Lev., chap. 25.
[8] Deut. 23:9, 10.
[9] Lev., chap. 15.
[10] Deut. 24:8; Lev., chaps. 13, 14.
[11] Deut. 22:13; Lev., chaps. 18, 20.
[12] Deut. 18:2; Num. 18:20 ff.

c) That the P code was known *ca.* 621 B. C. can be further demonstrated, and this time to a certainty. It is admitted on all hands that Josiah's reforms were carried out after the Book of Deuteronomy was found in the temple, in 621 B. C. It cannot be denied that these reforms were called forth by the Book of Deuteronomy. But it is misleading to claim that all of his reforms were based solely on that book. The following facts should be taken into consideration:

1. Josiah broke down the "high-places of the satyrs."[1] The law on satyr-worship is found *only* in the P code [2]

2. When Josiah destroyed the high-places of Judah, their priests were not permitted to serve at the altar in Jerusalem. But he permitted them to receive their portion of the unleavened bread of the temple.[3] The law on the priest's portion of the unleavened bread is found *only* in the P code.[4]

3. Josiah destroyed the high-places of Judah,[5] Jerusalem,[6] and Bethel.[7] But Deuteronomy has no law whatever on high-places, and the word (in this technical sense) does not occur in a single instance in the whole D code. The P code, however, has a law forbidding them.[8]

4. Josiah put away those who had familiar spirits, and the wizards. These are the only two kinds of witchcraft mentioned in the reform.[9] The P code has a law confined to these two kinds of witchcraft.[10] It is true that

[1] II Kings 23:8. The Hebrew reads "gates," but the same word with different points means "satyrs," and as satyr-worship was very common, the text should be so pointed.

[2] Lev. 17:7.	[5] II Kings 23:8.	[8] Lev. 26:30.
[3] II Kings 23:8, 9.	[6] II Kings 23:13.	[9] II Kings 23:24.
[4] Lev. 6:14–18.	[7] II Kings 23:15.	[10] Lev. 20:27.

Deuteronomy has a law on witchcraft, but it mentions not less than eight different kinds. The wording in II Kings most naturally identifies the reform with the law in Leviticus.

5. Josiah forbade Molech-worship.[1] Molech is not mentioned in D. But the P code has two laws forbidding his worship.[2]

d) We have already called attention to the reference by Isaiah to certain institutions of the P code regularly observed in his time. It is then interesting to notice that Hosea also[3] puts into the mouth of Yahweh the words, "Although I write for him my law in myriads of precepts." This indicates that the written law of Yahweh existed in the time of Hosea (ca. 730 B. C.).

e) According to I Kings,[4] Solomon offered a meal-offering at the consecration of the temple. The meal-offering is an institution of the P code,[5] and is found *only* in that code. This carries us back to the time of the united kingdom (ca. 960 B. C.).

f) In I Samuel[6] we read that before Saul visited the witch at Endor he had put away all those who had familiar spirits. As it evidently was an innovation on his part to do this, we cannot suppose that he would have dared to take so important a step unless he had behind him a law recognized as valid among his people. Now, the E code has a single law on sorcery.[7] As for D, the passage in I Samuel betrays no affinity either in thought or in language with it. But I Samuel does come very close indeed to the provisions of the law regarding witchcraft

---

[1] II Kings 23:10.   [4] I Kings 8:64.   [6] I Sam. 28:3-9.

[2] Lev. 18:21; 20:2-5.   [5] Lev., chap. 2.   [7] Exod. 22:18.

[3] Hos. 8:12.

in P,[1] where, as we have seen, only two kinds of witches are forbidden, those having familiar spirits and wizards. The conditions of the time, as we know from contemporary history, so strongly favored astrology and all kinds of witchcraft that Saul would not have dared undertake his reform except with the explicit support of a well-known law. And the law, in this case, could only be the one found in what we now call the P code.

g) Gen. 36:31 says that eight kings of Edom ruled before there reigned one in Israel. This gives a *terminus a quo* for this P portion in Genesis. This *terminus* is the reign of Saul, the first king of Israel (*ca.* 1050 B. C.).[2] If Gen. 36:31–39, which gives the history of the kings of Edom, was written in the time of Ezra or of Ezekiel, it is impossible to explain why only eight Edomite kings should be mentioned, and this history end abruptly with Hadar. In the case of the first seven kings, it is stated that each one of them died, but no such remark is added about Hadar. The only legitimate inference is that this history of Edom was written, when Hadar was yet reigning, either before or in the early part of Saul's (or David's) reign. But there is no reason why the P codes should not have existed before the P document, and no reason why this statement should not be regarded as a redactorial note.

VI. "Law of Yahweh"

Thus far we have found instances throughout the historical books indicating that the laws of the P code were in operation as far back as the time of Saul. We have

---

[1] Lev. 19:31; 20:6, 27.

[2] It should be noted, however, that the Greek here reads "Jerusalem" for "Israel," which would put the *terminus* forty-seven years farther on.

seen that reforms were carried out on the basis of this code, and that in the nature of the case such reforms must have been based on codified laws, since the practices that were reformed were the things that naturally rested upon traditions. A reform is, then, something new, and presupposes, not a tradition, but a definite law which enables a ruler or a priesthood to overrule traditions and bring in a new order of things. As surely as the reforms of Josiah were based upon written laws, so were the reforms of Hezekiah, Jehoshaphat, and Saul based upon written laws, laws which the people must have bound themselves to obey. At this late day it cannot possibly be objected that written laws were not possible at so early a date. The Amarna letters (1400 B. C.) are more than enough evidence for the universal use of writing at that time. Writing in the time of Saul must have been as common as in the time of Josiah.

The Bible furnishes, however, evidence that the P code existed in written form long before the time of Ezekiel:

a) In II Chron.[1] we read, "He [Hezekiah] appointed also the king's portion of his substance for the burnt-offerings, to wit for the morning and evening burnt-offerings, and the burnt-offerings for the Sabbaths, and for the New-moons, and for the set feasts, as it is written in *the Law of Yahweh*. Moreover, he commanded the people that dwelt in Jerusalem to give the portion of the priests and the Levites, that they might give themselves to *the Law of Yahweh*."

Here we have two references to *the Law of Yahweh*. And it is obvious that here the phrase is a technical term

[1] II Chron. 31:3, 4.

for a law that was written. What law could this have
been? The mention of "priests and Levites" points to
the P code. So does the mention of the morning and
evening burnt-offerings, the Sabbaths, the New-moons,
and the set festivals. In fact the whole passage betrays
evidences of the language and institutions of P. Referring, then, back to the P code, we find that the first reference of our quotation gives the substance of the law in
Num., chap. 28. No similar law is found elsewhere
in the Hexateuch. The second reference refers us to
Num. 18:8–24. Nor is this law found elsewhere in the
Hexateuch. The term, *Law of Yahweh*, may then be
assumed to be the technical term for the P code in the
time of Hezekiah.

The objection that this passage is found in Chronicles,
which came from priestly hands, cannot be much regarded,
for it is impossible to show that the matter referred to is
not historically true. And, furthermore, we shall presently show that the same technical term is used in the
same sense by other authors of whom no one would dream
of saying that they belonged to the priestly school. Moreover, in this passage we have the confirmatory evidence
of Kings, which says of Hezekiah that "he kept (or
enforced) the commandments which Yahweh commanded
Moses."[1] The language here points to the P code.

b) In II Chronicles we read, "Now the rest of the acts
of Josiah, and his good deeds, according to that which is
written in the Law of Yahweh, and his acts, first and last,
they are written in the Book of the Kings of Israel and
Judah."[2]

Again we deal with the same technical term, *the Law*

---

[1] II Kings 18:6.   [2] II Chron. 35:26, 27.

of Yahweh. The expression, "good deeds" or "benefactions," presents to us unmistakably the language and spirit of the P code. We noticed above that the reforms of Josiah were based both on the D and P codes. We know that the D code existed then in written form. What more likely than that the P code did also?

c) Jeremiah was a contemporary of Josiah. He refers also to this law, *the Law of Yahweh*, although he accuses the scribes of making changes in it, even at that early time. The charge was undoubtedly well founded, and is one which should be constantly remembered in considering the manuscripts transcribed by the scribes from 600 B. C. onward. He says, "How do ye say, We are wise, and *the Law of Yahweh* is with us? But, behold, the false pen of the scribes hath wrought falsely."[1]

Wilful corruptions of the text, then, date back at least to the days of Jeremiah!

d) We noticed above that the P code was known by the technical term, *Law of Yahweh* in the time of Hezekiah. This, of course, is the time of Isaiah. And he, too, knew of *the Law of Yahweh*. He says, "Because they have rejected *the Law of Yahweh of Hosts*, and despised the word of the Holy One of Israel."[2] *Yahweh of Hosts* belongs to the language of P, and *Holy One of Israel*, while characteristic of Isaiah, has for its basis, too, the language of the P code, especially that of the Holiness Code.

Again he says, "For it is a rebellious people, lying children, children that will not hear *the Law of Yahweh*."[3] And in another place, "Seek ye out of *the Book of Yahweh*."[4]

[1] Jer. 8:8.　　[2] Isa. 5:24*b*.　　[3] Isa. 30:9.　　[4] Isa. 34:16.

Here is an explicit reference to a *Book of Yahweh* which must have been well known to the people. It occurs in a prophecy in which Isaiah predicts the doom of Edom for its unkindliness toward Israel. The prophet desires to call the people's attention to the fact that Edom had always been treacherous to the children of Israel, and he gives for proof a reference to *the Book of Yahweh*. It is in the P document[1] that we find proof of Isaiah's veracity.

The Book of Yahweh, then, it would seem, is the P code and document, and is identical with *the Law of Yahweh*, except that we here find it referred to as *a book*, while the Chronicler merely says that it was *written*. The Hebrew word for "book," *Sepher*, means a complete, independent treatise. It is possible that *the Law of Yahweh* in *the Book of Yahweh* was merely the P code of our Exodus-Numbers, but it is not improbable that at this time the P sections of Genesis already belonged to it.

e) The home of Amos was south of Jerusalem. Therefore, if the P code, which evidently belonged to the priests in Jerusalem, existed in his time, he would probably know of it. He prophesied in Bethel, a city of the Northern Kingdom, where we would not expect to find traces of the P code. Nor does Amos allude to it, save in a single paragraph, which, significantly enough, is his oracle against Jerusalem, where he says, "Thus says Yahweh, For three transgressions of Judah, yea for four, I will not turn it away, but because they have rejected *the Law of Yahweh*, and have not kept his statutes, and their lies have caused them to err, after the which their fathers did walk,   "[2]

Is it not significant that of all his oracles Amos should

---

[1] Num. 20:14–21.   [2] Amos 2:4.

make mention of *the Law of Yahweh* only in that against Judah? We are almost forced to admit, as a logical consequence, that *the Law of Yahweh* is a technical term for a law-book existing in Judah and Jerusalem, and that this book existed there in the time of Amos.

f) II Kings refers us again to *the Law of Yahweh*. "But Jehu took no heed to walk in *the Law of Yahweh*, the God of Israel, with all his heart; he departed not from the sins of Jeroboam, wherewith he made Israel to sin."[1]

Here it is not the Chronicler, but the Deuteronomic compiler of Kings, who uses this term, *the Law of Yahweh*. Now Jehu was in the Northern Kingdom, and therefore, if we have been correct in our conclusions, not under *the Law of Yahweh*. But the editor, living in Jerusalem, judged him to have been a bad king simply because he did not accept the law-book of Judah. At any rate, the term is not one coined by the late Chronicler.

g) Going back to the time of Jehoshaphat, we read again, "And they taught in Judah, having the book of *the Law of Yahweh* with them; and they went about throughout all the cities of Judah, and taught among the people."[2]

The reference is to Levites who are teaching "the book" of *the Law of Yahweh*. And here we get the welcome information, which we anticipated when examining the passage from Isaiah, that the "Book of Yahweh" was "the book" of *the Law of Yahweh*. Now, this teaching began in the third year of Jehoshaphat (873 B. C.). We must admit that the term, *the Law of Yahweh*, seems to be a technical term, with the same meaning as in other passages in Chronicles.

[1] II Kings 10:31. [2] II Chron. 17:9.

It is of great importance that we here find the Levites out on missionary work, introducing *the Law of Yahweh* to the people of the cities of Judah. This preaching pre-supposes two things: first, that before this time it had not been well known outside of Jerusalem proper, and second, that the Aaronic priesthood, whose code this was, were now in the ascendancy, eager to propagate the peculiar tenets of their creed.

h) Asa, father of Jehoshaphat, was equally a zealous supporter of the P code. We read, "And he [Asa] com-manded to seek Yahweh, the God of their fathers, and to do the law and the commandments."[1] And again, "Now for a long time Israel had been without the true God, and without a teaching priest, and without Torah."[2]

The "teaching priest," "law," "commandments," are all well-known expressions of the P code. *Torah* may mean "teaching," as so many modern scholars would have us believe, and in many cases it undoubtedly does mean this; but when it is used in a technical sense, as it evi-dently is here, it can refer only to a collection of oracles or laws. Furthermore, we must assume from the nature of the case that it was in written form. We have no warrant for the assumption that *Torah* may mean an oral tradition, when used in a technical sense. If the P document was, as we have seen, in book form in the time of Jehoshaphat, it would be unwarranted to assume that it was only oral tradition in the time of his immediate predecessor, Asa.

i) The dying David prays for his son, Solomon, saying, "Only Yahweh give thee discretion and understanding, and give thee charge concerning Israel; that so thou mayest keep *the Law of Yahweh*, thy God."[3]

[1] II Chron. 14:4.   [2] II Chron. 15:3.   [3] I Chron. 22:12.

The phrase, "Yahweh thy God," looks Deuteronomic at first glance, and we might suppose that possibly the reference was to the D code; but this code is never elsewhere referred to as *"the Law of Yahweh."* This reference may not be pressed as a certain reference to the P code, but this seems the most likely explanation. But we have another instance recorded in regard to David.[1] In this other case, David assigns different orders of priests to the different sanctuaries: Asaph and his brethren to minister before the Ark of the Covenant of Yahweh in Jerusalem, as every day's work required, and Zadok the priest and his brethren, before the Tabernacle of Yahweh in the high-place at Gibeon, these latter "to offer burnt-offerings morning and evening, even according to all that is written in *the Law of Yahweh*, which he commanded unto Israel."

This passage is of the utmost importance if we desire to understand the religious situation of the time. Here we have the Ark of the Covenant, with a certain priesthood, set up in Jerusalem, and the Tabernacle of Yahweh, with another priesthood set up in Gibeon. The Ark of the Covenant is peculiarly the expression of the E and D codes, while the Tabernacle of Yahweh is peculiar to the P code. In this passage they are plainly distinct. Moreover, the ceremonies before the Ark of the Covenant are simple and undefined, just as the D code leaves them. The ceremonies before the Tabernacle of Yahweh, on the other hand, are those defined in the P code.[2] And before this Tabernacle, it is explicitly stated, the daily morning and evening holocausts were offered, "according to all that is written in *the Law of Yahweh*." Further-

---

[1] I Chron. 16:37-40.　　　　[2] Num., chap. 28.

more, it is said that this law was in *written* form in the
time of David. We must understand that *the Law of
Yahweh* here, as elsewhere, means the P code.

We found above that Saul carried out reforms based
upon the P code. And here we find that this code exists
in written form a few years after Saul's death. The
origin of the book of the P code can hardly be placed later
than the reign of Saul. On the other hand, we have no
warrant whatever, derivable from the Bible, for placing
the codification of the laws of P very much earlier. It is
true that there is a reference to *the Law of Yahweh* in
Exod. 13:9, but critical scholars seem to prefer that this
and the preceding verses be assigned to the D document
and it is thought that these verses have strayed in, in quite
lonely fashion, among P and J sections. The passage
has probably been misplaced.

There are three more references to *the Law of Yahweh*,
in Ezra,[1] in Nehemiah,[2] and in Daniel.[3] These, however,
are quite late, and are of no use, therefore, in determining
the *terminus a quo* for P. What we have already shown
is, we think, superabundant evidence that *the Law of
Yahweh* is the technical term for the P code and document
and that that code and document existed in written form,
a book, as early as the time of David, and, most probably,
in the days of Saul.

B. EXTERNAL EVIDENCE

a) To this internal evidence we are now able to add
some of an external sort. In 1907 Dr. Rubensohn discovered at Elephantine three documents written in 408
B. C. by a certain Jedôniah, a priest of the temple of Yah-

---

[1] Ezra 7:10.   [2] Neh. 9:3.   [3] Dan. 9:10.

weh in the city of Elephantine, in southern Egypt. One of these documents is a letter, or the copy of a letter, addressed to the governor of Jerusalem, asking his permission to rebuild the Jewish temple in Elephantine. In this letter it is stated that this temple had existed when Cambyses came to Egypt to conquer it, in 525 B. C. It adds that when Cambyses destroyed all the temples of Egypt, he left this one alone standing. The temple later on, through the influence of Egyptian priests, had been destroyed. The Jews now wished to have it rebuilt. In this letter there are several remarkable statements in regard to the temple ritual, by which it is plain that the services were conducted according to the elaborate ritual of the P code. References are made especially to the burning of incense, holocausts, and meal-sacrifices. The tone of the whole letter indicates that these services had been carried on ever since the temple had been founded.

Now, it was existing in 525 B. C., and the probability is that it had existed a long time before that. Isaiah[1] speaks about a "pillar of Yahweh" on the border of Egypt, and of worship in the Canaanite tongue (Galilean Aramaic) in five cities of Egypt. Four of these places are mentioned by Jeremiah,[2] and the fifth city may, perhaps, have been Elephantine. If the temple was founded in the time of Isaiah (ca. 700 B. C.) it was probably by fugitives from Galilee, fleeing after the conquest of Zebulun and Naphtali by Tiglath-pileser IV. This is perhaps the most probable date for the beginning of Jewish services in Egypt. We have here, then, a welcome testimony to worship with a P ritual in pre-Josianic times.[3]

---

[1] Isa. 19:19.   [2] Jer. 44:1.

[3] For the contents of the Elephantine letter, see Appendix I.

b) The Documentary Hypothesis assumes that the P document and code is later than D, and that the compilation of the four documents, J, E, D, and P, took place in the time of Ezra. Is it not strange that in this compilation no notice is taken of Deuteronomy? The first four books of the Hexateuch are closely fused, with hardly a trace of Deuteronomy, which latter is hung on to the completed JEP document in such a manner that the Greek title, "the Second Law," or Deuteronomy, becomes especially fitting. The fact that J, E, and P are combined and D added to the result seems to point to a date for the compilation of the JEP documents before the D document was discovered in 621 B. C. And if at that time P was combined and sometimes fused with J and E, it must, of course, have existed at that time.

C. CONCLUSION

In view of all these considerations it seems almost impossible to agree with those advocates of the Documentary Hypothesis who assign the P document to the time of Ezra, or indeed to any late date. The evidence, on the contrary, all seems to point unmistakably to a very early date, most probably to about the time of Samuel, Saul, and David.

CHAPTER III

The Unity and Contents of the P Document

I. FRAGMENTS AND DOUBLETS

The P document should, according to the Documentary Hypothesis, be one complete document. Still it gives, in many places, no complete story whatever. For instance:

a) Gen. 19:29 must be placed immediately after Gen. 13:12 in order to give it any meaning that is reasonable. The P redactor is thus charged with a wilful mutilation of the document. But even if this be admitted, P has no story of the overthrow of Sodom, and Gen. 19:29 presupposes such a story in the document. This story must have been omitted from the P narrative when that narrative was incorporated into the Hexateuch.

b) Gen. 25:19, 20, 26*c* cannot be understood by themselves, because the P document nowhere tells of the birth of Esau and Jacob.

c) P does not know that Jacob ever came to Laban. Still, it is said, it informs us that Laban gave Zilpah as handmaid to Leah,[1] that he gave Rachel to Jacob as wife,[2] and Bilhah as handmaid to Rachel. But the document nowhere tells us that Leah was the wife of Jacob. These two verses do not fit together, nor do they give the same meaning.

d) It is impossible to understand Gen. 30:21 otherwise than that Dinah is a daughter of Bilhah, if we read the P document by itself; but when we read the passage as a

---

[1] Gen. 29:24.   [2] Gen. 29:28*b*, 29.

whole, as it stands in the Bible, she appears to be the daugh ter of Leah.   The best way to explain this is on the hypoth esis that that portion of the P document which dealt with Leah has been lost.

e) Gen. 31:18b does not fit together with Gen. 30:21, which precedes it immediately in the P document, so called.

f) Gen. 37:2a shows no connection with Gen. 41:46 which is supposed to follow it in the document.

g) Gen. 47:5-11 cannot be understood without the preceding history of Joseph in Egypt, which, however, is not to be found in this document.

Gen. 26:34; 28:9; and 36:1-14 cannot all have come from the same document.   Modern criticism assigns these sections dealing with the genealogy of Esau all to the P document, nevertheless.   As they contradict one another, and as the same author should hardly have felt the need of recording the genealogy three times in three different ways, such an assignment seems very improbable, if there be but one P document.

Lev., chaps. 18 and 20, contain similar laws, on the same subject, but in detail quite divergent.   It is not easy to see how these laws could both have been promulgated at the same time and belong to the same document.

Nor is it easy to see why the same code should contain such a large number of laws on the Sabbath.

In Lev. 1:3—6:7 is a code dealing with the sacrifices. In Lev. 6:8—7:34 the same code is given again, covering the same ground.

These examples could be multiplied many times over, but they are sufficient to show: first, that the P document as we have it now is not complete; second, that there must have been more than one P document, or several documents, similar in language and contents, from which the P document was made up. Several portions of this P document were then left out when it was compiled with the other documents, wherever these other documents presented the more complete story on a given point.

II. CHANGE OF NAMES

It is assumed on the basis of Exod. 6:2 that when God revealed himself in a theophany under a new name, that new name should constantly be applied to him until another new name was given. Now, in Gen. 17:1, God revealed himself to Abraham and announced that his name was El-Shaddai. The significance of this name formed the basis for the covenant of circumcision which was then commanded. Again, in Exod. 6:2, El-Shaddai appeared to Moses and told him that he had revealed himself to the Patriarchs under the name of El-Shaddai, but that his real name was Yahweh; and he further told him that this was to be his everlasting name. The P document, consequently, uses Yahweh after Exod. 6:2. But how does this correspond to Gen. 17:2—Exod. 6:1? We would certainly expect that the P document should here constantly use El-Shaddai. But we find on examination that this is not the case. On the contrary, this name is used only four times.[1] Otherwise, the name used is Elohim, in exactly the same way that it was used of him before the theophany of the seventeenth chapter.

This observation is of importance for a better understanding of the P document in Genesis. Either our interpretation of Exod. 6:2 is faulty, or else there are several

[1] Gen. 28:3; 35:11; 43:14; 48:3.

P documents in Genesis, only one of which knows of the El-Shaddai theophany. We shall presently see that the latter assumption is quite probable.

This change of name applies not only to God, but also to some of the patriarchs. Abram's name was changed to Abraham,[1] and we find that from this time on this patriarch is known by this name. Jacob's name, too, was changed to Israel. Genesis gives a double account of this. In the J document this patriarch is known from this time on by the latter name.[2] The P document is generally supposed to relate the same event;[3] but here we find, as a matter of fact, not a single instance after the change of name of the use of the name Israel. Again, we may suppose that we have two P documents to deal with, the one of which knows of the change, the other of which does not. We must not, in this connection, lose sight of the fact that in ancient times the bestowing of a new name connoted elevation to a higher office. On the Egyptian monuments we find not only that a king at his coronation received a "throne name," but also that individuals, when they were taken into favor by the king, received a second or "beautiful" name. A glance at Egyptian inscriptions will inform us that kings sometimes call themselves by their throne names, sometimes by their birth names, and that they are so addressed by others. Favored individuals also could be addressed either by their birth names or by their beautiful names. Thus we might assume that the J document uses the beautiful name or the throne name perhaps, if Israel is to be regarded as a king, while the P document uses the birth name.

[1] Gen. 17:5.   [2] Gen. 32:28.   [3] Gen. 35:10.

Thus we may admit that in the case of Jacob-Israel
there was but one P document. Still, however, the diffi
culty with the names El-Shaddai and Yahweh is such that
we are almost forced to assume two P documents. It
seems improbable that the Hebrew text, the Samaritan
text, and the Septuagint version should all have undergone
such wholesale corruption that the name El-Shaddai
should be changed to Elohim in every case in P from Gen.
17:2 to Exod. 6:2, with only the four exceptions noted
above.

III. THE FOUR COVENANTS

When the Development Hypothesis was first advanced,
Wellhausen assumed that the P document was arranged
according to four great covenants, one in Gen., chap. 1, a
second in Gen., chap. 9, a third in Gen., chap. 17, and a
fourth at Sinai (Exod., chap. 34). There is, however, no
covenant at all in Gen., chap. 1. There could not be,
for there was neither a theophany nor a divine promise.
There is no mention in the chapter of anything resembling
a covenant. Nor is there any theophany recorded in Gen.,
chap. 9. Further, it seems very uncertain that there is
any covenant at Sinai recorded in the P document. J and
P are here hopelessly fused, and it seems more than probable that the covenant was a part of J. If so, there was no
P covenant at Sinai, and Lev. 26:9, which could be the
only reference applicable here, refers to a covenant to
come in the future. Furthermore, if a new covenant was
vouchsafed at this time, it should have been mentioned
in Exod. 6:2, where Yahweh revealed his new name to
Moses. Most modern critics, in view of all these facts,
have given up the idea that P is based on four covenants.

IV. THE TEN TOLEDOTH

More important is the assumption that the P document should consist of ten *toledoth*, each introduced by the formula, "These are the generations of. . . . ." The word *toledoth*, or "generations," corresponds somewhat to our idea of historical records, or genealogies, and the formula does occur ten times in Genesis.   But it is important to note that it does not occur elsewhere in the books of the Hexateuch.   Of equal importance is the fact that the histories of Abraham, Joseph, and Moses, the most important personages mentioned in the P document, are none of them introduced by this formula.   It has been assumed that in P this formula stood at the beginning of the history of each patriarch, or else as a title over each section of the document.   But the formula is not found in Gen. 1:1 in introducing that section which tells of the creation.   This omission is significant.   Modern criticism assumes that it has been misplaced by a later redactor, and put at the beginning of the Paradise story in Gen. 2:4, a story which belongs to the J document.   The case is not so simple, however.   The Septuagint reads in this latter place, "This is *the book* of the generation of Heaven and Earth." The word "book" presupposes that we deal here with an independent document, a volume by itself.   The Hebrew word *sepher*, Assyrian *shipru*, English "book," can only be so used.   The most likely explanation is that the P document did have a Paradise story, of which this was the superscription, which was crowded out by the J story of the Paradise when the P and J documents were in later times combined.   The superscription of the old P story, therefore, now stands over the J story.   If this be so, of course it was not transferred from Gen. 1:1, where, by the way, it does not fit.

The second *toledoth* section is to be found in Gen., chap. 5. Here the formula reads, even in Hebrew, "This is *the book* of the generations of Adam." Again we remark the word *sepher* as evidence that once this section was an independent work. We can no longer speak of the P document, but rather of the P documents or the P fragments.

In the case of the history of Jacob, the *toledoth* formula appears only when the patriarch is old, when all his children have been born, and when over half of his history has already been given.[1] No satisfactory explanation of this phenomenon has as yet appeared. One would certainly expect the formula to appear where the story of Jacob begins.[2]

The *toledoth* section introducing the genealogy of the sons of Shem[3] cannot possibly be a continuation of that *toledoth* section which introduces the sons of Noah,[4] because the sons of Shem have already been given.[5] If the latter genealogy belongs to the *toledoth* of the sons of Noah, then the P document has a useless repetition, which is entirely contrary to the theory according to which P is generally supposed to have been composed. Not more than one of these genealogies of Shem can have belonged to the *toledoth* sections. Either the genealogy given among the sons of Noah is not a part of the P document, or else there was a P document outside of the *toledoth* book. As the section under discussion is evidently to be identified with the P style, the latter alternative seems the more probable.

---

[1] Gen. 37:2.   [3] Gen. 11:10.   [5] Gen. 10:22-31.
[2] Gen. 27:46.   [4] Gen. 10:1.

V. THE FRAMEWORK OF THE HEXATEUCH

It is generally assumed that the P document forms the framework of the Hexateuch. This is but partly correct. In the book of Joshua the P sections are so few and so insignificant that they cannot possibly be regarded as forming the framework of the book. In Exodus and Numbers the P sections are more prominent; but most modern critics admit that even here P does not supply the framework. There remains, then, Genesis; and here it is evident that P is the framework into which the other sections, those of J and E, have been fitted.

But it is in this same book of Genesis that we find a number of *toledoth* sections. It seems, therefore, that it is not the whole P document, but merely the *toledoth* sections that furnish the framework for this book.

We come now to the important question, "Were these *toledoth* sections originally a part of what we call the P document?" The answer is, "No." Let us see why.

A. The Toledoth Book

Wherever we meet in Genesis with the formula, "These are the generations of," we find a peculiarity of language that is only rarely to be observed elsewhere in P. It is positively to be affirmed that the *toledoth* sections do belong to the P or Levitical style of writing. But their vocabulary, phraseology, and historical viewpoint show a marked divergence from the rest of P. And, on close examination, we find a difference in religious conceptions between the *toledoth* sections and other P sections, even others contained in the same book, Genesis. The *toledoth* sections—or let us call them, for the present, the *toledoth* Book—pay minute attention to chronological dates of a genealogical sort, of which none is to be found in other P sections. Both the ʝ and P documents do give genealogies, but they are always introduced with the formula, "These are the names of," or, "These are the sons of;" and nowhere in them do we find the expression, "These are the generations of."

The style and language of P is admittedly so peculiar, and offers such a marked contrast to the language of other sections of the Hexateuch that there can hardly be much well-founded doubt as to what are and what are not P sections. But even in the P document we find differentiations of language and style which can hardly be accounted for on any other hypothesis than the one which ascribes our P document to at least two different sources. In the *toledoth* Book, for instance, we find expressions like, "establish a covenant," here a technical term, while in the other sections of the P document we meet with the formula "give a covenant " In the *toledoth* Book we meet the word *rekush*, "substance," and, if we may trust the Septuagint, this word was not used outside that book.[1] The differentiation is apparent in words used both in the *toledoth* Book and in other sections of P, but with different meanings. Thus, in the *toledoth* Book,[2] the Hebrew word *kabod* signifies "honor," while everywhere else in P it is the technical term for the presence of Yahweh, and is rendered, in our versions, "glory."[3] Again, the *toledoth*

[1] In Gen. 15:4; 46:6; Num. 16:32; 35:3 the Greek is *aposkeve* and *ktene*, which presuppose Hebrew *miqneh*. When these passages have been corrected the word *rekush* occurs nowhere outside of the *toledoth* sections.

[2] Gen. 49:6.

[3] The ʝ document uses the same word (Gen. 31:1; 45:13), in the sense of "property."

Book uses for "handmaid" the Hebrew *shiphchah* in agreement with J.[1] The P document outside these sections, however, uses *amah*,[2] in agreement with the E and D documents. Many other instances of these linguistic differences between the *toledoth* Book and the rest of P might be noted. Perhaps one of the others worth particular mention is the use of Elohim, which is used in a plural sense frequently (perhaps always) in the *toledoth* Book, but always in the singular in the rest of the document.

We mentioned above that the P document contains two or three contradictory statements in regard to Esau's wives.[3] The style of the sections where these are given is admittedly that of P. But Wellhausen himself has admitted that if the Documentary Hypothesis be correct not more than one of these statements can rightly belong to P. The way out of the dilemma is to assign the latter of these statements[4] to the *toledoth* Book, with which it agrees in language, and the former[5] to the P document proper.

In a similar manner the two genealogies of Shem in Gen., chaps. 10 and 11, can be disposed of. In Gen., chap. 11, we have the language and characteristic formula of the *toledoth* Book. In Gen., chap. 10, the style is that of the P document proper.

Likewise the genealogies of the sons of Jacob who went down to Egypt[6] are to be explained. The former of these, with its reference to Paddan-Aram, betrays the language of the P document proper; the latter, although

---

[1] The only exception is Lev. 19:20, which in other respects offers a peculiarly ancient language.

[2] Lev. 25:6, 44.

[3] Gen. 26:34; 28:9; 36:1-14.

[4] Gen. 36:1-14.

[5] Gen. 26:34; 28:9.

[6] Gen. 46:8-25; Exod. 1:2-5.

it has not the characteristic formula of the *toledoth* Book, nevertheless belongs to it.

It certainly seems plain that there is not much internal unity between the *toledoth* sections and the rest of P.[1]

The language of the *toledoth* Book and its religious views, as well as its historical and archaeological notes, mark it as older in origin than the rest of P, and show it to have more affinity to the age and conditions of life set forth in the J document.

This *toledoth* Book seems originally to have been composed of a number of documents, still distinguishable by the references[2] to "the book" of generations. This being so of these documents where this phrase occurs in superscription, it is perhaps not unfair to assume that all the *toledoth* sections were originally independent documents. And we may even assume that, when these documents were compiled into one book, the *toledoth* Book, this resultant document contained the "generations" of Abraham, Moses, and Joseph, as well as those which we still have, sections which were later crowded out when J and P proper were combined with it.

B. The P Document Proper

The sections of the P document which remain after the removal of the *toledoth* Book show an unmistakable unity of thought and agreement in language. They contain, also, most of the laws of the P code. These laws in their present form are in the language of the P docu-

---

[1] The latest attempt of the critics to escape the difficulties in P is their theory that P is the product of a school and not of an author. This simply goes to show how inadequate the Documentary Hypothesis in its fulness has proven to be. It also shows how far from settled all these matters are.

[2] Gen. 2:4; 5:1.

sections of them, especially the so-called "statutes" and parts of the Holiness Code, seem to have been only older laws, probably pre-Aaronic, which were recast, fitted into the language of the P people, and embodied in the P document.

We have referred to *the book of the Law of Yahweh,* and we found that it was the technical term for the P code.. This code was at some time combined with the P document and with the *toledoth* Book. The resulting complex, then, made up of three originals at least, is our P "document," so called.

CHAPTER IV

The Language of the P Document

Some further consideration must here be paid to the language of the P document or documents.

It is assumed by many critics that P is a product of the age of Ezra, even though parts of it may go back to as early as the age of Ezekiel.[1] But if P had been written at that time it would surely represent the language of Ezra's age. While there are a number of similarities in vocabulary, phraseology, and thought between P and Ezekiel, similarities which the critics have greatly magnified, it should not be forgotten that there are almost as large a number of dissimilarities between them. The language of Ezekiel is rugged, and bears everywhere the imprint of the exilic period. Malachi belongs to the time of Ezra, and his style too shows affinity with the disintegrated language which came in with the Exile. The books of Ezra and Nehemiah, probably written a hundred years later, but still the product of the post-exilic period, add their witness to this disintegration. But when we turn to the P document and code not a trace of this disintegration is to be found. The vocabulary is in some respects similar to that of Ezekiel and Malachi. But the document moves in precise and stately expressions. The style is pure. The forms used are correct. Here and there are preserved archaisms. Not a single hint of exilic or post-exilic disintegration meets our eye. P belongs to an age of a purer language.

[1] Attention has been called to the apparent agreement in thought and expression between Ezekiel and P.

Still we must account in some way for the extreme difference in style and vocabulary between P and D.   If we assume that the dates usually, assigned by the critics for these documents are correct, how can we account for such an enormous change in language between 621 B. C., when, it is said, D was first promulgated, and 585 B. C., when Ezekiel began to prophesy, and the Holiness Code, at least, was in existence ?   We would have here a phenomenon with hardly a parallel in the history of language, at least so far as Semitic philology can offer us comparative criteria.   But a far easier and a far more probable expla nation of the differences between the codes is possible.

Usually these documents are assumed to reflect differ ent stages in the life of the Hebrews.   Each stage is sup posed to have produced its peculiar document, with its peculiar style, vocabulary, etc.   This principle may in itself be sound.   But it is most unsound to deduce from these premises the dates of compilation of any of these documents, say of D and P, because there is not at our disposal any external literary standard by which we can determine their respective ages.   There are no remains[1] of the Hebrew tongue outside of the Old Testament. We have no other literature with which we can compare any of the documents, and so establish a *terminus a quo* for its date.

Because of this lack the critics have employed analogy, and have constructed a scheme for the development of the Hebrew language, according to which they pass judgment upon the respective ages of the various documents.

---

[1] The Siloah inscription, dating from *ca.* 700 B. C., is too short to be of any appreciable help to us.   Other inscriptions are from the exilic and post-exilic periods.   The Mesa inscription is in the dialect of Moab, and therefore cannot help us.

This scheme may seem attractive, but it is, none the less, based purely upon supposition.

Hebrew Dialects

It is far simpler, and more probable, to suppose that these various documents differ in language and style, not because they represent different periods of development, but because *they represent different contemporary, or nearly contemporary, dialects.* These dialects may have been spoken by neighboring peoples at the same time, and the language of one dialect may have progressed or decayed rapidly. Therefore they may vary greatly from one another. This principle of dialects is so well known, and established by comparative philology with such certainty, that there can be no dispute concerning it. Such phenomena mark the history of every cultivated language of the globe. It was so in Greece and Rome. It is so today in England, Italy, Germany, and Sweden—even in the United States. The modern Arabic dialects show that the same principle applies among the Semites. And that dialects were in use among the Hebrews we know from the fact that in ancient times the Ephraimitic pronunciation differed from that of the Gileadites. The Gileadites said Shibboleth, the Ephraimites said Sibboleth.[1] This change from *sh* to *s* is common between the Babylonian and the Assyrian, and between the Hebrew and the Arabic. It indicates that dialectic differences existed between the east-Jordanic tribes and the tribe of Ephraim.

Further, it can be shown that some of the tribes used Hebrew words in quite different senses from those given them by other tribes. Thus, e. g., *Ish-bosheth* and *Mephibosheth* in the Benjaminite dialect correspond to *Ish-baal*

[1] Judges 12:6.

and *Meri-baal* in the Jerusalemite dialect. Although *Bosheth* means otherwise "shame" or "confusion," among the Benjaminites it was used for *Baal*, meaning "lord" or "master."[1]

Again, we know of a Galilean dialect at the time of Christ.[2] This dialect existed, in all probability, from very early times. The Song of Deborah,[3] the Book of Jonah, and the Song of Songs are all of Galilean origin, and the peculiarities of style in them should be explained as peculiarities of the Galilean dialect, rather than as "Aramaisms." Their use of *sh* for the relative pronoun, instead of the Hebrew *asher*, is not an Aramaism at all. The Aramaic uses invariably *d* for the relative. The *sh* shows relationship with the Phoenician *s* or *asse*, and is doubtless a mark of the ancient Galilean dialect.

It is, therefore, more than possible that a certain document may have been the property of some one tribe, speaking its own dialect. The peculiarities of vocabulary and style of a document may then be ascribed to the peculiar dialect of the tribe which owned it. And if this is the case *we have in the language of the documents no criterion whatever of the comparative ages of those documents.* The differences in language and expression between the D and P documents, then, furnish absolutely no evidence in regard to the date of the P document.

Dialect of Levi

To what dialect are we to assign P? The document and code is a product of the Aaronic priesthood. The language, therefore, is naturally the language of the priests.

---

[1] Cf. I Sam. 20:30, where the same word is used by Saul, the Benjaminite.

[2] Mark 14:70; Luke 22:59; 23:6; Acts 2:7.

[3] Judges, chap. 5.

Now the Aaronic priests form a clan of the tribe of Levi. The language of the P code, then, it would seem, is that of the tribe of Levi. The language of the Toledoth Book is closely related to that of the P document proper, and is therefore also to be assigned to the tribe of Levi. Its minor differences from the rest of P indicate only a different age in the development of the dialect. In this case we must assume that it is the older of the two. The prophet Ezekiel was also a priest, perhaps of the Zadokite family. His language would then be that of the Levitical tribe. This explains sufficiently the connection and similarity between his prophecies and the P document. The differences between them are equally well accounted for, by the assumption that Ezekiel's language shows a later and more disintegrated stage in the development of the Levitical dialect. Ezra and Malachi belonged to this same tribe of Levi, and both their affinity with the P language and their evidences of disintegration receive adequate explanation.

If this assigning of the P document to the dialect of Levi is correct, other phenomena of this document can more easily be explained. The religious institutions, for instance, mentioned in the P code, may then rest on the traditions of the tribe of Levi, and the P code may be looked upon as the product of the religious development of that tribe. As the Levites in D, and the sons of Aaron with Levites in P, were put in charge of the worship and the sanctuary, we would expect that the traditions and laws of the tribe of Levi would exert a most pronounced influence upon the thought and literature of all Hebrew tribes that came to worship at the sanctuaries where they officiated.

In view of all these facts the most reasonable way to account for the linguistic peculiarities of the P document is to assign the document to the dialect and to the religious conceptions, not of the exilic, the post-exilic, or any other period, but rather of a particular tribe, the tribe of Levi.

CHAPTER V

Conclusions in Regard to the P Document

In view of the facts that we have adduced in the three previous chapters, the following conclusions in regard to the P document have been deduced:

Early Date of P

In regard to the document's date, we have found that it cannot be assigned either to the exilic or the post-exilic periods, that it was in part the basis of the reform of Josiah, 621 B. C., that it was appealed to in the time of Hezekiah, *ca.* 700 B. C., and was well known to the pro phets of that time, Amos and Isaiah, that it was the basis of a missionary propaganda by the Levites in the time of Jehoshaphat, *ca.* 873 B. C., that it was well known to his father, Asa, that Solomon and even David worshiped on the basis of its ritual, and finally, that Saul carried out a reform on the basis of its laws. The conclusion seemed inevitable that the P document and code existed in a written form as early as the time of Saul and Samuel.

Documents of P

We have further pointed out that the P document, as embodied in our Hexateuch, has no claim to be regarded either as complete or as a unit—admitting that the Documentary Hypothesis is correct. Here and there it is only fragmentary, and so fragmentary that it gives no sense if read by itself. We found that it contains doublets, in the genealogies of the sons of Shem and of the sons of

Jacob, and in its statements regarding the wives of Esau. Our conclusion from these premises was that the P document, as we have it, is only a collection of fragments. A consideration of the Toledoth Book, with its distinguishing marks, confirmed us in this conclusion.

Language of P

Again, in considering the language of the document, we found that certain sections differed in vocabulary and phraseology, as well as in characteristic formulas, from other portions. We saw that this phenomenon ran through all of Genesis and parts of Exodus and Leviticus. Analyzing these sections, we found that we had in them fragments of an old Toledoth Book, and that in addition to this there was in P another document, known in the Old Testament as the *Book of the Law of Yahweh*, or, more briefly, as the *Law of Yahweh*. We considered further the peculiarities of the Toledoth Book and of this other document or documents, comparing them with the later priestly writings, and this led us to conclude that these peculiarities pointed to a literary product of the tribe of Levi, written in that tribe's dialect, and further, that the laws and institutions of our P collections were the property, and were based upon the traditions, of the people of the tribe of Levi. From all these considerations, we concluded that the peculiarities of the P document could best be accounted for by assigning them, not to the exilic or post-exilic periods, but to this particular tribe of Levi.

CHAPTER VI

The Date of the D Document

A. EXTERNAL EVIDENCE

Critical scholars who believe in the Development Hypothesis, and several scholars of the old school, agree that the Book of Deuteronomy was the law-book found in the eighteenth year of Josiah, 622–621 B. C.   It is a part of the Critical Hypothesis that the D document is older than the P document.   And all internal evidence seems to point that way.[1]   In regard to the date for D just given, however, we must remember that the Bible states, not that D was then composed, but merely that then the book was "found in the temple."[2]

I.   Finding of the Book of Deuteronomy

Before entering upon the question of the real date of D, let us briefly review the story of the finding of the Book of the Law of Moses in the temple in the eighteenth year of Josiah.

It seems that King Josiah had ordered some repairs of the temple to be carried out under the direction of Hilkiah, the high-priest.   One day the king sent his scribe, Shaphan with an order to Hilkiah to count the money that had been taken in at the doors of the temple, and to pay it over to the workmen, namely, the carpenters, builders, and masons, and to buy, too, timbers and hewn stones with

---

[1] In religion, institutions, etc., but not necessarily in language.   The Toledoth Book, however, is seemingly as old as D.

[2] II Kings 22:8.

which to repair the breaches of the temple. It would seem, therefore, that the repairs were already under way. Certainly, the workmen had to be paid. When Shaphan came to the temple, Hilkiah informed him in the following words, "I have found the Book of the Law in the house of God."[1] Hilkiah then gave the book to Shaphan and he read it. On his return to the palace, Shaphan told the king of his discovery, and read the book before him. When the king had heard the words of the book, he rent his clothes, and ordered Hilkiah and Shaphan and two other men to go and inquire from Yahweh in regard to the contents of the book. These men went to the prophetess Hulda and communed with her. She answered and told them, "Thus says Yahweh, Behold I will bring evil upon this place, and upon the inhabitants thereof, even all the words of the book which the king of Judah has read: because they have forsaken me, and have burned incense unto other gods, that they might provoke me to anger with all the work of their hands."[2] When the king heard the answer from the prophetess, he gathered the elders of Judah and of Jerusalem to the temple and read there in their ears, "all the words of the Book of the Covenant, which was found in the house of Yahweh."[3] The Book of Kings then continues, saying, "And like unto him there was no king before him that turned to Yahweh, with all his heart, and with all his soul, and with all his might, according to all the Law of Moses."[4]

This book, thus found, is referred to as the *Book of the Covenant*[5] and the *Law of Moses*. In the reforms by

[1] II Kings 22: 8.

[2] II Kings 22:16, 17.

[3] II Kings 23:2.

[4] II Kings 23:25.

[5] So called because it contained the "Ten Words," or Decalogue (Deut., chap. 5.)

him undertaken it is fair to assume that Josiah was guided by the Book of Deuteronomy, for there are specific refer ences in this book on which he could have based his reforms.

II. Reforms of Josiah

a) Josiah destroyed all the vessels made for the worship of the host of Heaven.[1] The law forbidding this worship is found in Deut. 17:3.

b) He destroyed the Asherah in the house of Yahweh.[2] The law on Asherah worship is found in Deut. 16:21, 22.

c) Josiah broke down the house of devotees.[3] The law on devotees is found in Deut. 23:17.

Attention has often been drawn by the critical scholars to the fact that Josiah destroyed the "high-places" of Judah.[4] Now it is true that Deut., chap. 12, forbids idolatry, but, to be precise, we must observe that in this chapter the word "high-place" does not occur. Nor does it occur in any other place in Deuteronomy. As we stated above, the law on high-places is in Leviticus.

It has also been emphasized by modern critics that Josiah refers to the "abominations" of Judah,[5] and that this is peculiarly a Deuteronomic expression. They have thereby attempted to show that Deuteronomy exclusively was the basis of the reform of Josiah. Now it is true that the word "abomination" occurs some eighteen times in Deuteronomy, and some sixteen times in the original code of Deuteronomy, but it must not be forgotten that the P code in Leviticus uses the same term not less than six times. The term is not, therefore, exclusively the property of Deuteronomy. It is impossible to base any argument on this term.

[1] II Kings 23:4. [3] II Kings 23:7. [5] II Kings 23:24.
[2] II Kings 23:6. [4] II Kings 23:8.

As a matter of fact, as we have already seen, Josiah's reforms were based, in the greater number of cases, on laws found, not in D, but in P. Nevertheless, the fact remains that in certain of his reforms he enforced laws found solely in Deuteronomy. From this we must conclude that D is at least as old as his time.

III. D Not Written in Time of Josiah

But modern critics go farther than this and assume that the book was *written* at this time, or, at the earliest, in the time of Manasseh, or, possibly, Hezekiah. But there is no reason to believe that such a book should have been composed in the times of the idolatrous Manasseh. It is equally improbable that it was composed in the time of Hezekiah. For why should a man go to the trouble to write a book, only to lay it away in a corner of the temple where perhaps it might by chance be found, a century after it was written? There remains, then, to be considered, the hypothesis that it was composed in the time of Josiah, at the time of its supposed discovery.

There is not a single statement in the Bible that can be used as the basis for such a belief. Indeed, such a hypothesis is at complete variance with the facts as there set forth, unless we are to suppose that Hilkiah or some of his friends deliberately forged the book, and that this fact was completely unknown, indeed unsuspected, both by the king and by the author of the Book of Kings.

It is true that we are told by many critics that for a man to write a book himself, and then to claim that it was written by an ancient author, somewhat in the fashion of the author of the *Book of Mormon*, would not have been considered dishonorable in those days, as it is in ours. But those who advance these views have yet to adduce an instance from the records of ancient times of such an imposture being perpetrated and the action being justified. The assumption has originated solely in their imaginations. It is absurd to claim that the author of Deuteronomy, that book of highly exalted moral claims, could have lent himself to such dishonesty.

Furthermore, is it not remarkable that King Josiah, the scribe Shaphan, and the prophetess Hulda could all of them have been so completely deceived as to believe and claim that this was in very truth the Law of Moses, which the predecessors of the king had disobeyed? It is impossible to believe that such a book would have been accepted without the most severe scrutiny by both the civil and the ecclesiastical authorities. And yet they all pronounced it a genuine discovery of an older law. The imposture hypothesis is in the highest degree improbable, when examined with the usual care used in historical investigation.

B. INTERNAL EVIDENCE

I. D and Josiah's Reform

In the conclusion just reached, that the D code was not written in Josiah's time, we are supported by the internal evidence. For if it had been, there would have been contained in it laws designed to fit the conditions prevalent in that time. This is not the case in at least the following instances:

a) Josiah deposed the idolatrous priests known by the name of *Chemarim*.[1] These priests were known as early

[1] II Kings 23:5.

as the days of Hosea,[1] and had been ordained by the kings of Judah. But Deuteronomy does not know of the existence of any such- sort of priests, although it takes great pains to enumerate different kinds of idolatrous priests.

b) Josiah drove out the women that wove hangings for Asherah.[2] But Deuteronomy does not know of the existence of any such women.

c) Josiah broke down the high-places of the satyrs.[3] But Deuteronomy has no law on satyr-worship. P, as we have seen, is the only code which mentions it.[4]

d) Josiah permitted the priests of the high-places of Judah to get their portion of unleavened bread from the temple in Jerusalem.[5] The law on this, too, is found, not in D, but only in P.[6]

e) Josiah forbade Molech-worship.[7] Deuteronomy does not mention Molech once, although it forbids passing children through the fire.[8] It is the P code which mentions Molech and forbids his worship.[9]

f) Josiah took away the horses of the Sun, which the kings of Judah had given.[10] Deuteronomy has no law on the subject.

g) The high-places near by Jerusalem, dedicated by Solomon to Ashtoreth, Chemosh, and Milcom, were destroyed by Josiah.[11] These gods are not mentioned in Deuteronomy.

h) Josiah destroyed the high-place at Bethel, built by

[1] II Kings 10:5. Cf. Zeph. 1:4.   [2] II Kings 23:7.

[3] II Kings 23:8, where we should read "satyrs" instead of "gates." The change involves only a slight alteration in punctuating the Massoretic text.

[4] Lev. 17:7.   [7] II Kings 23:10.   [10] II Kings 23:11.

[5] II Kings 23:9.   [8] Deut. 18:10.   [11] II Kings 23:13.

[6] Lev. 6:14 ff.   [9] Lev. 18:21; 20:2 ff.

Jeroboam I.[1] As we have seen, Deuteronomy has no law on high-places. ·

i) Josiah defiled the sepulchres at Bethel, where the Northern Kingdom had offered ancestor worship at the gravestones.[2] Deuteronomy does not prohibit or even mention ancestor worship. ¯

j) Josiah forbade the Teraphim worship.[3] Deuteronomy knows nothing of Teraphim.

II. D ̱and the Age of Josiah

Furthermore, Deuteronomy does contain laws which could not have applied to the time of Josiah, laws of which he took absolutely no notice.

a) There is in Deuteronomy an injunction to destroy Canaanites[4] and Amalekites.[5] But neither of these nations existed in the time of Josiah, nor had they existed for three hundred years before him.

b) Deuteronomy has precise rules for military service,[6] for besieging foreign cities,[7] and for the arrangement of the camp,[8] all of them utterly unsuitable for the time of Josiah.

c) Deuteronomy warns the Israelites against choosing a foreigner for their king.[9] This would be, to say the least, needless, when the house of David, to which Josiah belonged, had reigned almost four hundred years.

d) Deuteronomy cultivates a warm friendship for Esau.[10] It does not mention Edom[11] once. Now Edom

[1] II Kings 23:15.
[2] II Kings 23:16–20.
[3] II Kings 23:24.
[4] Deut. 7:1, 2; 20:17, 18.
[5] Deut. 25:17–19.
[6] Deut. 20:1–9.
[7] Deut. 20:9–15, 19, 20.
[8] Deut. 23:10–14.
[9] Deut. 17:15, 16.
[10] Deut. 2:2–8.
[11] It mentions " Edomite " once (23:7), which shows that the Edomites were then entering Mount Seir, but had not yet dispossessed Esau of his land.

had driven away Esau long before Josiah's time. In his time the prophet Jeremiah[1] denounces Edom, as do Obadiah, Joel,[2] and Isaiah.[3] And even if, as some suppose, Edom and Esau are to be considered as two names for one people, there was not a people more hated in Judah in Josiah's time than were the Edomites.

e) Deuteronomy enjoins the Israelites to destroy the Anakim.[4] Joshua and Caleb really destroyed them.[5] They are not known to have existed from that time onward. On the contrary Deuteronomy does not once mention the Philistines, who for 450 years before Josiah had been harassing the Israelites and who were still a thorn in their side.

In these first two sections of the internal evidence we have seen that Deuteronomy agrees neither in what it does contain nor in what it does not contain with the conditions prevalent in the time of Josiah. As the book could not have been written later than his time, we must look farther back to discover its origin.

III.   D and Early History of Israel

Some conservative modern critics concede that the institutions and the laws contained in our Deuteronomy may have existed for some time before the age of Josiah, but they maintain that these laws were not codified until his time. We can find strong evidence, however, to the contrary.

a) In II Kings 14:6 we read, "But the children of the murderers he (Amaziah) put not to death: according to that which is written in the Book of the Law of Moses, as

---

[1] Jer. 49:8.
[2] Joel 3:19.
[3] Isa. 63:1-6.

[4] Deut. 1:28; (2:10, 11, 21; 9:2.)
[5] Josh. 11:21, 22; 14:12-15.

Yahweh commanded, saying, The fathers shall not be put to death for the children, nor the children be put to death for the fathers; but every man shall die for his own sin." The last part of this passage is an exact quotation from Deuteronomy.[1] The passage has been explained as a late addition to the Book of Kings by the Deuteronomic editor. But the fact remains that Amaziah did not put the children of the murderers to death, which was contrary to the usual procedure in those times. He must, therefore have had a law which restrained him. All traditions would have encouraged him to kill them. Furthermore the editor of Kings claims that Amaziah followed the written law of the Book of Moses. If such a book did not exist in the time of Amaziah, our author of Kings has told a plain untruth. That he has done so remains to be proved. The author of Kings refers again and again to a number of books or documents which he used in compiling his history of the kings of Judah and Israel. No one has as yet been able to show that he falsified his material. What errors there are seem to have been in his sources. Nor has it been shown that these source-documents were non-existent. Fair-minded scholarship accepts their existence in his time, and acknowledges that he made use of them. Now this Book of the Law of Moses was really one of these documents, and we have no reason to doubt that the author is correct here, as in other places, in his statement of the source of his quotation.

The authenticity of this passage is made still more plain, however, when we compare it with the Book of Chronicles. We know that the source used by the author of the Book of Kings for the reign of Amaziah was a book called, *The*

[1] Deut. 24:16.

Chronicles of the Kings of Judah.[1]   The Book of Chronicles
for this same period uses another authority, namely, *The
Book of the Kings of Judah and Israel.*[2]   Yet the statement
in Chronicles[3] is identical with that quoted from Kings,
and here again there is the reference to the law in the Book
of Moses.   Critics are agreed in saying that the editor
of Chronicles neither had Deuteronomic tendencies nor
used Deuteronomic materials.   We have, then, in Chronicles, true corroboration of Kings in the statement that
Amaziah refrained from killing the children of the murderers because of a written law, a law which we know to
be contained only in Deuteronomic legislation.

b) In I Kings, chap. 8, we have the prayer which Solomon offered at the consecration of the temple.   It not
only breathes the spirit of Deuteronomy through and
through, but its very phraseology from verse to verse is
that of Deuteronomy.   Compare the characteristic phrases
in the following, for example:

I Kings	8:24	and Deut.	8:18; 10:15
	8:23	"	4:39
	8:25	"	chap. 15
	8:27	"	10:14
	8:32	"	25:1
	8:33	"	28:25
	8:35	"	11:17
	8:37	"	28:22,38
	8:37	"	28:52
	8:40	"	12:1; 31:13

---

[1] II Kings 14:18.

[2] Of course the Chronicles referred to in II Kings 14:18 is not our Book of
Chronicles, nor is the Book of Kings referred to in Chronicles our book of
that name.   Both references are to earlier documents used by the authors.   See
II Chron. 25:26.

[3] II Chron. 25:4.

I Kings 8:41 and Deut. 29:21
   8:42 "   11:2
   8:43 "   28:10
   8:44 "   21:10; 20:1
   8:46 "   7:2, 23; 23:14
   8:47 "   30:1
   8:48 "   30:2

Modern critics assume, of course, that the Deuteronomic author of our Kings modeled this beautiful prayer as he wished, according to the tenets of the Deuteronomic code, and that it is not at all the one which Solomon really offered. Of course Solomon must have offered some prayer at the consecration of the temple. Again the charge brought against the author of Kings is one of falsifying records. But in this case, as in the one just discussed, the fallacy of such a charge becomes apparent when we compare the record of the event contained in Chronicles. In II Chron., chap. 6, the same prayer is given as is contained in I Kings, chap. 8, exactly the same, not only in thought, but even in mode of expression.[1] Again, we must emphasize the fact that the author of Chronicles is not accused of having had Deuteronomic leanings. Now the author of Kings gives as his authority in compiling his history of Solomon, *The Book of the Acts of Solomon.*[2] The author of Chronicles gives as his authorities for the same period the following: *The History of Nathan the Prophet, The Prophecy of Ahijah the Shilonite,* and *The Visions of Iddo the Seer.*[3] If then from his source the author of Kings derived a prayer of Solomon

---

[1] There are a few unimportant differences, such as the omission of an "and" or of an article, but there are none which would not be natural between two copies made by different hands from one and the same original.

[2] I Kings 11:41.   [3] II Chron. 9:29.

exactly the same, even in language, as that derived by the editor of Chronicles from his three quite different sources, it seems indisputable that this prayer given by both is the product of neither, but that it is derived from contemporary records made at the time the prayer was delivered—in other words, that it is actually the prayer which Solomon offered.

But there are some critics who maintain that this prayer was merely the product of certain Deuteronomic tendencies or traditions which were indeed current in Solomon's time, but which were not written down until the time of Josiah. How, though, can those who hold this view explain the fact that this prayer of Solomon exhibits not only the thought, but also the language, of that written Deuteronomy which we know?

Back in Solomon's time, then, the code of Deuteronomy certainly seems to have been extant, and that in a written, definite form.

IV. " Law of Moses "

We have already noticed that in II Kings 23: 25 there is a reference to the *Law of Moses*. We found, as indeed is admitted by everyone, that the phrase there referred to Deuteronomy, which was supposed to have been found in the temple just at that time. Again, in both Kings and Chronicles we found that Amaziah's sparing of the children of the murderers was due to a law contained in the *Book of the Law of Moses*. And in this case, too, we found that the reference was to Deuteronomy. These facts point to a belief that the *Book of the Law of Moses* was the technical term for Deuteronomy. Let us see what other references there are which point the same way.

First, in the Book of Deuteronomy itself,[1] we read, "Beyond Jordan, in the land of Moab, began Moses to declare this law," and again,[2] "And this is the law which Moses set before the children of Israel; these are the testimonies and the statutes and the judgments which Moses spake unto the children of Israel, when they came forth out of Egypt, beyond Jordan, in the valley over against Beth-Peor." These words are taken from the introduction to the code. In chap. 28, which is the conclusion of the code and an inseparable part of the same, we read,[3] "If thou wilt not observe to do all the words of this law, *that are written in this book*," and again,[4] "Also every sickness, and every plague, which is not *written in the book of this law*, them will Yahweh bring upon thee until thou be destroyed." Here, then, Moses asserts that he himself has written this book, for as the introduction tells us, all these are the words which Moses purports to speak.

Chaps. 29–31 are not a portion of the original D code, but are contemporary with it, and may possibly be supposed to have been written by Joshua. Here we read,[5] "These are the words of the covenant which Yahweh commanded Moses to make with the children of Israel, in the land of Moab, besides the covenant which he made with them in Horeb." The author then continues, and says,[6] "And Moses wrote this law and delivered it unto the priests, the sons of Levi, which bare the Ark of the Covenant of Yahweh, and unto all the elders of Israel." And again,[7] "And it came to pass, when Moses had made

---

[1] Deut. 1:5.
[2] Deut. 4:44.
[3] Deut. 28:58.
[4] Deut. 28:61.
[5] Deut. 29:1.
[6] Deut. 31:9.
[7] Deut. 31:24–26.

an end of writing the words of this law in a book, until they were finished, that Moses commanded the Levites, which bare the Ark of the Covenant of Yahweh, saying, Take this book of the law, and put it by the side of the Covenant of Yahweh your God, that it may be there for a witness against thee." We can easily see how, from these passages in Deuteronomy, the name *Law of Moses*, might easily and naturally come into use as the title of the work. This is especially true when we consider that in no other code is Moses put forward as the author of the law-book. In other codes we are told either that Yahweh himself wrote the laws, or that Moses proclaimed them in Yahweh's name. But in D we are specifically informed that Moses himself wrote and promulgated them. What more natural, therefore, than that the technical term, *Law of Moses*, should have been applied to the D code, just as we found *Law of Yahweh* to be the technical term for the P code?

But by further references this assumption can almost certainly be proved.

a) In Josh. 1:7, 8, we are told that Yahweh committed to Joshua the charge of being the successor of Moses with the words, "Only be strong, and very courageous, to observe to do according to all the law which Moses, my servant, commanded thee: turn not from it to the right hand or to the left, that thou mayest deal wisely whithersoever thou goest. This book of the law shall not depart out of thy mouth, but thou shalt meditate therein day and night, that thou mayest observe to do according to all that is written therein." Here we find that Joshua received in charge a written book, called the *Book of the Law*, of which Moses, not Yahweh, is given as the author.

b) When Joshua had finished the subjection of the eastern part of the land, he gathered the tribes of Israel to Mount Ebal and there[1] "Joshua built an altar unto Yahweh, the God of Israel, in Mount Ebal, as Moses the servant of Yahweh commanded the children of Israel, as it is written in the *Book of the Law of Moses*, an altar of unhewn stones, upon which no man had lifted up any iron: and they offered thereon burnt-offerings unto Yahweh, and sacrificed peace-offerings. And he wrote there upon the stones a copy of the *Law of Moses*, which he wrote in the presence of the children of Israel." The law mentioned as being written in the *Book of the Law of Moses* is found exclusively in Deut. 27:5-8, where we read that Moses said, "And there shalt thou build an altar unto Yahweh thy God, an altar of stones: thou shalt lift up no iron upon them. Thou shalt build the altar of Yahweh thy God of unhewn stone; and thou shalt offer burnt-offerings thereon unto Yahweh thy God, and thou shalt sacrifice peace-offerings, and shalt eat there; and thou shalt rejoice before Yahweh thy God. And thou shalt write upon the stones all the words of this law very plainly." Here we have then a reference to the *Book of the Law of Moses* which plainly is a reference to the Deuteronomic legislation.[2]

c) When Joshua bade farewell to his people, he said,[3]

[1] Josh. 8:30-32.

[2] Some critics are inclined to regard Deut., chap. 27, on which this passage in Joshua is so evidently based, as not an integral part of the D code. The objection is based mainly on the blessings and cursings contained in it. But this is a mistaken notion, for the Code of Hammurabi has shown us that blessings and curses were an integral part of ancient codes, as a proper affirmation of their tenets. The blessings and curses in this chapter in Deuteronomy are a necessary part of the conclusion of the D code, just as the threats in Leviticus (chap. 26) belong to the conclusion of the P code.

[3] Josh. 23:6.

"Therefore be very courageous to keep and to do all that is written in the *Book of the Law of Moses*, that ye turn not aside therefrom to the right hand or to the left." Although there is nothing in this passage to point out what book it is that is known by this name, the similarity in phraseology between this and the passage from Joshua just cited above makes the assumption justifiable that what is referred to here is the same as that referred to in other parts of Joshua, i. e., the D document.

d) The dying David charged his son, Solomon, saying,[1] "Be thou strong, therefore, and show thyself a man; and keep the charge of Yahweh thy God to walk in his ways, to keep his statutes, his commandments, and his judgments, and his testimonies, according to that which is written in the *Law of Moses*, that thou mayest deal wisely in all that thou doest, and whithersoever thou turnest thyself." The tone of this passage is decidedly Deuteronomic, and resembles closely our quotation above from Joshua 1:7. It is worth remarking that the prayer which Solomon made when he came to dedicate his temple was, as we have seen, entirely Deuteronomic. David, then, knew of a written *Law of Moses*, and when he spoke of it used definitely Deuteronomic language.

e) In II Chron. 23:18 we have another reference to the *Law of Moses*. "And Jehoiada appointed the offices of the house of Yahweh under the hand of *the priests the Levites*, whom David had distributed in the house of Yahweh, to offer the burnt-offerings of Yahweh, as it is written in the *Law of Moses*, with rejoicing and with singing, according to the order of David." The expression, "the priests the Levites" is Deuteronomic, and not priestly

[1] I Kings 2:2*b*, 3.

as we might naturally expect in Chronicles, the product of the priestly school. And these priests the Levites are definitely said to be fulfilling their functions "as it is written in the *Law of Moses*." The identification of Deuteronomy with the *Law of Moses* seems to be plain here, too, in the reign of Joash, at the time when he became king, 837 B. C.

f) Something similar seems to be implied in II Chron. 30:16, where, at the great Passover of Hezekiah, the order of the priests is again referred to as being "according to the *Law of Moses*." The "order" refers, of course, to the arrangement made by David, who divided the priests into classes when he established his worship of Yahweh, a worship which, as we have seen above, seems to have been on a Deuteronomic basis, or at least worship around "the Ark of the Covenant," an ark which, as will be fully shown later, belonged to the D code.

g) Further references to the *Law of Moses* are to be found in II Kings 21:8 (the time of Manasseh), Ezra 3:2; 7:6, Nehemiah 8:1; 9:14, Daniel 9:11, 13. Malachi admonishes the people, "Remember ye the *Law of Moses* my servant, which I commanded unto him in Horeb for all Israel, even statutes and judgments."[1] A law referred to Horeb would at first glance seem to be E, but the term "statutes and judgments" must refer to D.[2] As late as the time of Malachi, therefore, the term *Law of Moses* seems to refer to Deuteronomy.

We have thus seen that probably in the time of Malachi, and certainly in the times of Josiah, Amaziah, Joash (Jehoiada), Solomon, David, and Joshua, that is to say, in every reference to the *Law of Moses* where anything

---

[1] Mal. 4:4.

[2] Deut., chap. 5–11, refers exclusively to the legislation at Horeb and the events between Horeb and Moab.

at all is implied as to what is meant, there is implied that the law which we call the D code is meant. It seems in the highest degree probable that such a book did exist from the time of Joshua down. And if it existed this early, as the evidence persuades us to admit, there is no reason to doubt that Moses wrote the D code at the cove nant in the land of Moab, just as Deuteronomy itself asserts.

In concluding this section in regard to the *Law of Moses* just one other fact needs to be observed. The D code ordains,[1] "And it shall be, when he [the king] sitteth upon the throne of his kingdom, that he shall write him a copy of this law in a book, out of that which is before the priests the Levites: and it shall be with him, and he shall read in it all the days of his life, that he may learn to fear Yahweh his God, to keep all the words of this law, and these statutes, to do them." This explicit order to write a copy of the law in a book implies that the law existed in codified form, for a *copy* could not be made of mere traditions. If we now turn to the historical books, we find that this law was strictly obeyed when Israel came to choose a king. As soon as Saul was chosen, and Samuel had consecrated him, Samuel told the people God's ordinance for the kingdom, and wrote it down in a book, which was laid up before Yahweh.[2]

V. D and the Central Sanctuary

Against all these facts which seem to argue for an early date for D, critics advance the plea that D must be late

[1] Deut. 17:18, 19.

[2] I Sam. 10:25. Instead of saying with Dr. Driver (*LOT*, p. 87f.), that the Law of the Kingdom (Deut. 17:14 ff.) is colored by reminiscences of the monarchy of Solomon, it is equally possible to say that the monarchy of Solomon reflects the Law in Deuteronomy.

because it is the only code which teaches "a central sanc-tuary," by which phrase they mean "a single sanctuary." The argument is that since up to the time of Josiah there were many sanctuaries, and it was he who abolished them all save the one at Jerusalem, D could not have been in effect before his time. This argument is based upon the substitution in the minds of the critics of "Jerusalem" for the phrase in Deuteronomy," the place for the dwelling of my name." This argument seems at first glance very plausible, but it is not nearly so strong when examined carefully.

First of all we must observe that not in one single instance does Deuteronomy mention Jerusalem, and the implication that it means Jerusalem is a reading into the Bible of a personal opinion merely. It does speak, again and again, about the place which Yahweh shall choose for causing his name to dwell in. But that place may be anywhere. And, as we know, it was moved about to different places up to the time of David. In the time of the Judges the principal sanctuary certainly moved about from place to place. Yahweh's oracle to Nathan the prophet clearly shows that this was the case.[1]

Furthermore, *Deuteronomy does not prohibit other sanctuaries*. This statement may appear startling, but it is, nevertheless, true. It ordains that there shall be only one place for *his name to dwell*, and that is all. And this phrase is a technical term for Yahweh's presence at the central sanctuary. It does not prohibit other places and altars for "sacrifices," so long as those sacrifices are made to Yahweh. Deuteronomy may be searched from one end to the other without finding a single prohibition,

[1] I Chron. 17:2–6; II Sam. 7:5–7.

denunciation, or even reproof of altars of this sort. On the contrary, Deuteronomy, in the code itself,[1] orders the people to go to Ebal and ratify the covenant made in Horeb and Moab. And in Joshua we read that Joshua carried out this command by building an altar to Yahweh and sacrificing thereon, and writing the law of Deuteronomy upon twelve stones placed around the altar. Thus we see that D deliberately ordained at least one altar of sacrifice apart from Jerusalem or the ark.

The twelfth is the great chapter in Deuteronomy forbidding idolatry, and it is on this chapter chiefly that critics base their contention about the "single central sanctuary of the D code." But in this very chapter, in vss. 15 and 21 we find permission given for the killing of animals outside the sanctuary. At first glance it might appear that this killing was just ordinary slaughtering. But the Hebrew word here is *zabach*, which never has meant, and never can mean, anything else but a sacrifice. The Revisers have thus made themselves liable to the charge either of wilful misrepresentation or of almost unpardonable ignorance in translating this word with "kill" merely, because in both these verses we are dealing with sacrifices and sacrificing. Thus we see that, even in the very passage most cited against other altars than that of Jerusalem, Deuteronomy permits sacrificing to Yahweh at any and every place in which his people see fit to do it.

VI. D and the Priests the Levites

It is further objected by critics that a date as early as we have postulated for D is impossible because in the early history of Israel anybody was permitted to offer sacrifice, while the D code confines the sacrificing to the priests

[1] Deut. 11:29; 27:4–13.

the Levites. Of course it is true that D prescribes a Levitical priesthood, that it includes as priests the sons of Levi,[1] and that these sons of Levi are to be identified with the whole tribe of Levi.[2] But here again critics have been reading into the Bible something which it does not contain. *Deuteronomy nowhere confines the right to sacrifice to members of the tribe of Levi.* All that Deuteronomy does insist upon is that the Levites shall serve at that sanctuary where the Ark of the Covenant is, or, to use the technical term, "the place where Yahweh's name is dwelling."[3]

VII. Finding of the D Document

We have seen that there is every reason for believing, and none for disbelieving, that the D document originated at a very early date, and that the document was known right down through Hebrew history, at least down to the time of Hezekiah. What then was meant by the statement that the book was "found" in the temple in the eighteenth year of Josiah? The word for "find," *maza*, points to a discovery, not by any means to an invention. The book seemingly had been unknown to Josiah up to the time of its discovery. Shaphan, Hilkiah, and Hulda, seem all of them to have been equally surprised when they saw it. And indeed we cannot expect that it should have been otherwise. The historical books show no trace of it since the time of Hezekiah, nearly a century before. Now it will be remembered that, when we were discussing the P code, we noticed that in the time of Jehoshaphat, 873 B. C., the Levites went through the cities of Judah on

[1] Deut. 21:5; 31:9.   [2] Deut. 18:1.

[3] For the distinction between the D term, "the priests the Levites," and the P term, "the priests and Levites," see below, p. 195.

missionary work to teach the *Law of Yahweh*, i. e., the P code. May we not see in this an organized effort on the part of the Aaronic or P priesthood to undermine the D code in favor of that more particularly its own? If this be so, it is not hard to imagine a gradual decrease in influence on the part of the D code, until, some time in the reign of the idolatrous Manasseh, *ca.* 685 B. C., it sank entirely into disuse and finally disappeared from the common knowledge of the people.

At the same time we should expect that there would be a copy of this important law in the oracle place of the temple. Here only the high-priest could enter, and that only once in each year, with the blood that was to be sprinkled on the ark. This oracle place was completely dark. The high-priest could see nothing inside it, nor could he touch anything there. We have noticed above that in D itself there is an order that a copy of it be laid up before Yahweh, at the side of the Ark. This copy might very well, then, be in the oracle place in Josiah's time, and have been there since Solomon built the temple. For we have no good reason to doubt that Solomon complied with the law and placed the copy there as it required. It may have been quietly resting there those 340 years, while the people, and even the high-priest himself, may have been in these later times utterly ignorant of its existence.

Now, there were masons, carpenters, and builders making extensive repairs of the breaches of the temple. It is not too much to assume that these repairs extended to the oracle place. We are told, indeed, that the repairs were to breaches in "the house," i. e., in the temple building proper, consisting of the holy place and the oracle place. Since we have no reason to assume that the repairs extended over the two-thirds of the house devoted to the holy place but not to the other third, the oracle place, we have indeed every reason to assume that the repairs did extend to the latter. It is only natural that while this work was going on the book should have been found and turned over to the high-priest.

Naville has lately suggested that the book may have been found by the workmen under the walls of the temple.[1] He calls attention to the fact that in several temples of Egypt deposition documents have been found which had been placed there when the temples were built. When such temples were repaired, these documents were taken out, augmented with additions regarding the repairs, and then laid back in their places in the foundations. He suggests that Deuteronomy may have been found in this manner.

Professor Grimme, using Naville's suggestion as a basis, believes that there is a statement in the code itself to that effect. His view seems very plausible.[2] It is not necessary that the book should have been laid in the wall or in the cornerstone, however. His argument applies equally well if it had been hidden away in the oracle place. The passage which Grimme cites reads, "That which was hidden away unto Yahweh our God and which has been revealed to us and to our children forever, that we may do all the works of this law."[3]

The D code proper ends with the twenty-eighth chapter. The next chapter is doubtless a later addition. Whether it was made by Joshua or by some other person is hard to

[1] *PSBA*, Vol. XXIX, pp. 232–42.
[2] *OLZ*, 1907, pp. 610–15; 1908, pp. 188–93.
[3] Deut. 29:29.

decide. But in thought and language it corresponds very closely with the code itself. It was probably there when the book was discovered in Josiah's time. This verse which Grimme notes may then have been added at the time the book was discovered.[1]

VIII. Conclusion

All these facts in relation to the finding of the document only go to corroborate what we have concluded from the rest of the evidence, both internal and external. The early date which we have determined, namely, at least as early as the time of Joshua, seems not only plausible, but extremely probable.

---

[1] The contents of the verse seem to point to this meaning rather than to the rather pointless one of the R. V. translation, "The secret things belong unto the Lord our God: but the things which are revealed belong to us and to our children forever, that we may do all the works of this law." This passage, thus translated, shows no logical connection either with the preceding or with the following chapters.

CHAPTER VII

The Date of the E Document

I.   The E Code Precedes D

Almost all modern critics admit that the E document precedes the D document in date.   Indeed, it is a part of the Critical Hypothesis that this should be so, for the laws and institutions of the E code seem, at first glance, to belong to quite a primitive state of society, and to be both fewer in number and less minute than those of D.   The argument is well taken.   E is older than D.   Now we found above that D is to be dated from the legislation in Moab.   The Bible asserts that the E code was given forty years before that, at Horeb.   May this statement be accepted?

It may be objected that this time is too short to allow for a change in culture so great as that shown by a comparison of the two codes.   But two answers may be advanced to meet this objection:

a) First, it is not certain that we have the whole E code in our Hexateuch today.[1]   Further, the ʃ code, if there be one, claims to belong to the same time and occasion, but it is only one-sixth the length of the E code as it now stands.   We cannot therefore certainly say that the E code as it was originally was either much shorter or much simpler than the D code.

b) Second, even under the Critical Hypothesis there is assumed only a little more than a century between these two codes.   If such a change could have taken place in

[1] In Exod., chaps. 21–23.

so short a time in the later monarchy, with its settled state
of society, how much easier would have been such a change
and how much quicker, in the years between the legislations of Horeb and Moab, during which time we have
the graphic story of not less than four rebellions, numerous
trials, and the unparalleled training of a stubborn and
stiff-necked people.

When we have admitted, then, that our date for E
depends upon our date for D, it might seem as if there
were nothing further to say on the date of this document
and code. But there are some few points that need to
be touched on.

II. " Law of Elohim "

We have already seen that the Bible has technical
terms for the D and P codes. We have observed that the
Law of Yahweh meant P, and that the *Law of Moses*
meant D. Similarly, we might expect that the E code also
would have a technical term to denote it. Is this the case?

Modern critics claim that the E code had its origin in
the Northern Kingdom. And whether or not it arose
there, there can be little doubt that that was where it was
more particularly in force. Now Hosea was a prophet
to the Northern Kingdom, and when he reproved the
people of Samaria he did it in the following language:
" My people are destroyed for lack of knowledge; because
thou hast rejected knowledge, I will also reject thee, that
thou shalt be no priest to me; seeing that thou hast forgotten the *Law of thy God* [*Elohim*], I also will forget thy
children."[1] Here we have a reference to a *Law of God*
or *Elohim*. This law must have been one known to the
people, else Hosea could not very well have cited it in

[1] Hos. 4:6.

rebuking them. Now the E document contains a code which might very well have been in operation in Samaria, with its low ideas of Yahweh. At this time it seems that even the simple laws of the code which had been in effect were set aside for idolatrous practices. The prophet therefore rebuked the people for having no knowledge, i. e., of Yahweh as presented in this simple code, because they had "forgotten the *Law of Elohim*."

In Joshua we read,[1] "And Joshua wrote these words in the *Book of the Law of Elohim;* and he took a great stone, and set it up there under the oak that was by the sanctuary of Yahweh. And Joshua said unto all the people, Behold this stone shall be a witness against us; for it has heard all the words of Yahweh, which He spake unto us: it shall be therefore a witness against you, lest ye deny your God." The words referred to were the parting address of Joshua to Israel by the sanctuary of Shiloh,[2] where Joshua and the people made a covenant with Yahweh, that they should be his people and worship him only. When the people had agreed to this, Joshua informed them that he would write their words and answers in the *Law of Elohim*, to be a witness against them forever. There was, then, a *Law of Elohim* in existence at this time, and it must have been in codified form, capable of receiving an addition, else Joshua could not have added *in writing* the covenant agreement.

III. The Book of the Covenant

We have now seen that there was probably a *Law of Elohim*, known in the time of Joshua at the time when he made the covenant at Shiloh, and that this law was in

---

[1] Josh. 24:26, 27.　　　　　[2] See p. 132.

written form and so capable of receiving written additions. We will now see that at least a portion of the code was in written form before the covenant at Shiloh.

In Exod. 24:7 we have a reference to the *Book of the Covenant:* "And he took the *Book of the Covenant*, and read in the audience of the people: and they said, All that Yahweh has spoken will we do, and be obedient." It is to be noted that this document is a *book*, and therefore in written form. Let us now inquire what this *Book of the Covenant* contained.

Modern critics agree that the *Book of the Covenant* contained Exod. 21:1—23:19, i. e., the judgments at Horeb. This they call the *Greater Book of the Covenant*, while Exod. 34:13–26 they call the *Lesser Book of the Covenant*. This is a reading into the Bible which cannot be admitted. The laws in Exod., chap. 34, are not, and never have been, a part of the *Book of the Covenant*. We have only one *Book of the Covenant*. In order to determine just what was its original extent, let us review briefly the history of the theophanies at Horeb.

In Exod. 19:3 we are told that Moses went up unto God, and that Yahweh called to him out of the mountain. We find afterward that this mountain is Mount Horeb. God at this time commanded Moses to speak to the children of Israel, and remind them how he had brought them out of Egypt, and promised that if they would keep his commandments the kingdom of Israel should become a kingdom of priests and a holy nation. The covenant mentioned[1] is, of course, the covenant which Yahweh is about to establish with the people. Moses then came down from the mountain, called for the elders of the people

[1] Exod. 19:5.

and set before them the words of Yahweh, i. e., that he intended to make a covenant with them. The people answered that all that Yahweh had said they would do. Moses then returned to the mountain and reported the words of the people to Yahweh.[1]

Yahweh then informed Moses that he was going to appear in a thick cloud, and himself speak to the people. He therefore ordered Moses down from the mountain to sanctify the people, that they might be ready by the third day, on which Yahweh was going to speak from the mount. On the third day Yahweh appeared on the mountain, and called Moses up to him. There he gave instructions that bounds should be set around the mountain so that the people should not come near it. Moses objected, because he had already taken these precautions, but Yahweh ordered him down just the same, telling him that he and Aaron should come up afterward.[2]

When Moses had come down to the people, God spake to them *the Words*, i. e., the ten commandments contained in Exod. 20:2–17. The people heard the voice, saw the lightnings, trembled, and asked Moses that he, and not God, might speak with them, that they might not die.[3] The Ten Words or commandents, then, are represented as being, not the words of Moses, or the words of God as delivered through Moses, but the words of God himself, which he spoke with his own voice to the Israelites from Horeb.

At this request of the people, Moses went up once more into the mountain and drew near the thick darkness where God was, while the people all drew away from the mount.[4] Yahweh then spoke to Moses the words contained in

[1] Exod. 19:8.   [2] Exod. 19:24.   [3] Exod. 20:19.   [4] Exod. 20:21.

Exod. 20:22*b*–26. Then he commanded the "judgments" contained in Exod. 21:2—23:19. Yahweh then contin ued to speak to Moses, informing him how he would send an angel before them to bring them into the land of Canaan.[1] When these words had been spoken, Yahweh told Moses that he, Aaron, Nadab, Abihu, and seventy of the elders of Israel should come up to the mountain, but that only Moses should come near unto Yahweh.[2] "Moses then came down and told the people all the words of Yahweh, and all the judgments: and all the people answered with one voice, and said, All the words which Yahweh has spoken will we do. And Moses wrote all the words of Yahweh, and rose up early in the morning, and builded an altar under the mount, and twelve stones, according to the twelve tribes of Israel."[3]

"All the words of Yahweh" must include all that Yahweh had spoken to the people (Exod. 20:2–17), but not the judgments in Exod. 21:2—23:19. Having written down these things, Moses sent his officers who prepared for a sacrifice.

At this sacrifice they took half of the blood and sprinkled it upon the altar. Then Moses read the *Book of the Covenant* in the ears of the people. Again they answered, "All that Yahweh has spoken, we will do, and be obedient."[4] Thereupon Moses took the other half of the blood and sprinkled it on the people and said, "Behold the blood of the covenant which Yahweh has made with you concerning all these words."[5] The covenant at Horeb was thus marked by a sacrifice, at which the people formally accepted the *Covenant Book.*

---

[1] Exod. 23:20–33. [3] Exod. 24:3, 4. [5] Exod. 24:8.

[2] Exod. 24:1, 2. [4] Exod. 24:7.

Moses, Aaron, and the seventy elders then presented themselves unto the God of Israel on the mount, and there they beheld God, and did eat and drink.[1] The covenant sacrifice was thus continued in the very presence of God.

The *Book of the Covenant* was so called because it contained the covenant between God and the people, and this covenant is contained in the "ten words," i. e., the Decalogue. The *Book of the Covenant* is then an exact parallel to the *Tables of Covenant*, which, as we know, contained only the "ten words." The difference in name refers, then, to the different kinds of material, on which the covenant-words were recorded. Being called a "book," the covenant-words must have been written down by Moses, exactly as the Bible itself asserts.[2]

"Judgments" is a technical term for civil law. The analogy of usage at this time, as evidenced by the Code of Hammurabi in Babylonia and the Laws of Haremhab in Egypt—both of which were civil law-codes—requires us to assume that the "judgments" in Exod., chap. 21–23, must have been written and thus made accessible not only to the people, but for the judges that had been appointed a few days before.

When the covenant was thus consummated, God ordered Moses to come up into the mountain to receive tables of stone, and the law, and the commandment.[3] We have here new terms, and we have no right to assume that these new revelations have anything to do, either with the words of God to Moses, or with the "judgments." They are technical terms for various laws which Yahweh now was about to give.

[1] Exod. 24:11.   [2] Exod. 24:4.   [3] Exod. 24:12.

Moses and Joshua, his minister, then went up, as commanded, and God wrote on the tables. Moses stayed this time upon the mountain for forty days and forty nights. Suddenly Moses was ordered by God, to go down, for the people had made a calf and were worshiping it.[1] Moses and Joshua therefore descended, and when Moses found out what the people had done, in anger he broke the two tables. Moses rushed to the people, and, finding them in rebellion, he placed himself in the gate of the camp, and said, "Whoso is on Yahweh's side, unto me!"[2]

The sons of Levi immediately left the rebellious hosts, and joined him. Moses ordered them to take swords and restore order in the camp.[3] After a heavy slaughter, peace was restored. The members of the faithful tribe of Levi were ordered to consecrate themselves, and when they had been blessed Moses returned to the mountain to intercede for the people.

Yahweh was angry, but he finally acceded to Moses' request, and followed him to his tent—which is now called the Tent of Meeting—outside the camp. Yahweh ordered Moses to hew two more tables, like unto the first ones, with the promise that he would write on them the words which the first ones had contained.[4] The next morning Moses presented himself yet again on the mountain, and again stayed forty days, fasting. He pleaded that Yahweh would pardon the iniquity and the sin, and take the people for his inheritance.[5] Yahweh agreed to this, and said, "Behold, I am making a covenant: before all thy people I will do marvels, such as have not been created in all the earth, nor in any nation: and all the people among which

---

[1] Exod. 32:8.   [3] Exod. 32:27.   [5] Exod. 34:9.
[2] Exod. 32:26.   [4] Exod. 34:1.

thou art shall see the work of Yahweh, for it is a terrible thing that I do with thee. Observe that which I command thee this day: behold, I drive out before thee the Amorite, and the Canaanite, and the Hittite, and the Perizzite, and the Hivite, and the Jebusite."[1] There follows a section of commandments,[2] and then the text continues, "And Yahweh said unto Moses, Write thou these words: for after the tenor of these words I have made a covenant with thee and with Israel. And he was there with Yahweh forty days and forty nights; he did neither eat bread nor drink water. And he wrote upon the tables the words of the covenant, the Ten Words."[3]

We thus see that there was a second covenant made at Horeb, but that we have no record of the second covenant possessing anything like a Covenant Book. Yahweh had promised Moses "tables of stone," and "the law," and "the commandments."[4] From Exod., chap. 34, we found that Moses received the two "tables," inscribed with the Ten Words, and also some "commandments," contained in Exod. 34:12–26. As for "the law," the word used means also "instruction," and we have an instruction

---

[1] Exod. 34:10, 11.   [2] Exod. 34:12–26.

[3] Exod. 34:27, 28. From the account given in Deuteronomy we know that the words spoken at Mount Horeb by Yahweh, i. e., the Ten Words (Exod. 20:2–17) were identical with the words written on the two tables (Exod. 34:38). In Deut. 5:22 we read, "These words Yahweh spake unto all your assembly, in the mount, out of the midst of the fire, of the cloud, and of the thick darkness, with a great voice: and He added no more." From Deut. 9:9 we know that these tables were called the Tables of the Covenant: "When I was gone up into the mount to receive the tables of stone, even the Tables of the Covenant, then I abode in the mount forty days and forty nights; I did neither eat bread nor drink water." The last clause identifies these tables with Moses' last visit to the mountain (Exod. 34:28). For further references on the Tables of the Covenant, cf. Deut. 9:10, 11, 15, 17; 10:1–5.

[4] Exod. 24:12.

given in Exod. 34:10, 11, quoted above. The law and the commandment are, then, the records contained in Exod. 34:10–26, together with the Ten Words, which are not repeated here because they evidently were identical with those spoken by Yahweh himself, and recorded in Exod., chap. 20.

According to Exod. 34:27 Yahweh commanded Moses to "write down all these words," which may refer only to the "law and the commandments." We have no reason to assume that Moses did not comply with this command. The laws of Exod., chap. 34, were then written down.

Thus, after this long divergence into the records of the Horeb covenants, we see that there existed a book, called the *Book of the Covenant*, containing Exod. 20:2–17, which was made at Horeb, and also "judgments" (Exod. 21–23), and a law and a commandment, written at the same place, containing Exod. 34:10–26. The E code must then have contained both the *Covenant Book* and the laws in Exod., chaps. 21–23, and 34, the last of which is so generally considered as a J code.

But, however this may be, there can be no doubt that the Covenant Book (Exod. 20:2–17) is a portion of the E document. This document generally addresses God under the name of Elohim, and would quite naturally be, therefore, a part of the *Law of Elohim*. We have seen before that the *Law of Yahweh* is the P code, given at Sinai, and likewise that the *Law of Moses* is the D code, given in Moab. We shall therefore probably be not far wrong in assuming that the *Law of Elohim* is the E code, given at Horeb.[1]

---

[1] The confusion of the names Sinai and Horeb in Exod., chaps. 19, 24, 34 of J took place when J and P were combined. See p. 138.

IV. Date of the E Document

We believe, therefore, that the E code extends back in written form to the covenant at Horeb. The question then remains as to whether any of the document outside of the code existed at that early time. In Exod. 17:14 we read, "And Yahweh said unto Moses, Write this for a memorial in a book, and rehearse it in the ears of Joshua: that I will utterly blot out the remembrance of Amalek from under heaven."

The passage refers to the war with Amalek in Rephidim, and the account of that war is given in Exod. 17:8–16. It would seem, then, taking the internal evidence of the document itself, that at least this much of the E document was written down in a book as early as the events in Horeb.

V. Conclusion

We have seen that there existed in the time of Hosea, at least in the Northern Kingdom, a code called the *Law of Elohim*. Again, we found this same technical term used as early as the time of Joshua, and used in a way that denoted a code. As the Hexateuch has only three codes, and two of them have already been identified, we suggested that this *Law of Elohim* was the technical term for the only other one, the E code. We found, further, that a part of the E code was known as the *Book of the Covenant*, and that this included the first legislation at Horeb. This was called a "book," and had therefore been written down. We found, too, that the later legislation at Horeb was also written down. It seemed obvious, then, that the part of the E code which we now have existed in written form as far back as the time of the Horeb covenant. We found, too, that at least one part of the E document outside the code seems to have existed in written form from the same time as the code.   We shall probably not err very gravely in concluding that the whole E document, with the code, existed from a very early age, not later than the time of Joshua.   This last we concluded because the document was capable of receiving an addition in his time at the covenant at Shiloh.

CHAPTER VIII

The Unity and Contents of the E Document

I. Unity of the E Document

The Documentary Theory presupposes, as in the case of P, that the Hexateuch contains a *complete* E document, if only we are able correctly to disengage it from the other material. It is held, however, by most critics that no certain traces of E are to be found earlier than Genesis, chap. 20.[1] It is evident, though, that we have no complete history in the E document, even from the time of Abraham to that of Joshua, which is the period that E is generally supposed to cover. If we did not have the history of the J document and the Toledoth Book of P, the E document would be mere fragments, often utterly unintelligible. This applies especially to the Exodus story. It is not to be denied that there was once a complete E document. although of it we have only fragments preserved in our Hexateuch.

II. Unity of the E Code

But it is not only the document that is fragmentary. The code is undoubtedly fragmentary too. In Exod. 15:25–26 we read, "There he (Yahweh) made for them a *statute* and an *ordinance*, and there he proved them; and he said, If thou wilt diligently hearken unto the voice of Yahweh thy God, and wilt do that which is right in his eyes, and wilt give ear to his commandments, and keep all his statutes, I will put none of the diseases upon thee, which I have put upon the Egyptians: for I am Yahweh

---

[1] Some critics think that a few verses in chap. 15 and chap. 16 belong to it.

that healeth thee." The passage belongs to E. It refers
to the incident of the sweetening of the bitter waters at
Marah. Now a "statute" was given to the people at
Marah, and a "statute" means originally, in Hebrew,
"something engraved," either on stone or on metal. A
"statute" cannot be a mere oral law; it must be a written
law. The term "statute" became technicalized in the Old
Testament, and meant a "canonical" or "church" law.[1]
In contrast with the "statutes" are the "judgments," a
term which denotes a code of "civil and criminal laws."[2]
Now the E code contains several "judgments," but not a
single "statute," although, as we have seen, a statute was
given at Marah.

A day or two later, when the people were encamped
at Rephidim, at the foot of Mount Horeb, Moses received
a visit from his father-in-law, Jethro. This happened
before the legislation at Horeb took place. Of this visit
we read that Moses was sitting and judging the people

[1] The following laws in the Hexateuch are called "statutes": Day of
Atonement, Lev. 16:29, 31, 34; 23:31; sacrifices to he-goats, Lev. 17:7;
sheaf of firstfruits, Lev. 23:14; Pentecost, Lev. 23:21; Festival of Booths or
Tabernacles, Lev. 23:41; shewbreads, Lev. 24:9; use of the silver trumpets,
Num. 10:8; the tithe, Num. 18:23: water of separation, Num. 19:2-21; vows,
Num. 30:16; purification of spoil, Num. 31:21; the Passover, Exod. 12:14
ff.; 13:10; the lamp, Exod. 27:20, 21; Lev. 24:3; the breeches of the priest.
Exod. 28:42, 43; the priesthood, Exod. 29:9; the heave-offering, Exod. 29·28;
Num. 18:8-19; the laver, Exod. 30:21; fat of blood, Lev. 3:17; sacrifices
at consecration of priests, Lev. 6:22; 7:36; the wave-offering, Lev. 7:34;
10:13-15; and the temperance of the priest, Lev. 10:9.

[2] The only place where the term "judgments" is used as the title of particular laws is in Exod. 21:1, where it is in the superscription to the laws contained in Exod. 21:2—23:19. The term "judgments" corresponds exactly to
the term *danitu* used in the Code of Hammurabi (col. 40, l. 31), as the technical
term of that code. In Babylonian the word *dânu*, meaning "to judge," corresponds with the Hebrew *šaphaṭ*. From the Code of Hammurabi we know
that such codes did exist in written form. The Hebrew word *mišpaṭ*, "judgment," must be similarly understood.

who were coming in large numbers to plead their cases before him. Jethro asked Moses why he was doing all this judging himself. "And Moses said unto his father-in-law, Because the people come unto me, to inquire of God: when they have a matter, they come unto me; and I judge between a man and his neighbor, and I make them know the statutes of Elohim, and his laws."[1] Then Jethro counseled Moses to become only the supreme justice, taking the cases before God, and to appoint other judges to be a court of first instance: "Be thou for the people as Elohim, and bring thou the causes unto Elohim: and thou shalt teach them the statutes and the laws, and shalt shew them the way wherein they must walk, and the work that they must do."[2] How could he teach them "statutes," if he had none to teach? How could the judges of these lower courts decide if they had no basis for making decisions? It is necessary to hold well in mind the fact that a "statute" means something "engraved." The answer to these questions is plain when we consider what was stated above, that a "statute" had been given, two days before, at Marah. And still our E code has not one trace of a "statute," for its "judgments" on the festivals, in Exod. 23:14–17, belong to civil and not at all to canonical regulations.

How can such a disappearance be accounted for? Let us see.

The General Priesthood

After these "statutes" had been delivered, on the first day that God stood on the mountain, he said to Moses, "Now therefore, if ye will obey my voice indeed, and keep my covenant, then ye shall be a peculiar treasure

[1] Exod. 18:15, 16.   [2] Exod. 18:19, 20.

unto me above all peoples: for all the earth is mine: and ye shall be unto me a *kingdom of priests*, and an holy nation."[1] Whether the statutes already given were to this effect, or whether there were other statutes given three days later, we can never know; but it seems certain, at any rate, that a statute was given to this effect.[2] It was certainly the intention to make the whole nation a priesthood, and every man a priest. Yahweh based this remarkable statement on the condition that the people should keep his covenant which he was about to make with them. The covenant was established, the people accepting all the conditions of Yahweh: "All that Yahweh hath spoken, we will do."[3] Then Moses told the people all the words and the judgments of Yahweh, after they themselves had heard him proclaim the Ten Words, and the people again answered, and said with one voice, "All the words which Yahweh hath spoken, we will do."[4] The people thus complied with the conditions of Yahweh. The Covenant was established; the words and the judgments were given to them as their law. The whole people thus became a priesthood, appointed by Yahweh himself, and every Israelite, or at least every firstborn Israelite, of the Assembly, not only had a right, but was *de facto* constituted by Yahweh himself, to perform priestly functions. Consequently we read, "And Moses rose up early in the morning, and builded an altar under the mount, and twelve stones [so the LXX, but the Hebrew has "pillars"], according to the twelve tribes of Israel. And he sent young men of the children of Israel, which offered burnt-offerings, and

[1] Exod. 19:5, 6.
[2] If this be denied, it is certain at least that God proclaimed it to Moses.
[3] Exod. 19:8.   [4] Exod. 24:3.

sacrificed peace-offerings of oxen to Yahweh."[1] These young men were not Levites, nor were they heads of their fathers' houses, but were evidently picked, one out of each tribe. The twelve stones were in this case, as so often else, sacrificial places, corresponding to the later high-places. A general priesthood, consisting of all Israel was thus inaugurated.

The Levitical Priesthood

When this covenant was established, Moses, Aaron, Nadab, and Abihu, and seventy elders went up into the mount, and Moses staid there forty days. Aaron and the elders returned. In the meantime the people fell away into idolatry, requesting that Aaron would make them a golden calf to worship. Aaron complied with the request, and this gave Yahweh occasion to tell Moses to go down to the people. When Moses came down he found the people in revolt.[2] He then stood in the gate of the camp and called for volunteers. The sons of Levi presented themselves unto him. Moses ordered them to go out into the camp and put down the rebellion. They did so, slaying some 3,000 men.[3] Moses then turned to the Levites (for it is to them he is speaking in this passage), "and Moses said, Consecrate yourselves today to Yahweh, yea, every man against his son and against his brother; that he may bestow upon you a blessing this day."[4]

This passage is not translated perfectly, either in the A. V. or in the R. V. The LXX reads, "Fill your hands this day to Yahweh, every one against his son and against his brother, that a blessing may be bestowed upon you."

---

[1] Exod., 24:4, 5.

[2] Exod. 32:25.

[3] Or perhaps better, "three clans."

[4] Exod. 32:29.

This is not only the Greek, but it is a perfect translation of the Hebrew text as we have it in the Massoretic version today. Now "fill the hands" is in Hebrew a technical term for "ordain to the priesthood." Up to this time all the people had been priests, but now, after the rebellion with its worship of the golden calf, the people had forfeited their priesthood in the eyes of Moses. The tribe of Levi alone had turned to the side of Yahweh and fought for him. As a reward, Moses at that time constituted the whole tribe of Levi as the priesthood of Yahweh, to take the place of that of all the people, now forfeited. It is worth noticing that Moses did this without any express command from Yahweh. We have therefore, now, two ideas of the priesthood, one based on the covenant at Horeb, consisting of all the people, the other consisting of the Levites exclusively, constituted by Moses at this time. The first priesthood is that of the E code; the second, that of the D code!

The Levitical priests thus resulting received, forty years later, numerous "statutes" regulating their ritual, which are embodied in our Deuteronomy. When the old E code came to be compiled with the other codes, in later centuries, its "statutes," providing as they must have done for a general priesthood, were so radically different from the "statutes" of the other codes that they were omitted from the compilation. This seems a probable explanation of how the "statutes" came to be missing from the E code as it is today in our Hexateuch.

At any rate, as we have seen, there were "statutes" in the original code, and these "statutes" have since disappeared. The E code then, as it stands today, is not a complete code; it is fragmentary.

III. The History of the E Code

The point made above, that the E code provided for a priesthood which consisted of all Israel, has a very great and important bearing on two things: first, on the contention of many critics by which they seek to show that all codes, and the E code among them, were late; and second, on the restoration of the history of the E code.

a) It is maintained by critics that neither the E code nor any other code was in operation before 800 B. C., or perhaps even 750 B. C., or 700 B. C., because the history of Israel does not show us any traces of the operation of any code before this time. In proof of this it is asserted by the critics that up to the time of 950 B. C., at least, sacrifices were made in different places in Israel by men who were neither priests nor Levites, and that, moreover, not a single protest was made against it. The authors of Judges, Samuel, and Kings record such instances as commonplace matters of fact. Such actions, the critics claim, are contrary to the codes. Therefore, when such things were allowed, the codes could not have existed. But, as we have seen above, such a practice is *not* in contradiction to *all* the codes; it is in exact accordance with the E code. By the simple hypothesis that each of the non-Levites who sacrificed was a follower of the E code, which, as we have seen, ordained him a sacrificing priest, we solve the difficulty, and remove the force of the argument. The E code provides *that every Israelite is a priest,*[1] *and every place where Yahweh has caused his name to be remembered is a legitimate place of worship.*[2]

b) But let us examine these various instances of non-

---

[1] Exod. 19:6.

[2] Exod. 20:24

Levitical sacrifices, and so gain the outlines of the history of the E code.

1. In Judg. 6:19–26 we are told that Gideon, a man of the tribe of Manasseh, offered a sacrifice under the oak in Ophrah, in the presence of the "angel of Yahweh," who not only permitted it but received it favorably. Of course Gideon was not a Levite. In the tribe of Manasseh, then, it would seem that the E code was observed *ca.* 1300 B. C.

2. In Judg. 11:34–39, Jephtha offered a sacrifice, even of his daughter. Now Jephtha was a "Gileadite," probably of the tribe of Eastern Manasseh, certainly not of the tribe of Levi. Again we find that in the east-Jordanic territory non-Levites made sacrifices with the full approval of their people. The E code must have been in force there *ca.* 1210 B. C.

3. In Judg. 13:19 we read of Manoah, the father of Samson, of the tribe of Dan. He too offered a sacrifice to Yahweh, although not a Levite. In the tribe of Dan, too, the E code seems to have been observed *ca.* 1150 B. C.

4. In I Sam. 6:14, the people of Beth-Shemesh offered up kine for a burnt-offering to Yahweh. They belonged to the tribe of Judah. They did this, moreover, although there were Levites present, handling the ark. At least this portion of the tribe of Judah seems to have observed the E code, *ca.* 1075 B. C.

5. Of Saul it is recorded, in I Sam. 14:34 f., that he built an altar to Yahweh, around which both he and all the people slew sheep and oxen in a great propitiation sacrifice.[1] Now Saul was a Benjaminite. In Benjamin,

---

[1] This sacrifice was really a compromise of the E and P codes. E permitted Saul and all the people to sacrifice, but P restricted them from eating the flesh with the blood. This shows again Saul's anxiety for the P code.

too, the E code seems to have been recognized, *ca.* 1025 B. C.

6. In I Sam. 20:6 we read that it was the custom of the family of David to offer a yearly sacrifice at Bethlehem. David and all his family belonged to the tribe of Judah. This was about the same time as Saul's great sacrifice noted above, *ca.* 1025 B. C.

7. This was no novelty for David. In II Sam. 6:13, 18, we find David sacrificing oxen and fatlings as burnt-offerings and peace-sacrifices when the ark was brought to Jerusalem. And again, in II Sam. 24:25 we find David building an altar in Jerusalem, where he offered burnt-offerings and peace-offerings. In this case, though, it must be admitted that possibly there were Levites present, who offered the sacrifices at the command of the king. This was *ca.* 975 B. C.

8. In I Kings 1:9 we find a pretender to the throne, a son of David, offering oxen and fatlings by the stone of Zoheleth. He too was, of course, of the tribe of Judah. In this case, however, it may have been the Levites who sacrificed at the pretender's command. This was in 971 B. C.

9. About the same year Solomon offered sacrifices at Gibeon, as is recorded in I Kings 3:4. And again, he offered sacrifices at the consecration of the temple, as we know from I Kings 8:63. In both these cases, though, the possibility of Levitical sacrifices must be admitted. This was in 960 B. C.

These instances of non-Levitical sacrifice cover the entire period from Judges down to the kingdom of Solomon. They come from north, south, east, and west. Nowhere are the practices condemned. On the contrary they seem in many cases to have the divine approval. Now these practices are authorized in the E code. It would seem, then, that during this period the E code was the one in use, at least among the majority of the people.

But we are able to carry the history of the E code, not only up to the monarchy, but also on from the division of the kingdom after the death of Solomon. Jeroboam was the first king of the Northern Kingdom. One of the charges brought against him by the late Deuteronomic editor of Kings is that "he made priests from among all the people, which were not of the sons of Levi."[1] This is, as we have seen, only in strict accord with the provisions of the Horeb covenant, as recorded in the E code.

At the same time that this was going on in the Northern Kingdom, we well know the history of the Southern Kingdom. Under Rehoboam, their first king, they fell into idolatry, from which they were restored in the time of Asa and Jehoshaphat. These kings gave their preference to the Aaronic priesthood and therefore the P code.

It would seem then that after the separation of the kingdoms the E code found its home in the Northern Kingdom, while it was neglected in favor of the P code in the Southern Kingdom.

IV. The E Code and the Code of Hammurabi

Another thing worth noticing about the E code is its remarkable similarity to the Code of Hammurabi. Of all the Hebrew codes the E code is the only one which can be directly connected with the Hammurabi law-book. The following instances will make quite plain the connection between the two:

[1] I Kings 12:31.

E Code	Code of Hammurabi

Patricide

E Code

Exod. 21:15: And he that smiteth his father or his mother, shall surely be put to death.

Code of Hammurabi

195. If a son strike his father, they shall cut off his fingers.

Mansteading

E Code

Exod. 21:16: And he that stealeth a man, and selleth him, or if he be found in his hand, he shall surely be put to death.

Code of Hammurabi

14. If a man steal a man's son, who is a minor, he shall be put to death.

16. If a man harbor in his house a male or female slave who has fled from the palace or from a freeman, and do not bring him forth at the call of the commandant, the owner of that house shall be put to death.

19. If he detain that slave in his house and later that slave be found in his possession, that man shall be put to death.

Quarrels

E Code

Exod. 21:18, 19: And if men contend, and one smiteth the other with a stone, or with his fist, and he die not, but keep his bed; if he rise again, and walk abroad upon his staff, then shall he that smote him be quit: only he shall pay for the loss of his time, and shall cause him to be thoroughly healed.

Code of Hammurabi

206. If a man strike another man in a quarrel and wound him, he shall swear, "I struck him without intent," and he shall be responsible for the physician.

Miscarriage

E Code

Exod. 21:22, 23: And if men (strive together and) hurt a woman with child, so that her fruit depart, and yet no mischief follow: he shall be surely fined, according as the woman's husband shall lay upon him; and he shall pay as the judges determine. But if any mischief follow, then thou shalt give life for life.

Code of Hammurabi

209. If a man strike a man's daughter, and bring about a miscarriage, he shall pay ten shekels of silver for her miscarriage.

210. If that woman die, they shall put his daughter to death.

211. If, through a stroke, he bring about a miscarriage to the daughter of a freeman, he shall pay five shekels of silver.

E Code	Code of Hammurabi

212. If the woman die, he shall pay one-half mana of silver.

213. If he strike the female slave of a man, and bring about a miscarriage, he shall pay two shekels of silver.

214. If that female slave die, he shall pay one-third mana of silver.

Lex talionis

Exod. 21:24, 25: Eye for eye, tooth for tooth, hand for hand, foot for foot, burning for burning, wound for wound, stripe for stripe.

196. If a man destroy the eye of another man, they shall destroy his eye.

197. If one break a man's bone, they shall break his bone.

198. If one destroy the eye of a freeman, or break the bone of a freeman, he shall pay one mana of silver.

199. If one destroy the eye of a man's slave, or break a bone of a man's slave, he shall pay one-half his price.

200. If a man knock out the tooth of a man of his own rank, they shall knock out his tooth.

201. If one knock out a tooth of a freeman, he shall pay one-third mana of silver.

Goring

Exod. 21:28: And if an ox shall gore a man or a woman, that they die, the ox shall be surely stoned, and his flesh shall not be eaten; but the owner of the ox shall be quit.

Exod. 21:29: But if the ox were wont to gore in time past, and it has been testified to his owner, and he hath not kept him in, but he

250. If an ox, when passing through the street, gore a man, and brings about his death, that case has no penalty.

251. If a man's ox were wont to gore, and they have testified to him his habit of goring, and he have not protected his horns, or have not tied him up,

E Code

hath killed a man or a woman, the ox shall be stoned; and his owner also shall be put to death.

Exod. 21:30: If there be laid on him a ransom, then he shall give for the redemption of his life whatsoever is laid upon him.

Exod. 21:31: Whether he have gored a son, or have gored a daughter, according to this judgment shall it be done unto him.

Exod. 21:32: If the ox gore a man-servant or a maid-servant, he shall give unto their master thirty shekels of silver,[1] and the ox shall be stoned.

Code of Hammurabi

and that ox gore the son of a man, and bring about his death, he shall pay one-half mana of silver.

252. If it be the servant of a man, he shall pay one-third mana of silver.

Theft of animals

Exod. 22:1: If a man shall steal an ox, or a sheep, and kill it, or sell it, he shall pay five oxen for an ox, and four sheep for a sheep.

8. If a man steal ox or sheep, ass or pig, or boat—if it be from God or palace, he shall restore thirty-fold—if it be from a freeman, he shall render tenfold. If the thief have nothing wherewith to pay, he shall be put to death.

Burglary

Exod. 22:2: If the thief be found breaking in, and be smitten that he die, there shall be no blood-guiltiness for him.

22. If a man practice brigandage, and be captured, that man shall be put to death.

Unlawful pasturage

Exod. 22:5: If a man shall cause a field or vineyard to be eaten, and shall let his beast loose, and it feed in another man's field, of the best of his own field, and of the best of

58. If, after the sheep have gone up from the meadow, and have crowded their way out of the gate into the public common, the shepherd turn the sheep into the field,

---

[1] Equals ⅓ mana, but the Phoenician mana equals ⅔ of a Babylonian, and the value of the penalty is therefore identical in the two laws.

E Code	Code of Hammurabi
his own vineyard shall he make reparation.	and pasture the sheep on the field, the shepherd shall oversee the field on which he pastures, and at the time of harvest he shall measure out sixty *Gur* of grain per ten *Gan* to the owner of the field.

Deposit

Exod. 22:7: If a man shall deliver unto his neighbor money or stuff to keep, and it be stolen out of the man's house, if the thief be found, he shall pay double. Exod. 22:8: If the thief be not found, then the master of the house shall come near unto God, (to see) whether he have not put his hand unto his neighbor's goods. -	125. If a man give anything of his on deposit, and at the place of deposit, either by burglary or pillage he suffer loss in common with the owner of the house, the owner of the house who has been negligent and has lost what was given to him on deposit shall make good (the loss), and shall restore (it) to the owner of the goods. The owner of the house shall institute a search for what has been lost, and take it from the thief.

Storage

Exod. 22:9: For every matter of trespass, whether it be for ox, for ass, for sheep, for raiment, (or) for any manner of lost thing, whereof one saith, This is it, the cause of both parties shall come before God; he whom God shall condemn shall pay double unto his neighbor.	120. If a man store his grain in bins in the house of another, and an accident happen to the granary or the owner of the house open a bin and take grain, or if he raise a dispute about the amount of grain which was stored in his house, the owner of the grain shall declare his grain before God, and the owner of the house shall double the amount of the grain which he took and restore it to the owner of the grain.

Herding

Exod. 22:10: If a man deliver unto his neighbor an ass, or an ox, or a sheep, or any beast, to keep, and it die, or be hurt, or be driven	263. If he lose an ox or sheep which is given to him, he shall restore to their owner ox for ox, sheep for sheep.

E Code

away, no man seeing it, 11. the oath of Yahweh shall be between them both, whether he hath not put his hand unto his neighbor's goods; and the owner thereof shall accept it, and he shall not make restitution. 12. But if it be stolen from him, he shall make restitution unto the owner thereof. 13. If it be torn in pieces, let him bring it for witness; he shall not make good what was torn.

Exod. 22:14: And if a man borrow aught of his neighbor, and it be hurt, or die, the owner thereof not being with it, he shall surely make restitution. 15. If the owner thereof be with it, he shall not make it good: if it be an hired thing, it cometh into its hire.

Code of Hammurabi

266. If a visitation of God happen to a fold, or a lion kill, the shepherd shall declare himself innocent before God, and the owner of the fold shall suffer the damage (cf. 244).

245. If a man hire an ox and cause its death through neglect or abuse, he shall restore an ox of equal value to the owner of the ox.

Sorcery

Exod. 22:18: Thou shalt not suffer a sorceress to live.

2. If a man charge a man with sorcery, and cannot prove it, he who is charged with sorcery shall go to the river; into the river he shall throw himself. And if the river overcome him, the accuser shall take unto himself his house. If the river show the man to be innocent, and he come forth unharmed, he who charged him with sorcery shall be put to death. He who threw himself into the river shall take to himself the house of his accuser.

Perjury

Exod. 23:1: Thou shalt not take up a false report: put not thine hand with the wicked to be an un-

3. If a man, in a case, bear false witness, or do not establish the testimony that he has given, if that

E Code

Code of Hammurabi

righteous witness. 2. Thou shalt not follow a multitude to do evil; neither shalt thou bear witness in a cause to turn aside after a multitude to wrest judgment; 3. neither shalt thou favor a poor man in his cause.

case be a case involving life, that man shall be put to death.

Bribery

Exod. 23:6: Thou shalt not wrest the judgment of thy poor in his cause. 7. Keep thee far from a false matter; and the innocent and righteous slay thou not; for I will not justify the wicked. 8. And thou shalt take no gift: for a gift blindeth them that have sight, and perverteth the cause of the righteous.

4. If a man bear witness for grain or money, he shall himself bear the penalty imposed in that case. 5. If a judge pronounce a judgment, render a decision, deliver a verdict duly signed and sealed and afterward alter his judgment, they shall call that judge to account for the alteration of the judgment which he had pronounced, and he shall pay twelve-fold the penalty which was in said judgment; and, in the assembly, they shall expel him from his seat of judgment, and he shall return, and with the judges in a case he shall not take his seat.

The similarity between the two codes, which the examples given above serve to illustrate, has been noticed by many scholars, and some of them have consequently drawn the conclusion that the E code was based on the Code of Hammurabi, and that therefore the time when the former code was written must have been a time when Babylonian influence exerted itself in Palestine. This argument, it may be remarked, goes against the date usually assigned by critics to this code. For if the E code were written in the eighth century, Babylonian law codes could have influenced it little if at all. At that time Babylonia was a very weak state, and the history of Israel at that time shows how impossible any considerable Babylonian influence could have been.

But we have ventured to claim that the E code was delivered at Horeb, in the time of Moses, sometime in the fifteenth century. At this time there was a close connection between Babylonia, then in great power, and Egypt which the Israelites had so lately left and from which Moses had received his education. Intermarriages had taken place between the two royal houses.[1] Caravans were constantly passing from the one land to the other.[2] A Babylonian influence upon the E code would at this time have been quite possible.

But, in spite of the many similarities between the two codes, it is true that there are differences. These are accounted for by two things: (1) Over seven hundred years had elapsed since the time when the Code of Hammurabi as we have it today had been published in Babylonia, during which time, as we know, it had been modified even in Babylonia itself; (2) in promulgating a Babylonian code among the Hebrews it was of course necessary so to modify it as to fit the surrounding conditions and the Hebrew temperament.

V. Conclusion

We have seen in this chapter that the E document is not a document, but a collection of fragments of what was once a document; that the code too is not a complete code, but also fragmentary, and especially wanting in the "statutes" which once belonged to it but which have been lost; that the E code provided for a non-Levitical priest-

[1] Cf. Knudtzon, *Die El-Amarna-Tafeln*, Nos. 1–14.

[2] *Ibid.*, No. 8, ll. 11–41.

hood; that in the period of the judges and the early monarchy the presence of this non-Levitical priesthood shows
the general use of the E code all over Israel; that it is
probable that at the division of the kingdom the E code
with its non-Levitical priesthood became peculiarly the
law of the Northern Kingdom; and that the E code shows
a remarkable similarity to the Code of Hammurabi.   In
all of these things we can find no contradiction, but on
the contrary confirmation, of the theory reached in the
last chapter, that the E document is to be assigned to a
date much earlier than that génerally given by the critics,
and that quite probably it belongs to the time when it
purports to have been delivered, namely the stop at Horeb
when Moses and the people received it at Yahweh's hands.

CHAPTER IX

The Relation Between the E and D Documents

Everyone admits that D is later than and dependent upon E. Our analysis has shown that it is later, nor can it be denied that it is dependent upon it. But the interrelations of the two are worthy of more than a merely passing reference.

The Bible itself gives the reason for the similarity between the two, when it says that D was promulgated in the land of Moab forty years after E had been given in the Horeb mountain, and to the same people. Moses and Joshua are represented as acting together in both cases.

We saw in the last chapter that after the rebellion at Horeb had been put down there were two priesthoods, one authorized by the code and consisting of all the sons of Israel, the other authorized by Moses and consisting only of the tribe of Levi, which he wished to reward. But did the new order take effect immediately and over the whole army?

The Rebellion at Kadesh

Shortly after the events at Horeb the assembly started on its northward march. After a short stay in Hazeroth the assembly reached Kadesh-barnea. Here Yahweh commanded Moses to send out twelve spies to search the land, and Moses accordingly appointed one from each tribe, among them Caleb and Joshua.[1]

---

[1] This appointment of the spies is generally assigned to P, although the critics themselves are not agreed. If it be P, it belongs to the older Toledoth Book, or else it is a P redaction of an older document.

These spies went as far as the valley of Escol, and, after forty days, returned. Ten of them gave a most discouraging report, while Caleb and Joshua tried to encourage the people to go in and to take the land. The assembly, however, murmured and was dissatisfied. Yahweh, enraged, ordered Moses to tell the people to stay in the wilderness for forty years, until those who had murmured were dead.

When Moses promulgated this commandment of Yahweh, a great rebellion broke out. "They rose up early in the morning and got them up to the top of the mountain, saying, Lo, we be here, and will go up unto the place which Yahweh has promised, for we have sinned."[1] Moses tried to persuade them to desist from this undertaking, but in vain. "But they presumed to go up to the top of the mountain; nevertheless the ark of the covenant of Yahweh, and Moses, departed not out of the camp."[2]

Thus we see that there were now two camps of the children of Israel, one which went up into the highlands, the other which remained at Kadesh with Moses and the ark. These two parties were never entirely re-joined during the entire forty years between this and the conquest.

The First Conquest

The party which went up into the highlands suffered a crushing defeat at the hands of the Amalekites and Canaanites.[3] They were not, however, destroyed, but finally made a second stand at Zephat, where they routed the Canaanites, and in memory of their victory called the place Hormah.[4] This story is again given in Judg. 1:17 as a part of the story of the conquest of Canaan.

[1] Num. 14:40. The sin had been their not going up when ordered to do so.
[2] Num. 14:44.   [3] Num. 14:45.   [4] Num. 21:1-3; 14:45.

It is significant that it is *a conquest in which Joshua takes no part.*

It is to be noted that it is Judah and a part of Simeon which make this conquest in the Judges story. The punishment received at the hands of the Canaanites was sufficient to send many of the rebels cringing back to Moses at Kadesh.[1] *Judah, however, did not come back.* We conclude this from at least two circumstances.

In the first place, Moses, when blessing the people in Moab, at the slopes of Pisgah, prayed to Yahweh in the following words, "Hear, Yahweh, the voice of Judah, and bring him in unto his people: with his hands he contended for himself; and thou shalt be an help against his adversaries."[2] This shows that at the death of Moses Judah was still separated from his brethren.

In the second place, after Joshua had conquered a portion of Canaan, written the laws at Shechem, and located the Ark of the Covenant at Gilgal, "then the children of Judah drew nigh unto Joshua in Gilgal: and Caleb the son of Jephunneh, the Kenizzite, said unto him, Thou knowest the thing that Yahweh spake unto Moses the man of God, concerning thee and concerning me, in Kadesh-barnea."[3] In the history as told by the E document, Caleb, son of Jephunneh, does not appear once between Kadesh-barnea and this present occasion. Here at last, in Gilgal, according to E, the prayer of Moses is fulfilled, and Judah again takes its place in the confederacy of the tribes. In the meantime, apparently, the tribe had been living a free-booter life in the mountainous wilds of Judaea.

[1] Deut. 1:44–46. [3] Josh. 14:6.
[2] Deut. 33:7.

But was Judah the only tribe which seceded at Kadesh and did not return?

In Judg. 1:22–26 is a story about "the house of Joseph" which went up and occupied Bethel. It has been assumed that this house of Joseph was merely another name for the tribes of Ephraim and Manasseh. Some have included Benjamin in it, basing this upon I Sam. 9:21. In the time of David it is true that the name was applied to these three tribes. But originally the house of Joseph seems to have occupied middle Palestine, before the tribes of Ephraim and Manasseh had come into the country at all. This is quite the simplest way to explain Judg., chap. 1, where Ephraim and Manasseh and their conquests are mentioned directly after those of this house of Joseph.

We see that the house of Joseph conquered Bethel.[1] And from Judg. 1:34, 35 we learn that, when the Danites had been driven away by the Amorites, the house of Joseph came and subdued the conquerors and made them tributary. These two are the only mentions of any conquests on the part of the house of Joseph.

The conquests made by Ephraim and the half-tribe of Manasseh are told of, however, not only in Judg., chap. 1, but also in Josh., chaps. 16, 17. The same is true of Zebulon, Asher, Naphtali, and Dan, which are told of in Josh., chap. 19. We are told in Judg. 1:27–34 that none of these six tribes was able to effect a settlement at this time in Canaan. On the other hand, both Judah and this house of Joseph are said to have effected settlements and to have maintained strong positions.

What then is more reasonable to suppose than that this house of Joseph, like the tribe of Judah, was a Hebrew

[1] The Judges' account is the only account of this conquest in the Bible.

tribe long established and thoroughly at home in Canaan some time before Joshua and his invading confederacy appeared on the scene? And if this be true, what can be more likely than that it too was a tribe which seceded at Kadesh-barnea, not to rejoin the confederacy until after the conquest of Canaan had begun?

From the account in Numbers we are not able to say just what tribes seceded at Kadesh. All we can say is that of those which did secede some stragglers came back after the battles with Amalek and Canaan.[1] That any whole tribe came back we have no record. If, however, no whole tribe did come back, we must suppose that the remnants of the old tribes would reorganize on the basis of the old tribal lines and resume their place in the confederacy. We must also suppose that the portions which had left would do the same thing in the lands whither they had gone. Thus it is perfectly possible that after Kadesh there should have been the same number of tribes about Moses as before, while at the same time there were Hebrew tribes, bearing the same names, in Palestine, whither the rebels had fled.

Does not this throw some light upon that difficult passage, Judg. 1:1—2:5? This portion of Judges is conceded by scholars to be of a different source than the rest of the book. It describes several conquests, namely those of Judah, Simeon, Benjamin, the house of Joseph, Western Manasseh, Ephraim, Zebulon, Asher, Naphtali, and Dan. With what period of time does this passage deal?

It has been assumed that the reference corresponds to Josh., chaps. 7–21. But this cannot be admitted. The

---

[1] And this we learn from Deut. 1:45. No mention of any return is contained in Numbers.

history in the two passages is vitally different.   In Judges, in the first place, Joshua is not mentioned.   He does not appear.[1]   Secondly, in Judges the six tribes, Manasseh Ephraim, Zebulon, Asher, Naphtali, and Dan, do not effect a settlement.   In Joshua,[2] on the other hand, these same tribes do effect a settlement.

It is far more reasonable to suppose that the two passages refer to quite different events, and to quite different periods.   What can be more likely than that *in Judges we deal with attempts at settlement on the part of those portions of the tribes which had seceded at Kadesh and gone north, while in Joshua we have the record of the later and more effective settlements made by those portions of the same tribes which had remained at Kadesh under Moses' guidance?*

We left Moses and the Ark of the Covenant at Kadesh barnea.   Let us go back for a while and follow the adven tures of those with him.   We are still in the first year of the wandering, at least so far as E tells us.   We know that neither Judah nor the house of Joseph is longer with him.   Both have gone north and have settled in Palestine. Of the other six tribes mentioned-in Judg., chap. 1, portions at least remain around Moses, holding the old places in the confederacy of the tribes.   The three so-called "east-Jordanic tribes," Reuben, Gad, and Manasseh, since they are not mentioned in Judg., chap. 1, at all, seem to have remained intact at the secession and to have continued with Moses.[3]

[1] The mention of his name in Judges 1:1 is, of course, due to a redactor who wished to connect Judges with the preceding book. This is conceded by all.

[2] Josh., chaps. 16, 17, 19.

[3] The omission seems unexplainable on any other theory.

And it is these three last-mentioned tribes which play the most important part after Kadesh. The next event told of in E is the rebellion of Dathan and Abiram, which happened at Kadesh, after the great insurrection, but before the army had moved on. Both Dathan and Abiram, the leaders in this rebellion, are Reubenites.

After this, except for a brief notice of the death of Miriam, we have in E a blank of thirty-eight years. When the curtain again rises we find the people in the land of Moab. Here we have the great battles against Sihon, king of the Amorites, and Og, king of Bashan. Both of these the Israelites under Moses slew, and confiscated their lands. Then follows the incident of Balaam and his prophecies, as a result of which Balak, king of the Moabites, left the Israelites in undisputed possession of the lands which they had conquered.[1]

The Israelites were then abiding on the border of Moab, in Shittim. There they committed a sin by joining them-

[1] In Num., chap. 26, is recorded a "numbering" of the people in Moab. This is the second "numbering" known in the Book of Numbers, the first (Num., chap. 1) having taken place at Kadesh. Both of these "numberings" are allotted to the P document by most critics. The first undoubtedly does belong there. But the second "numbering," the one here in Moab, although evidently edited by a P redactor, shows unmistakable traces of an E original. Not only do we have here the names of Dathan, Abiram, Eliab, and Miriam, which are certainly E names, but the abrupt beginning of Num. 26:4 shows that the P editor used a document of another source. Without going farther into a discussion of the linguistic marks of this section, we can say that it is evident that we have here an older source which knew of a "numbering" in the land of Moab. Our translation, "numbering," of the Hebrew *paqad* is, however, inadequate. The word really means "mustering," "enrolling," or "passing in review." It is a military term. This mustering can imply only that a people, a company of soldiers, here were joined to Moses' army, i. e., mustered in. In this mustering were peoples from all tribes. These were probably deserters from other allied tribes round about, from those portions, possibly, of the tribes which had deserted at Kadesh. At any rate they were surely of Hebrew descent.

selves to Baal-Peor, the god of the mountain of Peor.   For
this they were afflicted with a plague.   But the offenders
were promptly punished, and the plague was stayed.[1]

It was at this point that Moses allotted the lands con
quered from Sihon and Og.   *It is significant that he gave
them to the three tribes which had apparently remained
intact with him, namely Reuben, Gad, and Eastern Manasseh.*

He did this with the proviso that the men of these tribes
should accompany their brethren of the other tribes over
the Jordan, and assist them to conquer the west-Jordanic
lands.   With these words ends the E document in the
Pentateuch.   We have no more of it until we get to the
Book of Joshua.

The Covenant in Moab

The history between the allotment of the lands and
the march over the Jordan is given in the D document.

From this we learn that Moses delivered a new law,
the law of Deuteronomy, and died.   In this new code the
priesthood was definitely confined to the tribe of Levi,
all of whom were made priests.   Thus we see that the
decision made by Moses after the rebellion at Horeb had,
during the forty years of wandering, become so engrafted
into the lives of the people that now it could be included
even in their official law-book.   This becomes easier of
explanation when we consider that a great portion of the
tribes to whom the E code had been given had left Moses
at Kadesh, and that the remainder had been overawed
both by the awful catastrophe to Dathan and Abiram
when they had ventured to question Moses' authority,
and by his great victories over Sihon and Og.   In the
people's eyes Moses had become the mouthpiece of God.

[1] Num. 25:1-5.

And so they were now willing to accept without question the new code given in Moab.

In essentials, outside of the question of the priesthood, it differs little from the E code. It simply amplifies and interprets it from a humanitarian viewpoint, and does it so beautifully that D has become the model for the codes of the civilized world. And even in regard to the priesthood, the old custom of the E code does not entirely disappear. For it is only the holocausts that are restricted to "the priests the Levites;" the other sacrifices, i. e., the peace-offerings, are still to be offered by any of the people.

The D code becomes, then, the code of Joshua and of the people who crossed the Jordan with him. That this is true is shown by the fact that the E passages in Joshua breathe the spirit of the D document.[1]

The Stay at Gilgal

The first halting-place after the crossing of the Jordan was at Gilgal, a city between that river and Jericho.[2]

[1] A few examples may suffice: "He is God," in Josh. 2:11 and Deut. 4:39; "the Living God," in Josh. 3:10 and Deut. 5:26; "Lord of all the earth," in Josh. 3:11 and Deut. 10:14; "the seven peoples," in Josh. 3:10 and Deut. 7:1; "in time to come," in Josh. 4:6, 21 and Deut. 6:20. More important is the fact that the punishment of Achan for stealing the devoted things at Jericho was based on a law found in Deuteronomy. Cf. Josh. 7:15 and Deut. 13:17.

[2] Joshua was here commanded to circumcise the people. The text here shows that we are dealing with the fusion of two accounts. In Josh. 5:2 we read," At that time Yahweh said unto Joshua, Make thee knives of flint, and circumcise *again* the children of Israel *the second time*." As we have not heard of a circumcision the words "again "and "the second time" deserve notice. The original account or accounts must have contained a distinct record of two events dealing with circumcision of Israelites in Gilgal. The text as it stands not only is an enigma to us, but was so to the D redactor, who added vss. 4–7, attempting to explain the passage by saying that circumcision had not been practiced in the wilderness. But this does not explain why the text says that the operation was performed *a second time*. The first circumcision must, of course,

At this point it is necessary to notice a remarkable passage in Judg. 2:1-5. Here we are told that a messenger of Yahweh came up from Gilgal to Bochim at Bethel. He reprimanded the inhabitants of Bochim for having violated the laws, contained in the E code, regarding the destruction of heathen worship. This moved the people so much that they began to weep, and then they made a sacrifice to Yahweh. In doing this they acted, it may be remarked, according to the E, and not according to the D code. How is this passage to be explained?

First of all it is to be remembered that we left the "house of Joseph" at Bethel. They of course had never received the D code. And this messenger is represented as speaking to a Hebrew people, one under the E and not the D code, and one which lived in Bethel. What can be more reasonable than to suppose that it is to this "house of Joseph" that the messenger spoke?

There is nothing in the Hebrew to indicate that this "messenger of Yahweh" was Yahweh himself, or indeed a supernatural being at all. He may have been, for all we are told, a mere man acting in the name of Yahweh. He may have been sent from Joshua's army to this near kindred people. He may have been Joshua himself.

The sacrifice implies that there was some agreement made between this messenger and the people of Bochim. Why not suppose that this agreement was an alliance between the people at Bethel and Joshua's army?[1]

It is to be noted that, while these people did make some

have been of the peoples who had joined Moses' army. Now, of course, people cannot be circumcised twice. Therefore, since there are two great circumcisions implied in the text, there would seem certainly to have been another accession of new people to the Israelite army.

[1] This new alliance naturally explains the "second" circumcision at Gilgal.

sort of an agreement with the "messenger of Yahweh," they did *not* abandon their E-code sacrifices. If our supposition be correct, then, we have a portion of the Israelite army which was not under the D code at all, but which, nevertheless, was in active alliance with that portion which was.

The Second Conquest

From Gilgal the army started out to conquer the land. The sequence of events in this conquest is perfectly plain through the conquest of Jericho and Ai, the alliance with Gibeon, and the war with the five kings, headed by the King of Jerusalem. From this place on everyone agrees that we have only fragments, and those not placed in chronological order. For example, the war against Jabin of Hazor, recorded in Josh. 11:1-15, belongs to the close of Joshua's life, while the meeting with Caleb,[1] and the conquest of the south country[2] are dated in the fifth year after the crossing of the Jordan. The conquest of middle Palestine is not mentioned at all in the Book of Joshua. Still, it must have taken place, because Joshua went up to Mount Ebal and erected there the altar and the twelve stones. There his people ratified and accepted the D code.[3] This event took place before he met Caleb. Consequently we are able to date the conquest of middle Palestine at some time before the fifth year of the conquest.

Directly after this conquest of middle Palestine, and before the meeting with Caleb, the Ark of the Covenant was settled in Gilgal. Of course this Gilgal cannot be the one between the Jordan and Jericho. It is doubtless the one in Ephraim, southeast of Shiloh and north of Bethel.

---

[1] Josh. 14:6.   [2] Josh. 11:16.   [3] Josh. 8:30-35.

This Gilgal is a central place and was well adapted for a base for the operations of Joshua. Further, it belonged to the territory of Joshua's own tribe, Ephraim.

The Reunion of Joshua and Caleb

Here, in the fifth year of the conquest, Joshua received Caleb, son of Jephunneh, and the tribe of Judah. Now, as we have observed, this is the first mention of Caleb since the secession at Kadesh. What more natural, then, than that Caleb's very first words should have referred to this event of forty-five years ago? "Then the children of Judah drew nigh to Joshua in Gilgal, and Caleb, the son of Jephunneh, the Kenizzite, said unto him, Thou knowest the thing that Yahweh said unto Moses the man of God, concerning me and concerning thee, in Kadesh-barnea. Forty years old was I when Moses the servant of Yahweh sent me from Kadesh-barnea to spy out the land; and I brought him word again as it was in my heart. Nevertheless my brethren that went up with me made the heart of the people melt: but I wholly followed Yahweh my God. And Moses sware on that day, saying, Surely the land whereon thy foot has trodden shall be an inheritance to thee and to thy children forever, because thou hast wholly followed Yahweh my God. And now, behold, Yahweh has kept me alive, as he spake, these forty and five years, from the time that Yahweh spake this word unto Moses, while Israel walked in the wilderness: and now, lo, I am this day fourscore and five years old. As yet I am as strong this day as I was in the day that Moses sent me: as my strength was then even so is my strength now, for war, and to go out and to come in. Now, therefore, give me this mountain, whereof Yahweh spake in that day; for thou heardest in that day how the Anakim were there, and cities great and fenced; it may be that Yahweh will be with me, and I shall drive them out, as Yahweh spake. And Joshua blessed him, and he gave Hebron unto Caleb, the son of Jephunnah, for an inheritance."[1]

The passage has been worth quoting in full. It is very evidently just the speech that a man would make who, "while Israel walked in the wilderness," had been living apart from Joshua. He now reminds Joshua, his old friend, of events in which, forty-five years before, they had borne their part together, calling his attention even to small details. He asks Joshua to assist him in keeping possession of the land granted him so many years before by Moses. And Joshua, touched, and perhaps only too willing to conciliate this powerful tribe of Judah and to amalgamate it into his own confederacy, consents, and grants him permission to occupy Hebron. No mention is made, however, at this time, of Judah's accepting the D code. It is to be supposed that the tribe still retained the E code, with which it had seceded at Kadesh.

The War with Jabin

After this, we know that Joshua went on conquering land after land, until finally he succeeded in overcoming Jabin, king of Hazor. In this conquest Joshua is represented as meeting his enemy in northern Palestine near the waters of Merom.[2] But we know that he was not alone in this war. Another army of Israelites, under the command of Deborah and Barak, met another army of this king Jabin of Hazor under the command of his general Sisera, in the valley of Jezreel.[3] In both battles,

---

[1] Josh. 14:6–13.   [2] Josh. 11:7–16.   [3] Judg. 4:1—5:31.

that in the north and that in the south, the hosts of Israel were successful, and Jabin was utterly routed.

It is to be noted that in this second army, under Deborah and Barak, there were not complete tribes, but only "remnants" of tribes. These remnants, moreover, were of Ephraim, Benjamin, Machir (a clan of Manasseh), Zebulon, Issachar, and Naphtali. Moreover, in the Song of Deborah, Dan and Asher are reproached for not coming up to help in the battle. Now all of these tribes, with the exception of Issachar, are mentioned in that passage in Judges[1] which, as we have seen, probably refers to Palestinian conquests after Kadesh but before the arrival of Joshua. Does not the suggestion naturally follow that most of the army of Deborah and Barak may have con sisted of those Hebrew peoples which had been in the land before Joshua came?

The Covenant in Shiloh

This war with Jabin of Hazor completed the conquest of Canaan. It would be the most natural thing in the world if, after such an event, the various Hebrew peoples of the land should meet together to form a more perfect coalition, both political and religious. The next thing we find in the E document is that such a meeting actually did take place.[2] The people met together at Shiloh,[3] which was an old sanctuary and at this time had a temple.[4]

---

[1] Judg. 1:1—2:5.   [2] Josh. 24:1–32a.

[3] Josh. 24:1, 25. It is true that the Hebrew text says Shechem. But all the old Greek texts give Shiloh, and as they are hundreds of years older than our Hebrew, they are, in a matter like this, to be accepted. We can see just when the corruption arose in the Hebrew text, for the version of Lucian, which may go back to a text as late as the time of Christ, is the first to have Shechem in this place. The Syriac Peshitta, of the same period as the Lucianic text, also gives the later reading.

[4] Josh. 24:26.

Here Joshua gathered together all the tribes of Israel, and recited for them their history from the departure of Abraham from the old Hebrew home in Eber-hannahar, telling of Abraham's conversion to the Yahweh worship, his settlement in the land of Canaan, his descendants, Isaac, Jacob, and Esau, Esau's taking possession of Seir, and how Jacob and his children went down into Egypt. Then he told how God sent Moses and Aaron, who plagued Egypt, and at last brought their fathers out of the land of bondage. He recounted how they came to the Red Sea, where Yahweh saved them. He then reminded them of the events of the conquest of the east-Jordanic lands, of the capturing of Jericho, and finally of the subduing of the Canaanitic peoples.

He then demanded of the people whether they would serve Yahweh or some heathen God. Now, we have no intimation of any lapse from faith on the part of the people who came in with Joshua. But we have seen that the people of Bochim had lapsed from their faith,[1] and that these people were probably among the seceders at Kadesh. If this were true of one of the seceding tribes, it may well have been true of the others.[2] If this be true, it gives additional point to Joshua's cry, "As for *me* and *my house*, we will serve Yahweh!"

The people with one accord accepted Yahweh's religion, and agreed to turn from their heathen gods. Joshua and the people thereupon made a covenant to that effect.[3] Then we read that Joshua "set them a statute and an ordinance" in Shiloh. Now a "statute," as we have seen, is a religious or ceremonial law. The word "ordinance" here is not a correct translation. The original is *mishpat*,

[1] Judg. 2:1–5.   [2] Cf. Judg. 4:1–3.   [3] Josh. 24:25.

meaning a "judgment," or a civil law. Joshua wrote these, though, not in the Book of the Law of Moses, i. e., Deuteronomy, but in the Book of the Law of Elohim, i. e., the E code.

It is easy to see why this should have been the case, for it is hard to believe that the tribes which seceded at Kadesh would ever have agreed at this time to accept the D code, which had been given long after they had left the tribes in the wilderness, and which had thus been given to only a portion of the original confederation.

The E code, then, became the law for all the confederated peoples which made the covenant at Shiloh, and it remained so at least for the rest of the period of the judges, as was observed in our consideration of the non Levitical sacrifices. The D code was for the time dis carded. It remained written on the stones at the moun tain of Ebal, and certainly other copies of it were in existence, but for the people as a whole it fell into disuse, at least for the time being.

Conclusion

We have now brought down the history of the E and D codes from the leaving of Egypt to the death of Joshua. We have seen that, for a large portion of the people—those who seceded at Kadesh—the E code was the only code acknowledged in this period, and that it was to the other portion only—those who remained with Moses—that the D code was given. Lastly, we have seen that after the conquest of Canaan, when all the tribes were reunited, it was on the basis of E, and not of D, and that D sank into disuse throughout the period of the judges, during which time the E code, non-Levitical sacrifices included, was in force among the people.

CHAPTER X

The Language of the E and D Documents

The E sections of the Hexateuch have a distinct vocabulary. We have postulated for the P document a P or Levitical dialect. The arguments then given for the existence of a dialect peculiar to the tribe of Levi will serve equally well here for the language of E. We find that Joshua, who had much to do with the E code, was of the tribe of Ephraim. The code was finally ratified in Shiloh, which was in the territory of Ephraim. In the E sections of Genesis and Joshua particular attention is paid to the enumeration of the cities of Ephraim. After the split of the kingdom, as we have seen, the E code was in force in the Northern Kingdom, and especially in Ephraim. These facts all point to one conclusion, namely, that the language of the E code was the tribal dialect of the tribe of Ephraim.[1]

Not only is the D code based upon the E code, but its

---

[1] Some sections of the E document are not so distinct in language as critical scholars generally assume when they assign them to E. This applies especially to Genesis, e. g., Gen. 20:1–18; 21:22–34; 26:1, 6–23; 26:26–33; 35:8; the E sections of chap. 37; 40:15; 41:38–40; 45:16–21; 45:27; 46:5; 50:15–21. It applies also to Joshua 24:32b, 33. In none of these sections is scarcely a word that is not found in the later P document and code, although some of the words may not be so common in P as in E. It is, however, evident that this E language was known to P. There seems to be no cogent reason, therefore, why these so-called E sections should not be ascribed to P. If they are to be called E, they ought at least to be separated from the early E, and called E2 sections. An exception to this must be made in the case of three words: the word for "pray," in Gen. 20:7, 17; the word for "on account of," in Gen. 21:25; 26:32; and the word for "dream," in Gen. 20:3, 6. These three words alone, of course, are not enough to separate these documents from the late P, or from the late E document.

language, too, comes nearest to that of E.   We found that the D code was finally recorded on the stones at Ebal and Gerizim, i. e., at Shechem.   May not the language of D be a local variation of the Ephraimite dialect, peculiar to the Shechem region?

CHAPTER XI

The J Document

It may be that there is no J code in the Hexateuch, but only fragments of a J document. The sections which have been ordinarily considered as making up that code, Exod., chap. 34, really seem to belong, as we have seen, to the E code. It is perfectly possible that there was a J code originally, but that it was so similar to the E code that it was dropped in favor of the latter at the time of the compilation. What little there is to be said about the J document may be divided into three heads: date, unity, and language.

I. Date

Modern critics generally assign the J document to *ca.* 850–800 B. C. It may, they say, have been a century earlier than this. It cannot, however, so they claim, have preceded the time of David, because there is, in a J section in Num. 21:14, 15, a quotation from the "Book of the Wars of Yahweh," and in the Book of Samuel there is a quotation from the same book regarding David. But this is really not conclusive, for this quotation may have been added from the "Book of the Wars of Yahweh" at the time when the documents were combined. There is no reason why J cannot be as early as E, namely the time of the Covenant at Horeb. There is nothing to show that it is earlier or later.

II. Unity

It cannot be denied that there was an original J document, but from the remains which we have of that document in our Hexateuch we are forced to say the same thing of it as we have already said of E and P, namely, that there have been only fragments preserved to us. It is admitted on all hands that in large sections of Genesis, Exodus, Numbers, and Joshua, J and E have been so fused together that it is now impossible ever to divide them. Nor is this necessary, for J and E relate the same history and the same events. Any attempt completely to divide these documents can only be for the satisfaction of a literary curiosity.

It is a fact of greater importance that we find J fused with later P passages, and borrowing from P, e. g., when J, in Exod. chaps. 19, 24, 34, uses Sinai for Horeb. It will be shown in a later chapter that these two mountains are not identical and cannot be considered as one. The occurrence of Sinai in a J document can be explained only on the supposition that the priestly redactor, in compiling J sections with P, assumed that any reference in J to the mountain of the law-giving must be to the Sinai of the P document. Other cases of the same sort, but of less importance, will be noted below.

III. Language

First of all, the language is the dialect of Judah. We have already seen that P represents the dialect of Levi, and E and D the dialect of Ephraim. J centers itself around places in Judah, especially around Hebron. That city was the first capital of David. Caleb, prince of Judah, received it as his inheritance and capital. At a later time it was granted to Aaron's family as a Levitical city. This last fact may account for a compilation of J and P in Hebron, and a fusion of those documents. Besides all this, the language is so distinct that it seems certainly a tribal dialect. We cannot go far wrong in assuming it to be the tribal dialect of Judah.[1]

The difficulty that the study of the Hebrew language offers to beginners is well known. The explanation of this difficulty is not to be found in its peculiar alphabet, because that is soon mastered. Nor is it to be found in the flexion of the words, nor in the syntax, in both which respects the Hebrew is far simpler than either Greek or Latin. Nor does Hebrew possess a large vocabulary. The real difficulty lies in the many and varied meanings that Hebrew words possess.

A close study of this difficulty reveals the fact that it arises from the fusion into one book of the literary products of many and varied dialects. This is the case, not only in the Hexateuch, but in most of the historical books, especially in Judges, Samuel, Kings, and Chronicles, which we know were compiled from a large number of original documents. It is also the case in some of the prophets, Isaiah and Zechariah especially. Proverbs and Psalms belong to the same class. They are compiled from a large number of documents, which originated in several tribes, and which bear, therefore, the dialectic peculiarities pertaining to those tribes.

By calling attention to these dialectic peculiarities we do not desire to be construed as denying the continuous development of the Hebrew language. But this law of development may be extended to dialects as well.

The study of these linguistic peculiarities in the Hexateuch seems to reveal the following facts:

I. Dialectical Denotations of Words

A single Hebrew word has often several denotations, each of which belongs to a different tribe; as, e. g.:

Yarek. In Judah (J and the Toledoth Book) it signifies "thigh"

---

[1] Some sections of the J document in Genesis differ from the other J sections in much the same way that we saw prevailing in the E document. As these sections, however, contain the name of Yahweh, they must come from a J source, but belong to later strata of the J literature

(euphemistic for *membrum virile*.)[1]   In Benjamin it meant "side" or "loin."[2]   In Levi it denoted "base," "seat," or "standard."

Paqad.   In Judah it meant "pay attention to," "attend to," "observe;" in Ephraim, "visit," "visit upon," "punish;" in Levi, "appoint," "muster," "pass in review."

Minḫa.   In Ephraim it signified "present;" in Judah, "offering;" in Levi, "meal-offering."

II.   Modifications of Meaning of Words

Words common to all the tribes are modified in their denotations in the course of the development of the language; e. g.:

Ḥaṭât.   In JED it equals "sin;" in P, "sin" and "sin-offering."

Maqôm.   In JED, "sanctuary;" in P, "place."

Mišpeʾah.   In Judah (J and P[1]), "kindred" (Greek συγγενεια); in Levi (P[2]), "clan" (Greek φυλη).

Yaraš.   In Ephraim (E[1]), "take possession of," "drive out;" in Levi (P[2] E[2]), "inherit."

'Aḥaz.   In Ephraim (E[1] J[1] ?), "seize;" in Levi, "to possess."

Mišpat.   In P[1] and JED, "judgment;" in P[2], "manner," "ceremony."

III.   Tribal Vocabulary

Each tribe has in a number of cases its own peculiar word to express a common idea; e. g.:

"Handmaid."   In Judah (J and P[1]), *šiphḥah;* in Ephraim and Levi (EDP[2]), *'amah.*

"Raiment."   In Judah and Levi (J and P), *beged;* in Ephraim (E), *salmah* and *simlah.*

"I."   In JEDP[1], *anoki;* in P[2], *'ani.*

"Prince."   In JED, *šar;* in P, *našî'.*

"Tribe."   In JED, *šebeṭ* (as also in P in the sense of a subdivision of a tribe); in P, *maṭṭe.*

"Dwell."   In J, *yašab;* in D, *(le)šakken;* in P, *šakan.*

"Thigh" (euphemistic).   In J, *yarek;* in P, *halaṣayim.*

---

[1] Exod. 1:5.

[2] Judg. 3:16, 21.

CHAPTER XII

Differences Between P and JED.—The Settlements in Egypt

Most critics claim, of course, that the discrepancies between the four documents are due to their being variants of one and the same story, due to different traditions. While this is doubtless sufficient explanation of such differences as exist between J, E, and D, it will not at all suffice to explain those between P and the other three documents. In a comparison of these four documents, such as we are about to undertake, it is impossible to commence before the thirty-ninth chapter of Genesis, because the D document begins properly only with the settlement in Egypt. Comparisons of the three documents visible before that time are not to be a part of this study, which from this point on will deal more particularly with the events of the Exodus and the conquest of Canaan.

The differences between what we may assume to be the composite narrative of JED and the narrative of P are of such a radical nature as to demand careful consideration. Some of the discrepancies are due, doubtless, to errors and interpolations which have crept into the modern Hebrew Massoretic text during the ages. This may be seen clearly when comparisons are made with the ancient versions, such as the LXX, the Syriac, and the Aramaic translations. But even this is not sufficient to explain the greater number of discrepancies. Let us see what some of these differences are. And, first of all, let us examine the accounts of the settlements in Egypt.

These are given in Gen. 46:28—47:12. It is almost impossible to accept our Hebrew text as it stands. Quite evidently there have been corruptions. The most accurate text which lower criticism is able to afford us is based chiefly on the LXX. For the sake of convenience the two accounts, according to divisions of this reconstructed text, are here presented side by side.

J

P

Gen. 46:28: And he sent Judah before *them*, unto Joseph, into the land of *Raamses*.

29. And Joseph made ready his chariots, and went up to meet Israel his father, *at Heroo-polis;* and he presented himself unto him, and fell on his neck, and wept on his neck a good while. 30. And Israel said unto Joseph, Now let me die, since I have seen thy face, that thou art yet alive. 31. And Joseph said unto his brethren, and unto his father's house, I will go up, and will tell Pharaoh, and will say unto him, My brethren, and my father's house, which were in the land of Canaan, are come unto me; 32. and the men are shepherds, for they have been keepers of cattle; and they have brought their flocks, and their herds, and all that they have. 33. And it shall come to pass, when Pharaoh shall call you, and shall say, What is your occupation? 34. that ye shall say, Thy servants have been keepers of cattle, from our youth even until now, both we and our fathers: that ye may dwell in the land of Goshen of *Arabia;* for

J

P

every shepherd is an abomination unto the Egyptians. 47:1: Then Joseph went in, and told Pharaoh,[1] and said, My father and my brethren and their flocks and their herds, and all that they have, are come out of the land of Canaan; and behold, they are in the land of Goshen. 2. And from among his brethren he took five men, and presented them unto Pharaoh. 3. And Pharoah said unto the brethren *of Joseph*, What is your occupation? And they said unto Pharaoh, Thy servants are shepherds, both we and our fathers. 4. And they said unto Pharaoh, To sojourn in the land are we come, for there is no pasture for thy servant's flocks; for the famine is sore in the land of Canaan: now, therefore, we pray thee, let thy servants dwell in the land of Goshen. 5. And Pharaoh said unto Joseph, In the land of Goshen let them dwell; and if thou knowest any able men among them, then make them rulers over my cattle.

6. And Jacob and his sons came into Egypt to Joseph. And Pharaoh, the king of Egypt heard (thereof). And Pharaoh spake unto Joseph, saying, Thy father and thy brethren are come unto thee; behold, the land of Egypt is before thee; in the best of the land make thy father and thy brethren to dwell. 7. And Joseph brought in

---

[1] Codex Alexandrinus (Greek) reads, "And Pharaoh went in and told Joseph."

J

Jacob, his father, and set him before Pharaoh: and Jacob blessed Pharaoh. 8. And Pharaoh said unto Jacob, How many are the days of the years of thy life? 9. And Jacob said unto Pharaoh,

The days of the years of my pilgrimage are an hundred and thirty years;[1]

Few and evil have been the days of the years of my life.

but they have not attained unto the days of the years of the life of my fathers in the days of their pilgrimage.[1]

10. And Jacob blessed Pharaoh, and went out from the presence of Pharaoh. 11. And Joseph placed his father and his brethren in the land of Egypt, *in the best land*, in the land of Raamses, as Pharaoh had commanded.

12. And Joseph nourished his father, and his brethren, and all his father's household with bread, according to their families.

These, then, are the stories of the settlement in Egypt. According to J and its kindred documents, Israel and his sons were settled in the land of Goshen. In P the settlement of Jacob is confined to the land of Raamses. These two districts are not by any means the same.

Land of Goshen

Goshen was the capital of the twentieth nome of Egypt, Arabia, and was that part of the Delta east of the Nile

---

[1] This passage, while P in character, evidently belongs to the Toledoth Book, because of the exactness of the date and its quaint language. We have shown above that this book is an early document.

and bordering on it, i. e., the district in the vicinity of Belbeis, Saft el-Henneh, and Abu Hamad.[1]

Land of Raamses

But in P it is not in Goshen, but in "the land of Raamses" that the people are settled. "The land of Raamses," of course, means the land around the city of Raamses, just as "the land of Goshen" means the land around the city of Goshen. We know that Ramses II built a city named after himself.[2] This city was rebuilt by Ramses III, though it was still called after the name of the former builder.[3] Petrie has advanced the suggestion that this city of Raamses was located at the modern Tel el-Rota bieh,[4] but his suggestion seems to be on not very sufficient grounds. In the manuscript of Gamurrini a pious woman relates that she left Heroo-polis to go to Goshen, which was sixteen miles away, and that on her journey she passed

[1] Pe(r)-Soped was the ancient name of the modern Saft el-Henneh, and was the old capital of the nome of Arabia. Cf. Naville, *Saft el-Henneh, p. 15.* In Coptic, Goshen, LXX *Gesem*, is called *Kos*, which the Greeks rendered *Pha-Kusa*, Latin *Phacusa. Pha* is the definite article. *Kos* or *Kusa* is an abbreviation of *Kesem*, which latter is found in Egyptian inscriptions. *Gesem* and *Kesem* are, of course, variants of the same name. Consequently *Goshen*, or *Kesem*, or *Gesem*, is the city-land of *Kesem* known in the monuments, i. e., the capital of the twentieth nome. Moreover, in the Arabic version of *Saadiah Gaon*, Goshen is rendered Sadir, which Quatremère locates at Abbaseh, in the region of the modern Saft el-Henneh. With this Abu Said agrees. Macrizi states that Belbeis is in this land.

[2] The city of Ramses II existed in the twenty-first year of that king, for the ambassadors of the Hittite king were received by him there in that year. Cf. Lepsius, *Denkmäler*, III, pl. 146, l. 2. According to Lepsius, *Denkmäler*, Text, Part IV, pl. 49, this city, "House of Ramses (II)—Meriamon" was again referred to in Ramses II's twenty-ninth year.

[3] Ramses III states, in Papyrus Harris, pl. 60, l. 2, " I rebuilt the great temple, (and) laboriously enlarged the same, in the House of Sutekh of Ramses (II)—Meriamon."

[4] Cf. *Hyksos and Israelite Cities*, p. 28.

through the city of Raamses, which was four miles from Goshen, the capital of Arabia. This would correspond to the location of the modern Tel el-Kebir, a great mound which has not yet been explored. Here we feel inclined to locate the city and "land" of Raamses. This location would tally perfectly with all the data in the monuments, the classical authors, and the Bible. If this prove to be correct, the city of Raamses must have belonged to the Nome of the East, the eighth nome of Lower Egypt, the capital of which was Pithom. At any rate, Raamses is not the same as Goshen.

Now if, as we have seen good reason for believing, the documents were composed within forty or fifty years after the leaving of Egypt, it is hard to believe that their authors should have been so confused and so forgetful that they confounded two city-lands so distinct and separate as Goshen and Raamses, and were ignorant as to which was really the Israelite habitat when in Egypt. There suggests itself at once the hypothetical question, *Were there two exodi, one from Raamses and the other from Goshen?*

CHAPTER XIII

Differences Between P and JED.—The Servitudes in Egypt

In the story of the oppression, the following sections should be assigned to P: Exod. 1:1-7,[1] 11b-14; 2:23-25. The other sections of the five first chapters of Exodus belong to JE.

In the JE account there are taskmasters appointed over the Israelites, and these force them to do field labor and to make bricks without straw. In the P document, they are forced to do a similar kind of serf labor, but there is nothing mentioned of anything like making bricks without straw. The P account further mentions—which is not touched on in JE—that they built store-cities for Pharaoh, Pithom, and Raamses.[2] Now the store-city of Pithom has been discovered by Naville at the modern Tel el-Maskhutah.[3] It is a city which, although dating from early times, was really built by Ramses II and rebuilt by

---

[1] This section, while P in character, belongs to the Toledoth Book: see above, pp. 54 f.

[2] Exod. 1:11b.

[3] Pithom, originally Pe(r)-Tum or Pe(r)-Atum, meaning "House of Tum," or "House of Atum," the city of the sun-god Tum or Atum, who was the predecessor of Re, the sun-god of Heliopolis, was the capital of the eighth nome of Lower Egypt, the civil name of which was the Eastern Nome. In later times the nome was also called "the Heroopolitan." On the eastern border of this nome was a city and a land called Succoth, the ancient name of which was "Door of the East." This city was located on the northern end of Lake Timsah, "Crocodile Lake." Naville has identified Pithom and Succoth, but on insufficient grounds. Succoth was several miles east of Pithom. Nor did Lake Timsah, on which Succoth was situated, extend west as far as Pithom in the Nineteenth Dynasty. The marsh land to the east of Pithom was, in the time of Mer-

Ramses III. There is nothing to show that the bricks of the city were made without straw. Raamses we have already located at the modern Tel el-Kebir.[1] To these

neptah, called "The Pools of Pithom," but this was a region quite distinct from Lake Timsah.

Naville assumes also that Heroo-polis, the Roman Ero, is identical with Pithom, because the Red Sea is called the "Heroopolitan Gulf." And indeed in the Bohairic version Heroo-polis is rendered Pithom, not because they were identical but because Pithom was the capital of the nome. It is certain that Heroo-polis was located on the shore (*clusma*), of that gulf. But it is not probable that the gulf extended up to Pithom at this time. Ptolemy the geographer asserts twice that Ero was only one-sixth of a degree from the head or upper end of the Arabian Gulf. Pliny and Strabo assert likewise that Heroo-polis was located on the Arabian Gulf. But when Ptolemy dug his soft-water canal, connecting the Nile with the Eastern Nome, it passed by Arsinoe, and still was not connected with the Bitter Lakes. This makes it impossible that the Arabian Gulf should have extended to Pithom in the time of Ptolemy. Furthermore, Herodotus says that it was one thousand stadia from Mount Casius. As we must admit that Herodotus used the shorter stadium (ninety-eight meters), his statement places the head of the Arabian Gulf near the northern end of the present Bitter Lakes. Here then Heroo-polis was located. It was here, according to the JE document, that Joseph met his father when he came into Egypt. It is of great importance that we bear in mind that the Arabian Gulf extended up to this point, and included the Bitter Lakes, which at this time stretched a little farther north than they do at present.

[1] It is interesting to note that in the Arabic version of *Saadiah Gaon* the land of Raamses, in Gen. 47:11, and the city of Raamses, in Exod. 1:11, are rendered as "the Well of the Sun" (*Ain-Šemes*). Now the Egyptian monuments know of a canal called "Water of Re" or "Water of the Sun." The name implies that it may have run close by the city of Heliopolis. This canal is not known before the eleventh year of Ramses III, when he slew the Libyan army on its banks. The same canal is again mentioned by the same king in Papyrus Harris (pl. 10, l. 8, and pl. 62a, l. 2). This canal can be nothing else than the old canal of Wady Tumilat, where lately the Ishmalieh Canal was dug. It started near Cairo, passed Heliopolis, Northern Heliopolis, and Belbeis, turned westward at Abbaseh, passed ¡Raamses (Tel el-Kebir), Tel el-Rotabieh, Pithom (Tel el-Maskhutah), and flowed into Lake Timsah at its northern end. "The Water of the Sun" thus flowed through all the land where in P we find traces of the Hebrew settlements. Furthermore this canal supplied water for all of the Eastern Nome, which Ramses II reclaimed for cultivation, and in which he built his magnificent cities, mentioned in P, cities which were afterward rebuilt by Ramses III, ostensibly because they had been destroyed in the period of anarchy which intervened between the Nineteenth and Twentieth dynasties.

the LXX adds the name of On, or Heliopolis. This, of course, cannot be the old city of Heliopolis, the history of which goes back to the time of the Fifth Dynasty. It must be the northern Heliopolis, modern Tel el-Jehudieh, the Roman Vicus Judaeorum.[1] At the time these cities were being built[2] there is not a mention in the monuments of Goshen, except in the geographical lists. It seems to have been favored neither by Ramses II nor by Ramses III. Merneptah seems to allude to it, only to say that it had been abandoned since the time of the ancestors and given up to pasturage. This implies, of course, that once, in the past, it had been a cultivated land.

The period of the servitude in Egypt, then, as known to the author of the P document, can clearly be determined. The people settled in the land of Raamses and helped build the cities of Raamses and Pithom. Before the reign of Ramses II no land of Raamses existed, for it was he who reclaimed the land from the swamps. And it was Ramses III who rebuilt these cities, so the monuments clearly say, and he did it with serf labor from Asia! And, of course, if they settled in Ramses II's reign, he could hardly have been the Pharaoh of the oppression. This Pharaoh must have been Ramses III. The date of the servitude, then, according to the evidence derived from P itself, seems to have been the reign of Ramses III, i. e., 1181–1150 B. C.

[1] We know from Papyrus Harris (pl. 29, ll. 8–12) that Ramses III built a temple in "the House of Re on the north of Heliopolis." This northern Heliopolis is not known on the monuments before the reign of this king, although it still existed in the time of Sheshonk I (Lepsius, *Denkmaler*, III, 253*a*, l. 12 This city has been identified with the modern Tel el-Jehudieh, the Roman Vicus Judaeorum, near Belbeis. This Vicus Judaeorum is not to be confused with another Tel el-Jehudieh, which in Latin is called Scenae Veteranorum, the place where Onias built his temple.

[2] I. e., the Nineteenth and Twentieth dynasties.

PAPYRUS HARRIS, P[l] 29, ll. 8–12

But what of the oppression in the JE document? In it there is no mention of the building of these great store-cities of Raamses and Pithom. Now if, as we have seen from our dating of the documents, there is no reason to doubt that JE was written forty years after the departure from Egypt, or less, can it be supposed that in this very short time all memory of the slaving on these cities, in which the people had suffered so grievously, should have utterly perished from the mind of the JE author? It seems fair and conservative to assume that the people among whom the JE document arose had had no connection whatever with the store-cities of Pithom and Raamses.

Furthermore, if the JE exodus came from the land of Goshen, as it did, it must have passed by these cities on the way to the Red Sea, *if they were then existent.* But, although we have full mention of the cities they passed from the Red Sea to Horeb, there is no mention at all of any cities before the Red Sea. Does it not seem likely, then, that the Exodus told of in JE must have taken place at a time before these cities were built, when the later "land of Raamses" was a waste marsh, uninhabited? And this probable conclusion is made practically certain by the remark, in Exod. 13:18, "But God led the people about, *by the way of the wilderness,* unto the Red Sea."[1] We are forced, then, from evidence furnished by JE, to date the servitude and exodus of which it tells before the time of Ramses II, who reclaimed the wilderness and built the cities.

[1] In R. V. this phrase is rendered "*by* the Red Sea." The Hebrew may mean either "*of* the Red Sea" or "*to* the Red Sea." It cannot be "*by* the Red Sea." The LXX, the Targum Onkelos, the Syriac version, and the Arabic version all unite in rendering it "*to* the Red Sea." The inaccurate Vulgate alone, outside of the English versions, renders it "*by.*"

CHAPTER XIV

Differences Between P and JED.—The Going-out from Egypt

Even if we felt inclined to think that the exodus of P were not different from that of JED in time, we would find it hard to believe that they were not different in locality and route.

Again we place the two accounts of the route out of Egypt in parallel columns:

JE

(They were) about 600,000 (or 600 clans) on foot that were men, besides children, 38. and a mixed multitude went up also with them; and flocks and herds, even very much cattle. . . . . .

13:17: And it came to pass, when Pharaoh had let the people go, that God led them not by the way of the land of the Philistines, although that was near; for God said, Lest peradventure the people repent when they see war, and they return to Egypt; 18. but God led the people about by the way of the wilderness to the Red Sea: and the children of Israel went up armed out of the land of Egypt.

P

Exod. 12:37: And the children of Israel journeyed from Raamses to Succoth;

20. And they took their journey from Succoth, and encamped in Etham, in the edge of the wilderness.

JE

P

21. And Yahweh went before them, by day in a pillar of cloud, to lead them the way; and by night in a pillar of fire, to give them light; that they might go by day and by night.

14:1: And Yahweh spake unto Moses, saying, 2. Speak unto the children of Israel, that they turn back and encamp before Pi-Hahiroth, between Migdol and the Sea, before Baal-Zephon; over against it shall ye encamp by the Sea. 3. And Pharaoh will say of the children of Israel, They are entangled in the land; the wilderness has shut them in. 4. And I will make strong Pharaoh's heart, and he shall follow after; and I will get me honor upon Pharaoh and upon all his host and the Egyptians shall know that I am Yahweh. And they did so.

5. And it was told the king of Egypt that the people were fled; and the heart of Pharaoh and of his servants was changed toward the people, and they said, What is this we have done, that we have let Israel go from serving us? 6. And he made ready his chariot, and took his people with him: 7. and he took 600 chosen chariots,

8. And Yahweh made strong the heart of Pharaoh, king of Egypt, and he pursued after the children of Israel: for the children of Israel went out with an high hand. `9` And the Egyptians pursued after them, all the horses and chariots

JE

P

of Pharaoh, and his horsemen and his army; and he overtook them, encamping by the Sea, beside Pi-Hahiroth, before Baal-Zephon.

10. And when Pharaoh drew nigh the children of Israel lifted up their eyes and behold, the Egyptians marched after them; and they were sore afraid: and the children of Israel cried out unto Yahweh. 11. And they said unto Moses, Because there were no graves in Egypt, hast thou taken us to die in the wilderness? Wherefore hast thou dealt thus with us, to bring us forth out of Egypt? . . . . 15. And Yahweh said unto Moses, Wherefore criest thou unto me?

Speak unto the children of Israel, that they go forward.

16. (And) lift thou up thy rod;

And stretch out thy hand over the Sea, and divide it, and the children of Israel shall go into the midst of the Sea on dry ground. 17. And I, behold, I will make strong the hearts of the Egyptians, and they shall go in after them: and I will get me honor upon Pharaoh, and upon all his host, upon his chariots, and upon his horsemen.

19. And the angel of God, which went before the camp of Israel, removed and went behind them; and the pillar of cloud removed from before them, and stood behind them; 20. and it came between the camp of Egypt and the camp of Israel; and there was the cloud and the darkness, yet gave it light

JE

by night: and the one came not near
the other, all the night.

P

21. And Moses stretched out his
hand over the Sea, and Yahweh
caused the Sea to go back by a
strong east wind all the night, and
made the Sea dry land, and the
waters were divided. 22. And the
children of Israel went into the
midst of the Sea upon the dry
ground: and the waters were a wall
unto them, on their right hand and
on their left. 23. And the Egyptians pursued, and went in after
them into the midst of the Sea, all
Pharaoh's horses, his chariots, and
his horsemen.

24. And it came to pass in the
morning watch, that Yahweh looked
forth upon the host of the Egyptians
through the pillar of fire and of
cloud, and discomfited the host of
the Egyptians. 25. And he bound
their chariot wheels, and made them
to drive heavily: so that the Egyptians said, Let us flee from the face
of Israel; for Yahweh fighteth for
them against the Egyptians.

26. And Yahweh said unto
Moses, Stretch out thy hand over
the Sea, that the waters may come
again upon the Egyptians, upon
their chariots and upon their horsemen. 27. And Moses stretched
forth his hand over the Sea,

And the Sea returned to its strength
when the morning appeared; and
the Egyptians fled against it;
and Yahweh overthrew the Egyptians in the midst of the Sea.

JE   P

28. and the waters returned, and covered the chariots, and the horsemen, even all the host of Pharaoh that went in after them into the Sea; there remained not so much as one of them. 29. But the children of Israel walked upon dry land in the midst of the Sea; and the waters were a wall unto them on their right hand and on their left.

30. Thus Yahweh saved Israel that day out of the hand of the Egyptians, and Israel saw the Egyptians dead upon the sea-shore. 31. And Israel saw the great work which Yahweh did upon the Egyptians, and the people feared Yahweh, and they believed in Yahweh and in his servant Moses.

15:22: And Moses led Israel onward from the Red Sea.

And they went out into the wilderness of Shur; and they went three days in the wilderness and found no water.

Another account of the P journeying at this time is given in Num. 33:5–8c: "And the children of Israel journeyed from Raamses and pitched in Succoth. They journeyed from Succoth and pitched in Etham, which is in the edge of the wilderness. And they journeyed from Etham, and turned unto Pi-Hahiroth, which is before Baal-Zephon: and they pitched before Migdol. And they journeyed from before Hahiroth, and passed through the midst of the Sea into the wilderness: and they went three days' journey into the wilderness of Etham."

The P Route

In the P account, the Israelites, after having left Egyptian territory, came to "the Sea." In no place ın P is this called "the Red Sea." When we attempt to identify it with "the Red Sea," we are reading into the P account something not contained there. Now, from both the Hebrew and the Greek usages, "the Sea," without further limitation, can mean only "the Mediterranean Sea." And the P document gives evidence that this is the meaning here.

When the Israelites had come to Succoth, they were told to *turn* and go to Pi-Hahiroth, between Baal-Zephon and Migdol. Now Succoth was on the northern end of Lake Timsah, and was located where now stands the village of Ishmailieh. From Lake Timsah to Lake Balah there was a line of Egyptian fortresses, called in the inscriptions "the Wall," and in Hebrew "Shur" (the Wall of Egypt). At the northern end of this "wall" was a great fortress called in the inscriptions "Tharu," which is an exact equivalent of "Shur," being the wall or fortress *par excellence*. The word in Egyptian for fortress is *khetem*. This is rendered in Hebrew *etham*[1]. When, therefore, the Bible speaks of "the wilderness of Etham," it means "the wilderness of the fort." This wilderness is, then, the same as that called "the wilderness of Shur," as, indeed, becomes quite plain when we compare with Exod. 15:22. Now we know from a number of other references in the Bible[2] that Shur was the wilderness to the east of the Egyptian border, between Lake Timsah and the Medi-

---

[1] Exod. 13:20; Num. 33:6, 7, 8. Egyptian *kh* corresponds sometimes to the Hebrew *aleph*. Cf. Brugsch, *Dict. Geog.*, p. 647.

[2] Gen. 16:7; 20:1; 25:18; I Sam. 15:7; 27:8.

terranean.   If, then, the children of Israel passed through this wilderness, when they turned it must have been to the north from Succoth, i. e., north from Lake Timsah.

From the inscriptions of Merneptah we know that the fortress of Succoth was very strong.   It is then easily seen that the turn to the north was made to avoid this powerful obstacle in the way.   But the fortress of Tharu or Etham was even stronger, and so they had to continue their march yet farther to the north.   They could not safely get between the fortresses, because the district between them was very thoroughly patrolled.   This we know because the commanders of the fortresses were required to send daily reports to Pharaoh of all who went into or out of Egypt at and around their posts.[1]

Pi-Hahiroth

Continuing northward, they encamped at Pi-Hahiroth, between Baal-Zephon and Migdol.   Fortunately we are quite able to locate these three places.   Pi-Hahiroth means "mouth of the *hiroth*," and this word *Hiroth*, Greek *eiroth*, means "lagoons."   As Brugsch has shown, this can refer, properly, only to the lagoons of the Delta, and in our account can mean only the lagoons of Lake Menzaleh.   The "mouth of the lagoons" would then be the place where Lake Menzaleh connects with Lake Balah. Between these two lakes there is now dry land, except for the artificial slip which starts the Suez Canal.   But formerly they were connected by shallow water, as geologists have been able to determine.   This place is indeed between Migdol, which lay to the east, and Baal-Zephon, which lay to the west.

[1] Cf. *ARE*, Vol. III, pp. 270–72.

Migdol

Migdol means in Hebrew "fortress," and it has been supposed by some that the Migdol mentioned here may have been any Egyptian fortress. But this is not the case. There was a fortress, evidently founded by Semites, to the east of Pi-Hahiroth. When it was taken over by the Egyptians they retained the Hebrew word for "fortress," by which it was called, as its proper name. Thus Migdol to the Egyptians meant, not any fortress, but this particular fortress. Both Ezekiel and Jeremiah mention Migdol in such a way as to imply, not only that it was a definite place, but also that it was the first Egyptian city to be met on a journey into that country.[1] In the classical references, we may call attention especially to the itinerary of Antoninus, which says that Magdolum was twelve Roman miles south of Pelusium.[2] Bir-Maqtal is its modern name. It is situated twenty-three miles northeast of Ishmailieh, in the desert. Some scholars, anxious to locate the Exodus in the south, say that there may have been a Migdol near Suez. In this regard it is necessary to remember that there never has been the slightest scrap of evidence advanced in support of this supposition. It is an assumption, pure and simple. From all the excavations, in the Delta and in other places in Egypt, and from all the inscriptions so far found, not one statement, not one intimation has been discovered of any Migdol near Suez, or anywhere else, for that matter, except south of Pelusium and east of Pi-Hahiroth. And this location answers every requirement both of the Bible and of the inscriptions.

[1] Ezek. 29:10; 30:6; Jer. 44:1; 46:14.

[2] "A Serapio Pelusio mpm LX Thaubasio VIII Sile XXVIII Magdolo XII Pelusio XII."

PAPYRUS HARRIS, P 10   12

Baal-Zephon

The name Baal-Zephon has never been discovered, exactly as it stands, in the Egyptian inscriptions. The name means "Lord of the Northland." But we know that Ramses III built a city in the northeastern Delta, which he called after his name and dedicated to "Amon of the Northland."[1] This name Zephon is changed by Ezekiel and Jeremiah to Tahpanhes.[2] This is identical with the name the Greeks gave to the city of "Amon of the Northland," i. e.; Daphnai, the modern Tel el-Defenneh. This city Petrie has excavated.[3] We know its exact location, and that it was founded by Ramses III. It is a few miles to the west of where the Suez Canal begins, i. e., a few miles to the west of where we have located Pi-Hahiroth.

An examination of the map will show that the only place where the Hebrews could hope to penetrate the natural and artificial fortifications on the border of Egypt and so pass out into the desert was across the shallow waters between Lake Balah and Lake Menzaleh. And it is not at all unlikely that a strong eastern wind[4] could so have driven back the waters from this narrow strip that the place would have become passable. The two lakes, Balah and Menzaleh, would then have been the two metaphorical "walls of water on either side," of the biblical account. Furthermore Lake Menzaleh is really

[1] Papyrus Harris, Pl. 10, l. 12. Cf. Pl. 8, ll. 2–8.

[2] Jer. 2:16; 43:7, 8, 9; 44:1; 46:14; Ezek. 30:18. Hebrew *tsade* often becomes *t* or *d* in Greek. Cf. Hebrew *Zoan* and Greek *Tannis*. Cf. again Typhon the God of Avaris, the Hyksos stronghold.

[3] Cf. *Tanis II*.

[4] On the other hand, an eastern wind on the Red Sea would rather increase than diminish the water at its northeastern end. An eastern wind on Menzaleh would have just the effect desired.

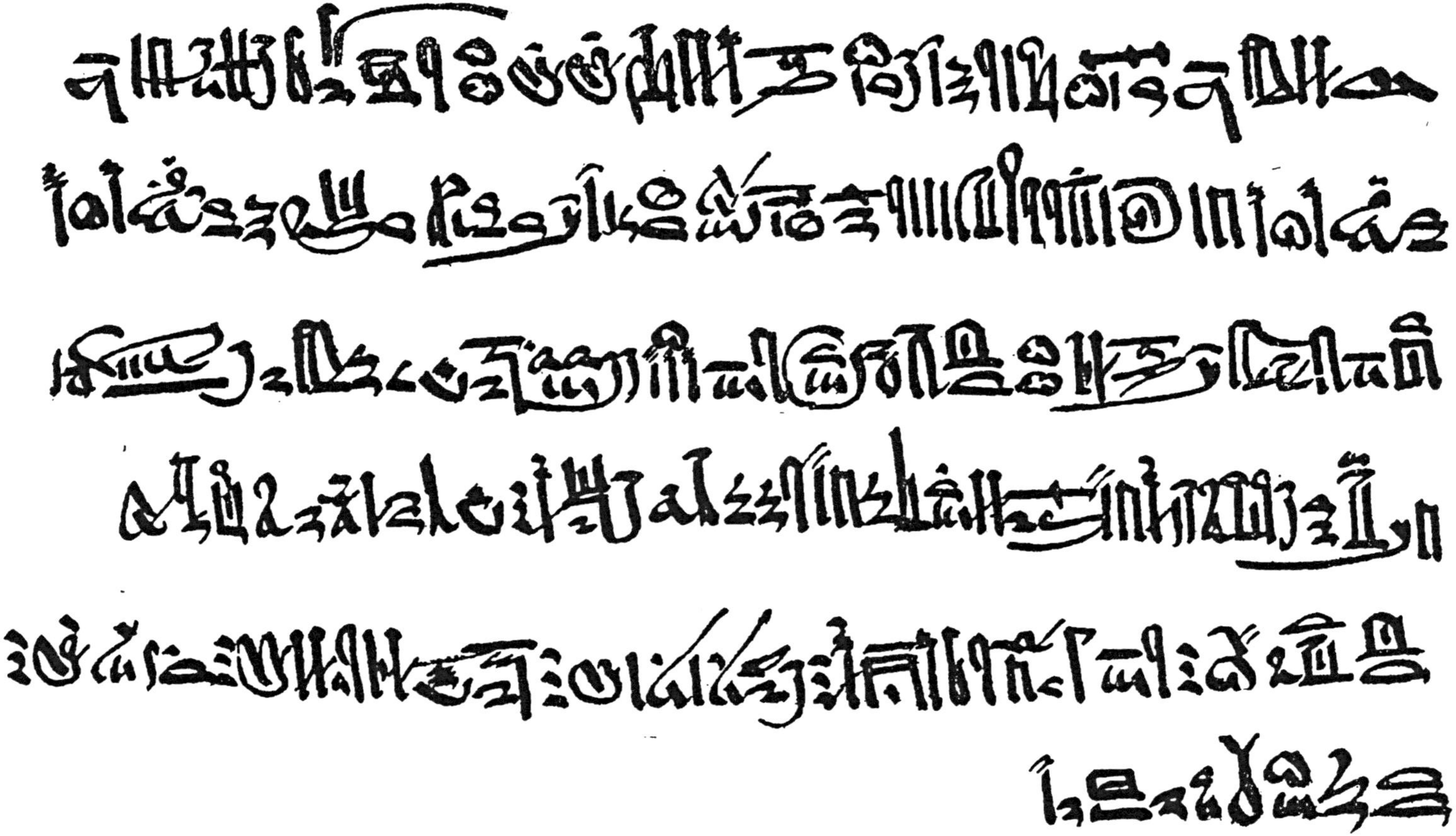

PAPYRUS HARRIS P 8, ll. 2–4

not a lake at all, but a bay, an arm of the Mediterranean, and it therefore is quite properly called "the Sea." Finally that this was the route of the P account is made the more plain by the statement that after leaving "the Sea" they came into the wilderness of Shur, which is, as we have seen, to be found in this locality and nowhere else.

The JED Route

The JED account, on the other hand, places the going-out quite definitely at the Red Sea. And furthermore, the JED account nowhere states that there was any passage through the Sea. The easiest explanation of the JED account, which may again be referred to in the parallel columns, is this. The Egyptians, pursuing the Hebrews, followed them out over the sand and mud flats uncovered by the ebbing tide, where the sand was moist and the chariots drove heavily, so that they could make little progress. There nightfall overtook them. Toward morning the tide rapidly returned, and, although they fled, overwhelmed them in the sea. And the Hebrews saw their bodies washed up on the shore. There is no supernatural phenomenon necessarily implied.

This Red Sea of JED cannot be placed in the north, any more than "the Sea" of P can be placed in the south. It is of course a mistake to place the Red Sea so far to the south as Suez, for Heroo-polis is mentioned as being on its shores, and we know that this city was north of what we now know as the Bitter Lakes. But though it extended this far north, it can never be confounded with the Great Sea or with Lake Menzaleh.

Only on the hypothesis of two exodi, one to the south, the other to the north, do the two accounts of the route out of Egypt become explainable.

PAPYRUS HARRIS, PL. 8, ll. 5–8

CHAPTER XV

Differences Between P and JED.—The Routes of the Exodus

From the JED documents we must route the journey of the Israelites as follows: (1) Red Sea; (2) Marah; (3) Elim; (4) Rephidim; (5) Horeb; (6) Taberah; (7) Kibroth Hattavah; (8) Hazeroth; (9) Kadesh-barnea; (10) Ezion Gaber; (11) Beeroth-bene-jaakan; (12) Moserah; (13) Gudgodah; (14) Jothbatha; (15) Zared; (16) Arnon; (17) Beer; (18) Mattanah; (19) Nahaliel; (20) Bamoth; (21) Pisgah; (22) Heshbon; (23) Jaazer; (24) Kedemoth; (25) Jahaz; (26) Edrei; (27) Beth-Peor; (28) Shittim in Moab.

From the P document we derive the following route: (1) Raamses; (2) Succoth; (3) edge of Etham; (4) Pi-Hahiroth; (5) the Sea; (6) the Wilderness of Shur; (7) Elim; (8) the Red Sea;[1] (9) the Wilderness of Sin; (10) the Wilderness of Sinai; (11) Sinai; (12) the Wilderness of Paran; (13) the Wilderness of Zin; (14) Meribah; (15) Kadesh-barnea; (16) Hor; (17) Oboth; (18) Ijje-Abarim; (19) Zared; (20) Plains of Moab; (21) Mount Nebo.

In these two routes there are only three places after Egypt was left behind that are the same: Kadesh-barnea, Elim, and Zared.

Of these Kadesh-barnea is the gateway for entrance into Canaan from the south, and any large number of people that wished to enter Canaan between the Philistine

[1] Here Gulf of Aqabah.

country and Mount Seir would find this spot the only convenient place to penetrate.

The second name, Elim, is one that occurs as the designation of several places in Palestine. The word is a plural form, and means "trees," especially oaks or terebinths.[1] In the itinerary according to JE,[2] Elim is placed between Marah and Rephidim. It had twelve wells of water, and three score and ten palms. These trees were undoubtedly regarded as sacred, and had given their name to the place. Probably it is to be identified with the modern Wady Gharandel, still known for its good water and its palm trees. The Elim of P,[3] on the other hand, can hardly be regarded as the same place. There was a place called by the feminine form, *Elath*, on the Eleanitic Gulf, which seems to fit well into the route as given in this document.[4]

Zared, the third point of agreement, is a brook or valley running westward into the Dead Sea through the land of Edom. Any army entering the east-Jordanic land from the south would have to cross this brook. It by no means follows that in the two accounts the crossings were at the same place. In other words, Zared is really not a point of agreement at all. In fact, from the routes

[1] Instead of the masculine *Elim* we often have the feminine *Elath*. The forms are used interchangeably.

[2] Exod. 15:27.   3 Exod. 16:1.

[4] Cf. Deut. 2:8, II Kings 16:6, and II Chron. 26:2. In all three places the Greek reads *Ailam* or *Ailon*, instead of *Elath*. In the two last instances we have a Greek form agreeing with the Hebrew plural *Elim*. In the first is used the Arabic masculine plural *Ailan*. The Eleanitic gulf has received its name from this Arabic form. The passages cited show that the name could be given either as a masculine or as a feminine. Pliny locates the place ten miles east of Petra and 150 miles southeast of Gaza (Pliny, V, 5, 11, 12). It is identical with *El-Paran* in Gen. 14:6. Jerome and Eusebius know it by the name of *Ailam* (the biblical *Elim*).

described, it seems very unlikely that the two armies did cross the brook at the same spot, for in P the route is far to the west of that in JED.

The other names of stopping-places are entirely different. It is a hopeless task to seek to identify them. We are not warranted in assuming that they describe the same route. Such an assumption cannot be allowed at all, for some of the principal names can be identified today, and the routes lie far apart.

CHAPTER XVI

Differences Between P and JED.—The Length of the Wandering

In the P account the available data for time consumed in wandering through the wilderness are as follows:

(1) The congregation of the children of Israel left Raamses on the day after the Passover, i. e., on the fifteenth day of the first month of the first year. The next day they marched from Succoth to Etham, and the next from Etham to Pi-Hahiroth.[1] (2) They then spent three days in the wilderness of Shur without finding water.[2] (3) They arrived in the Wilderness of Sin on the fifteenth day of the second month.[3] (4) They reached the wilderness of Sinai in the third month.[4] The day has fallen out of the text, but tradition has it that it was on the Day of Pentecost, fifty days after the Passover, the fifth day of the third month. (5) This is made the more probable by the next date. Moses was called up into the mountain on the seventh day,[5] which would be the last day of the Pentecostal festival. (6) Moses spent forty days on the mount.[6] This brings us to the twenty-second day of the fourth month. (7) The ordinance regarding the Passover was promulgated in the first month of the second year.[7] (8) The people were mustered in the wilderness of Sinai on

[1] Exod. 12:37; 14:2.

[2] Exod. 15:22. According to Num. 33:8 this wilderness is called the Wilderness of Etham.

[3] Exod. 16:1.   [4] Exod. 19:1.

[5] Exod. 24:16. This would then be the twelfth day of the third month.

[6] Exod. 24:18; 32:15, 16.   [7] Num. 9:1.

the first day of the second month of the second year.[1] The tabernacle had been made and was now being put up. (9) The journey from Sinai to the wilderness of Paran began on the twentieth day of the second month of the second year.[2] (10) The spies were sent from the Wilderness of Paran to spy out the land as far as the Pass of Hamath.[3] After their return the congregation journeyed and arrived in the wilderness of Zin in the first month.[4] The year has here fallen out, but the event is so closely connected with what has just gone before that the inference cannot but be that we now start the third year of the wanddering. After this time no more dates are given in P, except that the people mourned thirty days for Aaron in Mount Hor,[5] and that they wept a similar period for Moses in the plains of Moab.[6] As no new year is given in P, and as we remember the carefulness of the author in recording dates, we must assume that the arrival in the plains of Moab took place in the same year, i. e., the third. There is absolutely nothing in P to indicate that the journey from Egypt to Canaan took more than three years. But even though some may be inclined to doubt the certainty of this conclusion, there is no room for doubt in regard to the P chronology of the Exodus up to the arrival in the wilderness of Zin.

Now, what is true of the chronology of the JED account?

(1) The people left Egypt on the fourteenth(?) day of the month Abib.[7] (2) During the night of that same day they passed the Red Sea. (3) Outside of Egypt the first stop-

---

[1] Num. 1:1.

[2] Num. 10:11.

[3] Num. 13:21.

[4] Num. 20:1.

[5] Num. 20:29.

[6] Deut. 34:8.

[7] Exod. 13:4.

ping-place was Marah. The second was Elim.[1] The third was Rephidim.[2] They were now at the foot of Mount Horeb. We know this because while they were at Rephidim Moses was ordered to smite the rock of Horeb in order to get water for the people.[3] The journey up to this point would seem to have occupied three days. It will be remembered that when Yahweh appeared to Moses for the first time, the theophany took place at this same Mount Horeb.[4] There God commanded him, saying, "When thou hast brought forth the people out of Egypt, ye shall serve God upon this mountain."[5] The first objective point of the march, then, would be this mountain, in obedience to this command. And, further, when God commanded Moses to bring the people out, he said to him, "And thou shalt go, thou and the elders of Israel, unto the king of Egypt, and ye shall say unto him, Yahweh, the God of the Hebrews, has met with us: and now let us go, we pray thee, *three days' journey into the wilderness*, that we may sacrifice unto Yahweh our God."[6] And again we read that when Moses did appear before Pharaoh that was the request he made.[7] It would seem, then, that the distance from Egypt to the appointed place of sacrifice, Horeb, was three days' journey; and we have found that Rephidim, at the foot of Horeb, was the third station on the way. The stations so far, then, would seem each to have marked a day's journey. (5) When the people had left Rephidim, they were attacked by the Amalekites. After the battle Jethro visited Moses and offered a holocaust and a sacrifice at which Aaron and all the elders of Israel came to eat

[1] Exod. 15:27.   [4] Exod. 3:1.   [7] Exod. 8:27.

[2] Exod. 17:1.   [5] Exod. 3:12.

[3] Exod. 17:6.   [6] Exod 3:18

bread with him. The next day Moses spent judging the people. It is of course possible that these events took more than three days, but there is no indication to that effect in the context. The people were now encamped before the Mount of Yahweh, i. e., Horeb,[1] and had been on the way six days in all. (6) The third day Yahweh spoke to the people.[2] (7) Then Moses and the twelve chosen men performed the sacrifice in Horeb.[3] Next day Moses, Aaron, Nadab, Abihu, and the elders, went up into the mountain.[4] Moses stayed there forty days.[5] He then returned from the mount, put down the rebellion, and consecrated the Levites.[6] He then returned to the mount and stayed another forty days.[7] (8) The people then marched three days from the Mount of Yahweh.[8] The stations are mentioned as Taberah, Kibroth-Hattavah, and Hazeroth. This goes to substantiate our contention that in this narrative a single station means normally a single day's journey. (9) On account of Miriam's leprosy the people stayed for seven days at Hazeroth.[9] (10) It was eleven days' journey from Horeb to Kadesh-barnea.[10] As Hazeroth most probably belonged to the Horeb mountain-chain, this period is probably the time consumed from Hazeroth to Kadesh. Num. 33:18–30 seems to indicate that there were twelve stations from Hazeroth to Moseroth, but as we are not absolutely certain in identifying the names of the stations in that list, and as it was made up from the combined E and P

---

[1] Exod. 19:2.

[2] Exod. 19:16.

[3] Exod. 24:4–8.

[4] Exod. 24:9–11.

[5] Exod. 24:12–15a; Deut. 9:9–11.

[6] Exod. 32:29, 30.

[7] Exod. 34:28.

[8] Num. 10:33.

[9] Num. 12:3–15.

[10] Deut. 1:2.

lists at a late time, it is of minor value. (11) On arriving at Kadesh the twelve spies were sent to Escol. They returned after forty days.[1] (12) When the spies made their report the rebellion of Kadesh took place, and in punishment for it the people were condemned to a forty-years' wandering in the wilderness. Up to this time the period which had elapsed was about 183–190 days, i. e., about half a year.

The forty-years' wandering belongs to this JED story. It occurs in E sections; in Num. 14:33–34; 32:13;[2] 33:38,[3] and Josh. 5:6. D knows of nothing else than a forty-years' wandering.[4] Of the prophets, only Amos refers to it,[5] and he was the prophet of the Northern Kingdom, whose peculiar property, after the division of the kingdom, the E code was. In Ps. 95:10 there is also a reference to it. And these are all the references to such a wandering that there are in the Old Testament. Knowledge of such an event is confined to the JED account. The P account and its followers in their writings imply a three-years' wandering, and no more.

It is as impossible to reconcile the two chronologies of the wandering as it is to identify the two geographies.

[1] Num. 13:25; 14:34.
[2] A section redacted by P.
[3] An E statement recorded by a P editor.
[4] Deut. 1:3; 2:7; 8:2, 4; 29:5.
[5] Amos 2:10; 5:25.

CHAPTER XVII

Differences Between P and JED.—Horeb and Sinai

Are Horeb and Sinai mèrely different names for the same place?

We have already seen that in the JED account it took the people three days to march from Egypt to Horeb, where the Decalogue, the giving of the E code, and the institution of the Levitical priesthood all took place. We have also seen that in the P account it took at least forty-five days for the people to journey from Egypt to Sinai, where the Testimonies were given, the P code delivered, and the Aaronic priesthood instituted.

Horeb

Mount Horeb must then be sought in the immediate neighborhood of the Red Sea. Tradition has pointed out the Sinaitic peninsula, and especially Mount Serbal, as the place where the Decalogue was given and the theophany seen, a mount still called by the Arabs Et-Tur, "the Mount," the name being an exact equivalent for the Hebrew *zur*, used for Mount Horeb in the JED account. In the fifth century A. D. the Christian monks were driven from their monastery on Mount Serbal, and received a new monastic home from Justinian in Gebel Musa, a peak to the south of Serbal. The monks now stationed on Gebel Musa claim that this is the mount where the Decalogue was given; but their contention has no support from the old tradition. Mount Serbal has been singled out as the true mount by Jewish, Mohammedan, and

Christian tradition. It was a sacred mountain far back in ante-Christian times. Pilgrimages were made to it by the people living nearby, as the Nabathean inscriptions from the mount itself plainly testify. At the north end of it, lying at its foot, stretches the beautiful valley or Wady Firan, which would be the biblical Rephidim. A short distance to the north of this wady is Serbut el-Khadem, where Petrie in 1906 excavated and described[1] the great temple built by Queen Hatshepsut, which, perhaps, became the model for the Jewish temple idea. It is the only temple yet excavated which is like the Hebrew temples. There there were altars for holocausts and sacrifices, otherwise scarcely known to Egyptian temples, but well known to Hebrew rituals. There Petrie discovered a number of cow-images, from seeing which the people may have been inspired with their desire for the golden calf. The location of Mount Serbal fits perfectly the distance which could have been traversed in three days from Egypt. The biblical Marah, with its bitter waters, would be the present Ayn Musa, with its sweet and bitter springs. It lies a little to the south of the present Suez. If the E exodus took place to the south of Lake Timsah, it would then be just a day's journey from the passage of the Red Sea to this Ayn Musa. Another day would bring the army to Wady Gharandel, which we feel inclined to identify with Elim, still noted for its trees and good water. A short journey of half a day would bring them from there to Wady Firan, or Rephidim, on the north side of Mount Serbal. We shall not go far wrong if we identify Horeb with Mount Serbal, even as tradition urges us.

[1] Petrie, *Sinai.*

Sinai

As for Sinai, we have already noticed that it took forty-five, or perhaps fifty days for the army to reach it from Raamses. Although we may admit that some time was spent resting at Elim or Elath, nevertheless it is plain that we deal here with a mountain at a considerable distance from Egypt, and not, as was Horeb, at a distance of three days only.

Two passages in the Old Testament give clues as to the location of Sinai. In Deut. 33:2 we read, "Yahweh came from Sinai, and rose from Seir unto them; he shined forth from Mount Paran, and they came from the myriads of Kadesh: at his right hand was a fire, a law unto them." Again we read, in Judg. 5:4, 5, "Yahweh, when thou wentest forth out of Seir, when thou marchedst out of the field of Edom, the earth trembled, the heavens also dropped, yea, the clouds dropped water. The mountain quaked at the presence of Yahweh, even yon Sinai, at the presence of Yahweh, the God of Israel." In both passages Mount Seir and Mount Sinai are equalized. The parallelism peculiar to Hebrew verse presupposes that in these passages Seir and Sinai are to be regarded as one. Sinai is brought into connection with the fields of Edom. Ancient tradition has here located Sinai. And while this tradition has pointed out Mount Seir as Sinai, it has never identified it with Horeb. When all these facts are taken into consideration, the location of Sinai as a peak of Mount Seir is not only possible but probable.[1]

[1] The wilderness of Sin and the wilderness of Sinai are the oases of the Arabah, between the Seir ranges, from Ezion-Gaber to Petra. The wilderness of Zin is the oasis of Kadesh, and the wilderness of Paran is the great plateau

It seems conclusive, then, that Horeb and Sinai were two distinct and separated places.

south of Kadesh, west of Seir, north of Tih (northern mountain range of the Sinaitic peninsula), and east of the Wilderness of Shur.

Midian was the land on the western or southwestern slopes of Mount Seir. Madian (Greek Madiam) was the land on the western shore of the Gulf of Aqabah. The Amalekites lived in the wilderness of Paran, west of Midian.

While reading page-proof, the author received the last instalment of R. Weill's article, "Le séjour des Israélites au désert et le Sinai dans la relation primitive, l'évolution du texte biblique et la tradition christiano-moderne" (*Revue des Etudes Juives*, July, 1909, pp. 23–60). The author cannot but admire M. Weill's solid arguments for locating Sinai in the land of Edom. His criticism of some wild-cat theories of radical critics is also to the point and well taken. But when Mr. Weill proceeds to identify Horeb and Sinai, locating it in Edom, by totally discounting the value of the whole E Document on this point, we have in it only a new reminder of the narrow limitations within which modern biblical science labors. When facts do not fit theories, throw the facts away. Now, if anything is certain it is the fact, that in the JE Document, Horeb or "Mount of God" was situated at the distance of three days' journey from Goshen. But it is *absolutely* impossible for any army of 6,000 (or 600,000) men encumbered by women, children, and cattle, to march from Goshen in Egypt to Mount Seir in Edom in three days.

CHAPTER XVIII

Differences Between P and JED.—The Sets of Tables and the Arks

The Two Sets of Tables

At Horeb God gave Moses two Tables of Covenant.[1] These were broken by Moses, when he saw that the people were worshiping the golden calf.[2] But he was ordered to prepare new tables,[3] and on these God wrote the words of the covenant, "the Ten Words."[4] Deuteronomy knows of no other tables save these of the Covenant.[5] When Solomon built his temple, he placed in it these same Tables of the Covenant. "There was nothing in the ark, save the two tables of stone which Moses put there at Horeb, where Yahweh made a covenant with the children of Israel, when they came out of the land of Egypt."[6] The priestly writer of Chronicles records the same fact.[7]

At Sinai, on the other hand, in the P account, Moses received two Tables of Testimony. "And Moses turned, and went down from the mountain with the two tables of the testimony in his hand; tables that were written on both their sides; on the one side and on the other were they written."[8] Are these Tables of Testimony identical with the Tables of Covenant? We know that the latter contained the Decalogue. But there is no hint anywhere

---

[1] Exod. 24:12.   [3] Exod. 34:1.

[2] Exod. 32:19.   [4] Exod. 34:28.

[5] Deut. 4:13; 5:22; 9:9, 10, 11, 15, 17; 10:1-5.

[6] I Kings 8:9.   [7] II Chron. 5:10.   [8] Exod. 32:15.

in P of the promulgation of any decalogue. Further, it is explicitly stated that the Tables of Testimony were written on both sides, which would presuppose quite an extended document. It would hardly be necessary to use so much space for the short Ten Words. Furthermore, the Tables of Testimony must, of course, have contained "testimonies." The word is a technical one, denoting the theophany of Yahweh at a given place. The Tables of Testimony would therefore deal with Yahweh's theophany, or, more particularly, with the place where he would appear. Now immediately after the return of Moses from the mount with these tables,[1] we have a minute description of the pattern of the tabernacle which Moses built, and in which Yahweh dwelt.[2] Moreover we find that the instructions concerning the building of the tabernacle had been given to Moses while on the mount.[3] This section of instructions ends with these remarkable words, "And he gave unto Moses, when he had made an end of communing with him on Mount Sinai, the two tables of the testimony, tables of stone, written with the finger of God."[4] The inference is that God's communication to Moses on the mount was recorded in these tables, the "testimonies" of which were the ordinances on the tabernacle and the priesthood. From a consideration of the P code itself (the only way we have a right to consider the code historically) this is the only inference which can be drawn.

The tables delivered at Sinai, then, and those given at Horeb appear to have been two different things.

[1] Exod. 34:29.
[2] Exod. 35:1—40:38.
[3] Exod. 25:1—31:18.
[4] Exod. 31:18.

The Two Arks

In Deut. 10:1–8 Moses relates that he was directed at Horeb to make not only the two tables of stone, but also an ark. He made it of acacia wood, and put into it the Tables of the Ten Words, elsewhere known as the Tables of Covenant. This ark, from that time onward, was known as the Ark of the Covenant.[1] This became its usual name, evidently because the Tables of Covenant were inside it.

In the P code, on the other hand, we read that Moses was ordered at Sinai to make an Ark of the Testimony,[2] and that he did so.[3] It is to be assumed that this name was derived from the fact that the Tables of Testimony were kept within it.

The hypothesis may be advanced that these two arks were really one and the same. But this is difficult to believe in view of their subsequent history. Let us observe this briefly.

The History of the Ark of the Covenant

In the first place, in the march through the wilderness, according to the E document, the Ark of the Covenant was carried *in front* of the army,[4] while in the P document we constantly read that the Ark of the Testimony was borne *in the midst of* the host.[5] Why the difference?

When, according to E, the people broke up camp and set forth from Horeb, the Ark of the Covenant went before them, and at the secession at Kadesh, it remained with Moses by the camp.[6] It was still with Moses and his

---

[1] Deut. 10:8.

[2] Exod. 25:16, 21, 22; 26:33, 34; 27:21; 30:6, 26; 31:7.

[3] Exod. 39:35; 40:3, 5, 20, 21; Num. 4:5; 7:89.

[4] E. g., Num. 10:33.   [5] E. g., Num. 10:11–28.   [6] Num. 14:44.

people, the "priests the Levites" bearing it, when Moses delivered the D code in Moab.[1] When Joshua passed over the Jordan with his army, the Ark of the Covenant was carried over before them until they reached the midst of the river, where it was held until the army had passed over.[2] When Jericho was captured, the Ark of the Covenant was carried by the priests before the army in the march around the city.[3] It remained with the camp at Jericho until the whole army went up to take Ai.[4] When Joshua and his people went up to Ebal and Gerizim to read and record the D code, the Ark of the Covenant was with them.[5]

From I Chron. 17:5, 6 we learn that the Ark of the Covenant[6] was not placed in any permanent house of its own at this time, but that it was continually moved about from sanctuary to sanctuary, and from tent to tent. We know of the following stations where it was placed at different times: Bethel;[7] Shiloh[8] (in the time of Eli); the battle of Eben-ezer;[9] in the hands of the Philistines;[10] Ashdod in the temple of the Philistine god, Dagon;[11] Gath;[12] Ekron;[13] Beth-Shemesh[14] (where it was restored to the Hebrew people); Kirjath-Jearim;[15] the house of Obed-Edom (whither David removed it);[16] Jerusalem, the City of David, at the threshing-floor of Araunah or

[1] Deut. 31:9, 25, 26.
[2] Josh., chaps. 3, 4.
[3] Josh. 6:4–13.
[4] Josh. 7:6.
[5] Josh. 8:33.
[6] I Chron. 17:1.
[7] Judg. 20:27.
[8] I Sam. 4:3, 4.
[9] I Sam. 4:5.
[10] I Sam. 4:11.
[11] I Sam. 5:1.
[12] I Sam. 5:8.
[13] I Sam. 5:10.
[14] I Sam. 6:13–15, 18, 19.
[15] I Sam. 6:21; 7:1, 2; II Sam. 6:2–9; I Chron. 13:3–9.
[16] II Sam. 6:10–12; I Chron. 13:13, 14.

Ornan;[1] the temple at Jerusalem (whither Solomon removed it).[2] In every one of these cases it is the Ark of
the Covenant, not the Ark of the Testimony, with which
we are dealing. It was this same Ark of the Covenant
which, after all these wanderings, finally found rest in
the position of honor in the temple of Jerusalem.

The History of the Ark of the Testimony

Meanwhile the Ark of the Testimony had a very different history.

In Num. 4:5 the ordinance is given for the service of
the Levites in taking care of the Ark of the Testimony, and
in Num. 7:8, 9 we are told that Yahweh spoke to Moses
from upon this ark. In Josh. 4:16 we are told that this
ark was carried up from the Jordan when the P people
entered Canaan. Here all mention of the Ark of the
Testimony ends in the Old Testament.

Instead, there are frequent mentions of the Tent of
Testimony and the Tabernacle of Testimony, in which
the Ark of the Testimony was lodged. And instead of
the language, Tent of Testimony, we have, in a large
number of places, the term, Tent of Meeting. But this
latter term is not to be found in the Greek, which trans-
lates the places where the Hebrew has it with the term,
Tent of Testimony. And in this the Greek is probably
correct. In three places the term is used for the tent in
which the Ark of the Covenant was kept. But in P the
term in the original is different, the word being *mishkan*,
meaning "tabernacle" or "dwelling-place." By these

---

[1] II Sam 6:15–17; 15:24, 25, 29; I Kings 3:15; I Chron. 6:31; 15:1—
17:1; II Chron. 1:4.

[2] I Kings 6:19; 8:1–9; I Chron. 22:19; 28:2, 18; II Chron. 5:2–10;
6:11, 41; 8:11; 35:3.

terms we are able to trace the history of the Ark of the Testimony.

Now, we read in Josh. 18:1, "And the whole congregation of the children of Israel assembled themselves together at Shiloh, and set up the tent of meeting there, and the land was subdued before them." The words "congregation" and "tent of meeting" are expressions of the P document. We find, then, that when the conquest of Canaan described in P was over, the tent of meeting was set up at Shiloh. From Judg., chap. 21, and from I Sam., chaps. 1–4, we know that there was a temple or house of Yahweh in this place. Even though this temple may have been in Shiloh before the Tent of Meeting was set up there, we are not debarred from believing that the Tent of Meeting was placed there as well. It is to be noted, however, that nothing is said in this passage about the holocaust altar. In I Sam. 2:22 there is another reference to the Tent of Meeting m Shiloh. It is true, as has often been pointed out, that this statement is lacking in the Vatican codex of the Greek. This, though, does not necessarily mean that the statement contained in the Hebrew and the Alexandrian codex is incorrect. But even in these nothing is said about the holocaust altar. All we know is that at the end of the conquest the Tent of Meeting was at Shiloh, and, too, in the time of Eli. The altar of the holocaust, the "Altar of Yahweh" as it is called, may not, however, have been set up there. There are indications that it was placed among the Gibeonites.

Later, in I Sam. 14:18 we are told that the Ark of God was at that time in Gibeah.[1] The Ark of God referred

[1] The Greek in this passage, it is true, reads "ephod" instead of "ark," but both readings should be admitted, for where the ark was there naturally an ephod would be also.

to here can be only the Ark of the Testimony, because we
know that the other ark, the Ark of the Covenant, was at
that time in Kirjath-Jearim. Gibeah and Gibeon are
probably the same place, the modern Jeba.[1] In Gibeah-
Gibeon, therefore, we find under the priestly care of Ahijah, great grandson of Eli, the Ark of God, i. e., the Ark
of the Testimony.

When David arranged the courses of the priesthood,
he ordained as follows: "And Zadok the priest, and his
brethren the priests, before the tabernacle of Yahweh,
in the high-place that was at Gibeon, to offer burnt-offer
ings unto Yahweh upon the altar of burnt-offering con
tinually, morning and evening, even according to all that
is written in the Law of Yahweh, which he commanded
unto Israel."[2]   Here then we have an explicit reference
which states that the Tabernacle of Yahweh, as well as
the altar of burnt-offerings, was located in Gibeon.

And this is amply substantiated by the later history of
David and Solomon.

When David had numbered the people, his act dis-

---

[1] In the Old Testament we have three local names, Geba, Gibeah, and
Gibeon, which are often confounded. Gibeah and Gibeon were located close
by one another, possibly were the same place, Gibeah denoting the "hill-top,"
and Gibeon the city on the slopes of it. Saul is said to have resided at all three
places (I Sam. 10:26; 11:4; I Chron. 8:29-35; 9:35-41). The place is called
Gibeah of Saul (I Sam. 11:4), and again Geba of Elohim (I Sam. 10:5). Ahijah,
son of Ahitub, great-grandson of Eli, had an ephod there, which he as a priest
consulted (I Sam. 14:3). It was in Gibeah that Saul built an altar to Yahweh
(I Sam. 14:35), but Gibeon had a stone, and the probability is that this was the
altar which Saul consecrated (II Sam. 20:8). While Gibeah was Saul's capital,
Gibeon is referred to as the capital of Ish-bosheth, his son (II Sam. 2:12-24).
When David executed the seven sons of Saul in Gibeah, the Greek reads Gibeon
(II Sam. 21:6). Without denying that there may have been a Geba or Gibeah
farther west, the modern Jib, it seems certain that the Gibeah, Gibeon, and Geba
of Saul and his sons were but different names for the same place.

[2] I Chron. 16:39, 40.

pleased Yahweh, and an angel with sword drawn appeared before him in the threshing-floor of Araunah.[1] This angel prevented David from going to Gibeon to make sacrifices there. Because of this, David bought the place where the angel had stood, and consecrated there an altar of burnt-offering for Israel. "At that time, when David saw that Yahweh had answered him in the threshing-floor of Ornan the Jebusite, then he sacrificed there. For the Tabernacle of Yahweh, which Moses made in the wilderness, and the altar of burnt-offering were at that time at Gibeon. But David could not go before it to inquire of God, for he was afraid, because of the sword of the angel of Yahweh. Then David said, This is the house of the Lord God, and this is the altar of burnt-offerings for Israel."[2] We have thus two altars of burnt-offerings, one at Gibeon and the other in Jerusalem. The latter statement is verified by II Sam. 24:25. We have also a Tabernacle of Yahweh in Gibeon, at the same time that the Ark of the Covenant rested in the city of David in Jerusalem, in a dwelling-place which David made especially for it.

That there was one Ark, that of the Testimony, with its tent and altar at Gibeon, while another, that of the Covenant, with its tent and altar, was placed in Jerusalem, is plain from an incident in Solomon's reign. In I Kings 3:4, 5 we are told that when he became king he left the city of Jerusalem and went up to Gibeon "to sacrifice there; for that was the great high-place. A thousand burnt-offerings did Solomon offer upon that altar. In Gibeon Yahweh appeared to Solomon in a dream by

[1] II Sam. 24:16; I Chron. 21:15.
[2] I Chron. 21:28—22:1.

night." Then follows the story of Solomon's dream and the gift of wisdom. Then we read, "And Solomon awoke, and behold, it was a dream, and he came to Jerusalem, and stood before the Ark of the Covenant of Yahweh, and offered peace-offerings, and made a feast to all his servants."[1]

This account is also contained, a little more fully, in Chronicles.[2] "So Solomon, and all the congregation with him, went to the high-place at Gibeon; for there was the *Tent of Meeting* of God, which Moses the servant of Yahweh had made in the wilderness. But the *Ark of God* David had brought up from Kirjath-Jearim to the place that David had prepared for it: for he had pitched a tent for it at Jerusalem. Moreover the brazen altar that Bezalel, the son of Uri, the son of Hur had made, was there[3] before the Tabernacle of Yahweh: and Solomon and the congregation sought unto it. And Solomon went up thither to the brazen altar before Yahweh, which was at the *Tent of Meeting*, and offered a thousand holocausts upon it." Then follows the same account of the dream, and of the return to Jerusalem.[4]

The historicity of this account in Chronicles has been doubted, on the plea that the author was of the late priestly school, and so untrustworthy, But this can hardly be maintained in the face of the fact that the author of Kings, a man of the Deuteronomic school, and using quite different sources, gives us substantially the same account.

The passage is valuable, for it gives us quite plainly the information that in Solomon's time there were two arks. We are told that the Ark of the Covenant was in

---

[1] I Kings 3:15.   [3] I. e., in Gibeon.
[2] II Chron. 1:3-6.   [4] II Chron. 1:7-13.

Jerusalem. Yet we are informed that the brazen altar at Gibeon was "before Yahweh," a phrase which can mean, and does mean, only "before the Ark of Yahweh." As we know of only two arks among the Hebrews, and as the Ark of the Covenant was at Jerusalem, and as there was evidently another one at Gibeon, this latter must have been the Ark of the Testimony. And this is made the more certain by the use of the word "tabernacle" in the passage, a word found only in P, the document wherein this latter ark was given to the Hebrews.

When Solomon built his temple, it was the Ark of the Covenant which he placed there [1] It is explicitly stated that "there was nothing in the Ark save the two tables of stone which Moses put there at Horeb, when Yahweh made a covenant with the children of Israel, when they came out of the land of Egypt "[2] Nothing is mentioned of the Ark of the Testimony at the consecration of this temple. What was the further history of this latter ark is not pertinent to this present inquiry. Perhaps it may be taken up in some later study.

The point which we have endeavored to prove is that the Ark of the Covenant and the Ark of the Testimony are two different things, with two different histories, that they cannot be considered as identical, and that they form one of the great differences between the Exodus of JED and the Exodus of P.

[1] I Kings 8:6.
[2] I Kings 8:9.

CHAPTER XIX

Differences Between P and JED.—The Legislations at Horeb and Sinai

If, now, we turn to the laws promulgated at Horeb and Sinai, i. e., the laws of the E and P codes, we find not only a great difference in phraseology, which might be accounted for as the result of varying traditions, but a great difference in content. The enactments are often so contradictory, so divergent in tone, purpose, and wording, that it seems impossible that more than one of the codes could have been given or accepted at one time.

I. Laws of P Contrary to Laws of E

First of all let us compare some of the laws which differ from one another:

a) In regard to the place of sacrifice the E code ordains, "An altar of earth thou shalt make unto me, and shalt sacrifice thereon thy burnt-offerings and thy peace-offerings, thy sheep, and thine oxen: in every place where I cause my name to be remembered I will come unto thee and I will bless thee."[1] The P code says, "And thou shalt say unto them, Whatsoever man there be of the house of Israel, or of the strangers that sojourn among them, that offers a burnt-offering or sacrifice, and bringeth it not unto the door of the tent of meeting, to sacrifice it unto Yahweh, even that man shall be cut off from his people."[2]

These laws are so entirely contrary to each other that it seems almost impossible that they are variants of one

[1] Exod. 20:24.   [2] Lev. 17:8, 9.

original commandment. Even though we may be willing to admit that the P law refers to the wandering in the wilderness, and the E law to conditions after the settlement, the laws cannot have developed out of one original, common to both.

b) The E law on Hebrew slaves[1] differs so radically from the P law on the same subject[2] that it is hard to see how they could once have been the same.

c) In E[3] any sanctuary ("place") or altar is acceptable as an asylum, but in P[4] certain cities are appointed for that purpose.

d) The law in E on sorcery[5] is quite different from those in P.[6]

e) The offerings in the E code belong to Yahweh,[7] but in P they are handed over to Aaron.[8]

f) In E every Israelite is forbidden to eat the flesh of an animal that has been torn. Such flesh must be thrown to the dogs.[9] But in P the Israelite is permitted to eat such flesh, but it is provided that if he does he shall be ceremonially unclean until even.[10]

g) Other laws like those on the Sabbath and the Passover show the same marked differentiation.

It is argued that discrepancies and contradictions such as these are to be accounted for by the lapse of time between 800 and 444, when the two codes are said to have been promulgated. But that hypothesis is impossible to us, who have seen that both these codes were in operation at least three hundred years earlier than either of

---

[1] Exod. 21:2–11.

[2] Lev. 25:39–46.

[3] Exod. 21:13, 14.

[4] Num. 35:9–29.

[5] Exod. 22:18.

[6] Lev. 19:26*b*, 31; 20:6, 27.

[7] Exod. 22:29*a*; 23:19*a*.

[8] Num. 18:12, 13.

[9] Exod. 22:31.

[10] Lev. 17:15; cf. Lev. 11:40.

these dates, and have concluded that they were most probably promulgated during the wanderings in the wilderness, even as they themselves say.   It would seem then that the legislations of Horeb and Sinai were two different things.

II.   P Laws not Found in E

Admitting the fallacy of the argument from silence, it is nevertheless worth noting that P has a large number of laws not found in E.   We have shown above that E has lost its "statutes" or ritual laws,[1] and so a comparison of the codes in this realm cannot be undertaken.   But even the "judgments," or civil laws, are found to be less complete in E than in P.

For instance, although the E document knows that Moses' hand became leprous, and that Miriam was so smitten with the disease that the camp was delayed for seven days,[2] still E has no law on leprosy; but P has a very complete law covering the subject.[3]

E has no law on Nazirites, but P defines that order minutely.[4]   P has laws, too, on clean and unclean animals,[5] on disfigurement in mourning,[6] tithes,[7] mazzebas and stones,[8] rights and revenues of the tribe of Levi,[9] Molech-worship,[10] admixtures overstepping the boundaries of nature,[11] tassels,[12] adultery,[13] incest,[14] cleanliness in camp,[15] vows,[16] gleanings,[17] just weights,[18] etc., of none of which we have a trace in E.

[1] Pp. 101–103, 106.
[2] Num. 12:15.
[3] Lev., chaps. 13, 14.
[4] Num. 6:1–21.
[5] Lev. 11:2–47.
[6] Lev. 19:28.
[7] Lev. 27:30–33.
[8] Lev. 26:1a.
[9] Lev. 7:32–34; Num. 18:1–20.

[10] Lev. 18:21; 20:2–5.
[11] Lev. 19:19.
[12] Num. 15:37–41.
[13] Lev. 18:20; 20:10.
[14] Lev. 18:8; 20:11.
[15] Num. 5:1–4.
[16] Num. 30:2 ff.
[17] Lev. 19:9, 10; 23:22.
[18] Lev. 19:35, 36.

III. Laws of E not in P

On the other hand, E has the Decalogue, of which P has not a trace. This law was such an important factor in the life of the Jews that it is hard to see how P could have omitted it from the code, if the code were the same as that of Horeb.

In like manner, E has laws on seething a kid in mother's milk,[1] straying animals,[2] seduction,[3] pledges,[4] and man-stealing,[5] of none of which P shows any trace. Some of these laws we have already found to be very old, as old as the Code of Hammurabi. But why should they be left out of P, otherwise so circumstantial and full, which so often repeats one law over and over?

IV. Similar Laws in E and P

It is also true that there are a number of laws in which E and P agree, and where P certainly seems to record the same legislation as E does. Compare, e. g., the laws on idolatry,[6] manslaughter,[7] cursing of parents,[8] *lex talionis*,[9] lying with beasts,[10] strangers,[11] usury,[12] perjury,[13] the sabbatical year,[14] annual pilgrimages,[15] and the Feast of Unleavened Bread.[16]

[1] Exod. 23:19b; cf. 34:26b.
[2] Exod. 23:4, 5.
[3] Exod. 22:16, 17.
[4] Exod. 22:26, 27.
[5] Exod. 21:16.
[6] Exod. 20:23 (E); 20:4 (E); 34:17 (J); Lev. 19:4 (P).
[7] Exod. 21:12 (E); Lev. 24:17, 21b (P); Num. 35:16 (P).
[8] Exod. 21:17 (E); Lev. 20:9 (P).
[9] Exod. 21:23–25 (E); Lev. 24:19, 20 (P).
[10] Exod. 22:19 (E); Lev. 18:23 (P); 20:15 (P).
[11] Exod. 22:21 (E); 23:9 (E); Lev. 19:33, 34 (P).
[12] Exod. 22:25 (E); Lev. 25:35–37 (P).
[13] Exod. 23:1–3 (E); Lev. 19:15, 16 (P).
[14] Exod. 23:10, 11 (E); Lev. 25:1–7 (P).
[15] Exod. 23:14–17 (E); 34:18b, 22–25 (J); Lev., chap. 23 (P); Num., chaps. 28, 29 (P).
[16] Exod. 23:15 (E); 34:18 (J); Lev. 23:6 (P).

But we have pointed out above[1] that some of the laws of P have both the viewpoint and language of the Toledoth Book, and if we assign that book to the period of the JE code or codes, we may well assume that there were older P laws, which indeed were promulgated at Horeb and which descended through certain Levitical clans (the Mosaic) and were finally merged with the Aaronic laws of Sinai.

[1] P. 56..

CHAPTER XX

Differences Between P and JED.—The Priesthoods

To be able to conclude that a man was a priest it is not necessary to rely alone on the fact that he was called a priest. If we find him performing the acts of a priest, we may safely conclude that he was one.

Now in the E code there are mentioned two men, Moses and Aaron. The latter is neither called a priest, nor do we find him performing any priestly acts, except in the worship of the golden calf, which was admittedly illegal. But we do find that Moses, though not called a priest, does perform priestly acts. For instance, it is he, not Aaron, who offers sacrifices;[1] it is he who inquires from Yahweh;[2] it is he who intercedes for Miriam in her leprosy,[3] as well as at other times;[4] all of these were priestly acts. That they were all the priestly acts of the E code we cannot say, because, as we have seen, the ritual laws of this code have been lost. This much, however, is certainly true, that in E it is Moses, not Aaron, who acts as the priest. And the same thing is true of D and J. Incidentally, it may be interesting to note that in this tradition Aaron is the *younger* brother of Moses.

In the P code, on the contrary, Aaron is the *elder* brother of Moses. Moses ordains him to the priesthood, whereupon Moses ceases to perform priestly functions. Aaron from this time onward is the priest. And not only does he perform the priestly acts, but from the

[1] Exod. 24:5–8.
[2] Exod. 33:7–11.
[3] Num., 12:13.
[4] E. g., Exod. 32:30–34.

time of his ordination onward he is spoken of as "the priest," and his sons and successors are called "the sons of Aaron, the priests." This is plainly a very different state of affairs from that we found existing in JED.

Possibly this, by itself, might be explained as a mere difference in tradition. If, though, we were to find that there were two distinct priesthoods among the Hebrews in later generations, it would throw confirmatory light upon the hypothesis that it is a difference in fact, and not in mere tradition, that exists between the two stories. And since we have already found so many differences between them which can hardly be explained as due to mere varying traditions, the search for such distinct priesthoods is quite legitimate. What, then, do we find to be true of the priesthood in later generations?

"Priest," a Technical Term in P

First of all we wish to emphasize—as has already been noted—that in the P document the title "the priest" is affixed to Aaron's name, and this so uniformly that it becomes almost a part of the name itself. Further, when Aaron dies, and Eleazar, his son, is ordained to the high priesthood, to his name also the title of "the priest" is affixed. And this name, as a title, we find never used in JED. In E, of course, all the people are spoken of as priests when they perform priestly acts, and in D all the Levites are so spoken of when performing their official duties; but the name is *not* used as the title of any one man. When, then, in later periods we find men bearing this title affixed to their names, it is only natural to associate them with the priesthood of which Aaron was the founder.

In the P document and code we find, again and again,

in vital connection with this Aaronic priesthood, the expression, "priests *and* Levites." It is indeed so common that whenever we find the expression we are safe in assuming that the passage has at least been influenced by a P author or editor. In the D code we find the expression, "the priests the Levites," i. e., "the Levitical priests." When we find this phrase we may with equal certainty assume a D author or editor. It has long been felt that the two expressions are by no means synonymous, and that in all probability they stand for quite different ideas and institutions. We have already seen how the Levitical priesthood in D had its origin and development. It is now to be our attempt to trace the origin and development of the Aaronic priesthood, in its triple order of high-priest, priest, and Levite.

Early History of the Aaronic Priesthood

According to the P document, the army that left Egypt seems to have been exceedingly small. In fact we do not know of how many men it was composed, because the second half of Exod. 12:37 belongs, apparently, to E. There it is stated that there were about six hundred clans on foot, but the expression "about" betrays no connection with those of the early compiler of P. We are therefore left entirely without data in regard to the size of the P army. We do know that there were three tribes represented in this exodus,[1] Reuben, Simeon, and Levi. It is possible that these made up the great bulk of the army. We need not, however, understand this passage as implying that all the people of these tribes at this time came out of Egypt. The P editor takes great pains to enumerate just what families of each of them had been in Egypt. Of

[1] Exod. 6:14–26.

the tribe of Levi there had been only three families, Gershom, Kohath, and Merari. Of these Gershom and Merari had but two clans each. The family of Kohath had four, the oldest of which was Amram. To this clan of Amram belonged Aaron and Moses, the latter of whom became the leader of the people, while the former was chosen to head their priesthood.

Aaron had four sons: Nadab, Abihu, Eleazar, and Ithamar. The P editor, and later P writers, including the Chronicler, say that both Nadab and Abihu died early in life. It might even possibly be supposed that these two were not the sons of Aaron according to P at all. The JE document mentions them as sons of its Aaron, but knows nothing of either Eleazar or Ithamar.

It was this people that came to Sinai and received the ordinance to build the Ark and Tent of the Testimony. Aaron was appointed high-priest, and placed in charge of the worship which was conducted in that tent. His two sons, Eleazar and Ithamar, but no other Levites, were appointed to the second order, the priesthood, with a right for the firstborn of succession to the high-priesthood. The Levites as a whole were given the menial offices connected with keeping up the worship.

In the second year of the Exodus, then, according to P the hierarchy of the Aaronic priesthood consisted of one high-priest, Aaron, two priests, Eleazar and Ithamar, and a few Levites from the other nine Levitical clans. We know that the Levitical clans of Izhar and Uzziel had only three members each. Thirty Levites would then be a fair estimate of the number of the third order, this being probably about as many Levites as there were in the army. The dimensions of the court around the Tent of

Meeting, 50×100 cubits, presuppose that there was a very small number of people to be ministered to. A church 80×160 feet would hardly hold more than, say, 1,500 people, after allowance was made for the brazen altar and for the Tent of Meeting. Three priests could very well have handled the services for a congregation of such a size, and thirty odd Levites could easily have taken care of the tent and its furniture.

The Mustering at Sinai

Just after the ordination of Aaron and his sons, and when the Tent of Meeting had been reared in the wilderness of Sinai, Yahweh ordered Moses to take the sum of the congregation of the children of Israel. Aaron and Moses complied.[1] This "numbering" was not a mere "numbering," but, as the Hebrew word invariably means, a "mustering-in" of an army. Since there would have been no point in mustering in an army already in active service, there must have been new forces to be enrolled. In other words, Moses' army must have been augmented at this time.

From whence did these new troops come? We can, of course, state that they were Hebrews, and that they belonged to eleven tribes of the children of Israel. How many of them came? We must, of course, discard at the outset the absurd statement of the P compiler that there were 603,550. Petrie has shown satisfactorily[2] that the word translated "thousands" should here be rendered, as in many other places it is, "clans" or "tents." According to this, undoubtedly the correct exegesis, all the people now numbered 598 clans, or 5,550 soldiers. In the

---

[1] Num., chap. 1. [2] *Sinai*, pp. 207-15.

original P document it stated how many clans and how many fighting men each tribe had furnished. The compiler, taking the word *alaph*, "clan," in its other meaning "thousand," added the number of "thousands" and the original number of men together, and got 603,550.[1]

Among these tribes which were "mustered in" were some Levites, fugitives, we conceive, from Palestine. They were not numerous enough to make up a tribe, and so, when the other tribes were "numbered," they were not included.[2] But later on[3] the Levites had so increased that they could be "mustered in." Then they included 21 clans—1,300 persons.

The Rebellion of Korah

These Levites we assume had a hereditary right to the priesthood. But when they placed themselves under Moses they were put in the charge of Aaron and his sons, the priests, on a standing equal to that of the Levites who had been in the army from the beginning. Thus they were still concerned with the worship, but were reduced from their strictly priestly functions. At first they seemed content to acquiesce in this arrangement, apparently satisfied to receive the protection which Moses and his army afforded them. But this state of content did not last long, and soon there were murmurs because they had been reduced to their menial position. This discontent was headed by one Korah, a Levite. He approached Moses and Aaron, saying, "Ye take too much upon you, seeing all the congregation is holy, every one of them, and

---

[1] The fact is that in the older books of the Bible numbers of people are everywhere spoken of by the use of the word meaning "clans" instead of "thousands."

[2] Num., chaps. 1, 2.   [3] Num. 3:15.

Yahweh is among them. Wherefore, then, lift ye up yourselves above the assembly of Yahweh?"[1]

Now, as we have seen, this conception of the entire people as a consecrated priesthood was a part of the E idea. Consequently this demand of Korah and the two hundred and fifty princes who were with him, may be explained as nothing more than a demand that the nation revert to a régime previously in force and under which the people, or a considerable portion of them, had long been living. Now, when we remember that there was no sign of such murmuring until after the mustering-in, what is more natural than to suppose that these ideas were propagated by the new portions of Moses' troops, and therefore that these recruits came from people then living under the E code?

The demand was refused by Moses, and the resulting rebellion was put down. Korah and his company at length perished in a plague. Thereafter the Levites fell back unquestioningly into that place to which Moses wished to relegate them. They became the temple servants, under the control of the Aaronic priesthood so lately established at Sinai. They were "joined to" the Aaronic priesthood.[2]

The Mustering-in of Levites

It is not to be assumed that all Levites then existing joined Moses and Aaron in the wilderness of Sinai and were thus reduced to this lower grade of ministrations. We mentioned above that when the eleven tribes were mustered in there were few Levites among them. Shortly after, these Levites were enrolled. They had grown to

[1] Num. 16:3b.

[2] Num. 18:2. The word *nilwah* is a pun on the name *Levi*.

the number of 21 families, 1,300 persons.[1]   These Levites
were enrolled from a month old, and upward.   They were
accepted to redeem the firstborn[2] of the other tribes from
serving at the Tent of Meeting.

A few days later there was a new mustering of Levites.
Here the text uses the word for "muster"[4] instead of the
phrase "enroll by numbering" with which we have been
dealing.   This time the mustering is concerned with men
from thirty to fifty years of age, and is evidently for military
purposes.   They comprise at this time seven clans, 1,580
soldiers.   The difference between the numbers of the
Levites here and at the previous "numbering" is remarkable.   The great increase can be accounted for only if we
assume that between the two there was another large
increase of Moses' forces.

But, large as is this number of Levites who joined
Moses and Aaron at Sinai, we still have every reason to
suppose that the greater portion of the Levitical tribe still
remained in Palestine, never accepted the Sinaitic code,
and therefore still remained Levitical priests.   We have
no reason to assume that all the tribe of Levi ever accepted
the P code.

After the rebellion of Korah, the P document gives but
a scanty record of the proceedings in the wilderness, until
the people left the plains of Moab.   The only exception
to the general silence is the record of the death of Aaron
the priest at Mount Hor and the investiture of Eleazar
the priest as high-priest in his father's stead.[3]   In the

---

[1] Num. 3:22–43.

[2] The underlying idea of the universal priesthood in E presupposes that the
firstborn son of each family is to be regarded as the priest of that family.

[3] Num. 4:36–48.   [4] Num. 20:22–29.

plains of Moab this Eleazar the priest led the princes of the congregation and the army in the war against the Midianites. Since we saw that the Levites were "mustered in,"[1] we would naturally expect to find them doing military service; and here we find the leader of the Aaronic Levitical priesthood in truth the leader of the army.

The Aaronic Priesthood in Joshua and Judges

In the early part of the Book of Joshua we have only a fragment of the P document, enough to indicate that the Ark of the Testimony, carried by the priests, passed over the Jordan with the army, and that the people encamped and celebrated the Passover. This encampment took place on the tenth day of the first month, in, as far as we know, the fourth year of the wandering. Later in Joshua we have an account of the alliance of this people with the Gibeonites, by which these Gibeonites became hewers of wood and drawers of water to all the congregation.[2] The latter part of Joshua describes the division of the land under the oversight of Eleazar the priest and Joshua, son of Nun. Just as Aaron is so often mentioned in the P document before Moses, so now we find that Eleazar the priest seems to take precedence over the civil governor. Then we are told that the whole congregation of the children of Israel assembled themselves together at Shiloh, and set up the Tent of Meeting there.[3] In an addition to the Book of Joshua we are informed that "Eleazar the son of Aaron died; and they buried him in the hill of Phinehas, his son, which was given him in the hill country of Ephraim."[4]

[1] Num., chaps. 3, 4.
[2] Josh. 9:15b, 17-21.
[3] Josh. 18:1.
[4] Josh. 24:33.

The Book of Judges gives us only a few traces of the institutions of the P code, and those all in the latter part. At the time of the war against the Benjaminites at Gibeah, we are told, Phinehas, the son of Eleazar, the son of Aaron, stood before the Ark of God at Bethel.[1]

The High-Priesthood of Eli

The first four chapters of I Samuel give us the history of Eli and his two sons, Phinehas and Hophni. This Hophni is unknown, save in these chapters.[2] Eli also is unknown outside of them, except in I Sam. 14:3, where Phinehas is again named as the son of Eli the priest, and in I Kings 2:27, where Solomon deposed Abiathar and thereby cut off the house of Eli from being priests. The reason for this deposition was that they had greatly abused the office, and had thereby provoked the anger of Yahweh against the whole house.

The High-Priests

Who is this Eli? The Book of Chronicles knows nothing of him. We have three lists of the high-priests in Jerusalem: one in I Chron. 6:50–53; another in I Chron. 6:3–15; and a third in Ezra 7:1–5. The lists by no means agree, and there is a serious question as to whether any of them is worthy of our entire reliance. *But in none of them does the name of Eli appear.*

The lists are as follows:

I Chron. 6:50–53	I Chron. 6:3–15	Ezra 7:1–5
Aaron	Aaron	Aaron
Eleazar	Eleazar	Eleazar
Phinehas	Phinehas	Phinehas
Abishua	Abishua	Abishua

[1] Judg. 20:28. The Greek says "ephod" instead of "ark." Both agree that Phinehas was there in Bethel at that time.

[2] I Sam. 1:3; 2:34; 4:4, 11, 17.

I Chron. 6: 50–53	I Chron. 6: 3–15	Ezra 7: 1–5
Bukki	Bukki	Bukki
Uzzi	Uzzi	Uzzi
Zeraiah	Zeraiah	Zeraiah
Meraioth	Meraioth	Meraioth
Amariah	Amariah (I)	
Ahitub	Ahitub (I)	
Zadok	Zadok (I)	
Ahimaaz	Ahimaaz	
	Azariah (I)	
	Johanan	
	Azariah (II)[1]	Azariah
	Amariah (II)	Amariah
	Ahitub (II)	Ahitub
	Zadok (II)	Zadok
	Shallum	Shallum
	Hilkiah	Hilkiah
	Azariah (III)	Azariah
	Seraiah	Seraiah
	Jehozadak[2]	Ezra

The third list has two evident lacunae. Six names are lacking betwen Meraioth and Azariah (II), and one between Seraiah and Ezra. In this list Ezra comes next to Seraiah, while in the second list Jehozadak is placed there. Now Jehozadak went into captivty, not later than 587 b. c., while Ezra came to Jerusalem at the end of the captivity, 458 b. c. There is, then, in this place in the third list a lacuna of *ca.* 130 years.

In the second list, which seems to be the most complete, we notice the repeated recurrence of the same names. There are three Azariahs, two Amariahs, two Ahitubs,

[1] I Chron. 6:10 states that this Azariah executed the high-priestly office in the house that Solomon built in Jerusalem. But as his son, Amariah, was high-priest in the time of Jehoshaphat, *ca.* 870 b. c., this Azariah cannot have been identical with Azariah, son of Zadok, in the time of Solomon (I Kings 4:2).

[2] I Chron. 6:15 remarks that Jehozadak went into captivity when Yahweh destroyed Jerusalem by the hand of Nebuchadrezzar.

and two Zadoks. There is no reason to doubt the correctness of these names. They only go to show that the same names were often repeated in a given family, a phenomenon which we might expect from common Semitic practice [1] This fact is to be emphasized, for it is to be supposed that in later times scribes, finding lists with the same names, may often have mixed them up, and identified entirely different persons merely because they were called alike. We shall presently revert to this fact, in the case of the descendants of Eli, and the priests in the time of David and Solomon.

But the name of Eli, as we have said, occurs in none of these lists. It is necessary here for a moment to anticipate the conclusions reached in the next chapter, and to state that in our opinion the evidence in P conclusively points to a date 1144–1141 B. C., for the Exodus and entrance into Canaan therein described. Now the priesthood and judgeship of Eli took place 1118–1079 B. C. [2] A comparison of these dates shows that between the arrival of the P migration and the beginning of the Eli period there was a period of only 23 short years.

Now 20 of these are to be set down, according to our theory, to the judgeship of Samson, a period of the greatest disorder, during which the chaos caused by the entrance of the P people, as well as the Philistines, was gradually being resolved into order. At the end of the period we find that the land was subdued, and that the ark was

---

[1] Cf. the Gospel of Matthew, *in re* John the Baptist's name.

[2] We can hardly allot Samuel a shorter judgeship than twelve years, and as he died, an old man, in the time of Saul, and as it seems necessary to give Saul forty years, Samuel's birth must have been at least seventy years before Saul's death. And thus the dates assigned above to Eli's priesthood do not seem at all improbable.

placed at Shiloh, in the charge of Eleazar. But we know that Eli was priest, in charge of the ark, also at Shiloh. It is our contention, and we think not an unreasonable one, in view of what we are convinced is an identity of chronology, that *Eli and Eleazar were one and the same priest.*

Identity of Eli and Eleazar

The chief reasons for this identification, aside from the assumed identity in chronology, are these:

1. Both Eli and Eleazar, son of Aaron, had sons by the name of Phinehas. This in itself would not indicate an identity of the fathers, it is true, but the identity becomes more probable when we note that Phinehas is an Egyptian name.[1] It hardly seems probable that an Egyptian name would have been bestowed upon the son of one of the leaders of a people who had been three hundred years out of Egypt, as Eli and his son have conventionally been supposed to have been. It is even more improbable when we remember that Eli was high-priest, and that Phinehas is a heathen name. In the case of Eleazar, son of Aaron, these objections would not apply, for he might have named the son Phinehas, assuming, as is perfectly possible, that the latter was born in Egypt before the Exodus began. If we conclude that Eli and Eleazar were one, all difficulty in regard to the name disappears.

2. Furthermore, we read in I Sam. 2:27–31 that "there came a man of God unto Eli, and said unto him, Thus says Yahweh, Did I reveal myself unto the house of thy father, when they were in Egypt, in bondage in Pharaoh's house? And did I choose him out of all the tribes of Israel to be my priest, to go up unto mine altar, to burn

[1] I. e., *Pa-nekhsi,* "the negro."

incense, to wear an ephod before me? And did I give
unto the house of thy father all the offerings of the children
of Israel made by fire?   Behold, the days come that
I will cut off thine arm, and the arm of thy father's house,
that there shall not be any old man in thine house." And
this prophecy was fulfilled in I Kings 2:27: "So Solomon
thrust out Abiathar from being priest unto Yahweh; that
he might fulfil the word of Yahweh which he spake concerning the house of Eli in Shiloh." Now this Abiathar
was a great-great-grandson of Eli, the genealogy running
Eli, Phinehas, Ahitub, Ahimelech (LXX, Abimelech),
Abiathar.

As the text stands we have no reason to reject a literal
interpretation. The father of Eli had been in Egypt, in
bondage to Pharaoh, and had been chosen by Yahweh
as his priest. But the house which had been chosen in
Egypt by Yahweh was, as we know, the house of Moses
and Aaron. It was Aaron, the father of Eleazar, who,
in the P document, was chosen to be Yahweh's priest. It
is only the P document which knows of any calling in
Egypt. The JED document knows of one only in Horeb,
and in that it is Moses, not Aaron, who is called to be
priest.

It is true that in the Old Testament the word "father"
sometimes stands for what we would translate "fore
father." But there is nothing in the passage which would
seem to indicate that this is the meaning here.

From the considerations of chronology, from the similarity in the name of Phinehas, and from the prophecy
against the house of Eli, with its reference to the father
called in Egypt, we feel it safe to assume that Eli and
Eleazer were one and the same man.

The fact that in the Hebrew the name Eli begins with a different radical from that which stands at the beginning of the name Eleazar can hardly be taken as a good argument against this identification. We know that in the Galilean and Samaritan dialects all gutturals except ḥ were treated as in Assyrian, i. e., they were practically unpronounced. The difference in spelling might then be explained as due to slight dialectic differences. Nor can there be any legitimate objection raised to the shortening of the name from Eleazar to Eli. Such abbreviations are not an uncommon thing in Hebrew.

If Eli and Eleazar were the same, then we know that the house of Eleazar was the one cut off from the high priesthood in the time of Solomon, when Abiathar was deposed. But this seems to be contrary to all the priestly lists, which go back to Phinehas, Eleazar, and Aaron.

Confusion of Eleazar and Eliezer

Now we know that the Moses of the E document had a son whose name was Eliezer, and since he was the son of the man who in this document is the priest, it is but natural to suppose that he was a priest as well. This Eliezer had a brother, Gershom, whose son, Jonathan, became high-priest in Micah's house, and later in the sanctuary of Dan.[1] We know that in the ancient Hebrew script the vowel letters were very seldom written out, and in these old documents there would be absolutely no difference whatever between the appearance of the names Eliezer and Eleazar.

A later tradition, therefore, promulgated chiefly by the priests, who knew very well about Eleazar, son of Aaron,

[1] Judg. 18:30.

and very little if anything about Eliezer, son of Moses
would naturally identify the descendants of these two men.
It is our contention that in the priestly lists of the Chronicler
the names from Abishua down are not those of Aaronic
priests descended through Eleazar and Phinehas, but of
descendants of Moses, priest according to JED, through
Eliezer and his descendants, and that the confusion of the
two lines was due either to ignorance on the part of the
Chronicler, or, as seems more probable, to a desire on
the part of the later priests to connect themselves
with Aaron the high-priest, to whom greater privileges
had been given than to the priesthood of the JED exodus.

That in this case the Chronicler should have been so
confused as to be utterly unreliable is not improbable
when we consider how mixed he is in other portions of
his priestly lists.   In fact, in the later periods the succes-
sions and genealogies of the priests and high-priests seem
to have been pretty well mixed up in all the historians'
minds.   Perhaps a portion of these confusions is due to
the mistakes, either wilful or accidental, of those who
transcribed the original writings of such books as Samuel
Kings, and Chronicles.

Confusion of Ahimelech and Abimelech

In one case, at least, we can see that this is so, and even
point' out the time when the confusion arose.   In many
cases in our Samuel and Chronicles we read of an Ahimelech.   Sometimes he is the son of Ahitub and a descendant
of Eli, and has a son by the name of Abiathar.   At other
times he is a son of Abiathar, and has a son by the name
of Jonathan.   There seems at first glance a hopeless confusion here, and modern critics have advanced all sorts

of ingenious guesses to explain it. But when we look at the Greek text we find that this confusion has come into the Hebrew since the time that the LXX was translated. When "Ahimelech" in the Greek is spoken of as the son of Ahitub, he is always called "Abimelech." When the son of Abiathar is mentioned, the name "Ahimelech" is retained. Thus there are seen to have been two men who have, since the translation of the LXX, become confused in our Massoretic text. And this distinction becomes the plainer when we note that, whenever the one called in Greek Abimelech is mentioned in our Hebrew, the title "the priest" is affixed to the name, and whenever the one called in Greek Ahimelech is mentioned in the Hebrew, the title is omitted.

And this is the more significant when we remember that "Abimelech the priest" is a descendant of Eli—his great-grandson. As we have seen, the title "the priest" is a P title and reserved for the high-priesthood of Aaron and his sons. This Abimelech was a high-priest, although he is not mentioned in the list in Chronicles. This seems to show that the high-priestly line of Eli was left entirely out of consideration by the Chronicler.

At any rate, if confusion such as this between Abimelech and Ahimelech could arise in later years among the transcribers of Samuel and Chronicles, why need we wonder that the high-priestly lists in the latter book should show as one line a composite of what were originally two lines? This hypothesis alone explains the mysteries involved in the lists as they stand.

It will be seen, then, that there is nothing in the history of the times of Samuel and Eli which interferes with the hypothesis that there were two lines of priests among the

Jews, that of Aaron (P) and that of Moses (JED). In fact it may even be said that the history of these times seems to point in that direction. Let us now pass on to the priesthood in the time of David and Solomon.

The Priesthoods in the United Monarchy

Most modern critics admit that the division of the priesthood into courses by David, as recorded in I Chron., chaps. 23, 24, is a correct bit of history. For not only is this division attested by Josephus, but by both Ezekiel and Nehemiah, who each bear witness to a pre-exilic division.[1]

David divided the priests as follows:

THE SONS OF ELEAZAR (?)	THE SONS OF ITHAMAR
16 courses	8 courses
Over each course a "prince of the sanctuary."	Over each course a "prince of Elohim."
Over these princes a superior priest, Zadok.	Over these princes a superior priest, Ahimelech.

Over all these priests we must conclude that there was appointed by David a supreme high-priest, Abiathar, son of Abimelech.[2] It is true that in the account of the division the Chronicler makes no mention of such a high priest; and consequently most critics have assumed that Zadok and Ahimelech were co-ordinately high-priests at this time. But this seems highly improbable in view of what happened when Solomon came to the throne. One of the first things that he did was to depose from the high-priesthood Abiathar son of Abimelech[3] (who, as we have seen, was the great-grandson of Eli). It was at this point

[1] Neh. 12:1-7, 12-21.
[2] Thus the name in the Greek.
[3] I Kings 2:26.

that Zadok was raised to the high-priesthood, in Abiathar's place. Even the Chronicler seems to imply that this was the case, for he says that at the time Solomon was anointed to be king Zadok was anointed priest. This certainly means that he became priest at this time in a sense that he had not been before, i. e., that he became high-priest. Moreover, the Chronicler knows of only one high-priestly line. If he meant to imply that in David's time both Zadok and Ahimelech were high priests, why did he not include them both in his high priestly lists?

In view of all these circumstances, it is our belief that the two lines of priests systematized by David were by him made subject to the high-priestly line of Eli or Eleazar, and that this state of things lasted until this line was abolished by Solomon, and the line represented by Zadok advanced to the high-priesthood in its stead.

If this be the case, we must suppose that when the Chronicler calls the line of which Zadok was the head "the sons of Eleazar," he has again merely fallen victim to his usual false identification of Eleazar and Eliezer, son of Moses, and that the line was properly called "the sons of Eliezer." In other words, we are convinced that *this line of Zadokite priests, advanced by Solomon to the high-priesthood, was not of Aaronic descent at all, but was of the Mosaic priesthood of JED.*

We then conclude that under David's arrangement of priests the Mosaic line—that of Eliezer—and the younger branch of the Aaronic line—that of Ithamar—were both placed in subjection to the elder Aaronic line—the house of Eli or Eleazar.

Our investigations have led us to suggest the following genealogies of priests as probable:

II

Moses		
Eliezer		
(several generations probably)		
Abishua		
Bukki	Aaron (high-priest)	
Uzzi	(high-priests)	
Zeraiah	Eli (Eleazar)	Ithamar
Amariah	Phinehas	?
(then:)	Ahitub	?
Ahitub	Abimelech	Abiathar
Zadok (high-priest)	Abiathar	Ahimelech
Ahimaaz (high-priest)		Abiathar
Azariah (high-priest)		Jonathan
and so forth, as in the Chronicler's high-priestly list.[1]		

But why, it may be asked, should David have united these various lines of priests? The answer is to be found by a consideration of the circumstances involved in the history of the beginning of the monarchy.

We know that the home of King Saul was at Gibeah or Gibeon, and that both of these were Levitical cities. In this city was located, as we have seen, the Tabernacle of the Testimony and the altar that Moses and Bezalel made at Sinai, both of them P institutions, and therefore con-

[1] The only objection which could possibly be raised to the intrinsic probability of this arrangement is the similarity in names in the different lines of priests. But of course we must remember that, so far as the two Aaronic lines are concerned, similarities in names are only natural. We know of many families where certain names were regarded as peculiarly the favorites of the whole clan. Between the Aaronic priesthoods and that of Moses there is only one likeness in names. There is an Ahitub present in each. But Ahitub we know to have been a common priestly name. There is a high-priest of that name, for instance, much farther down in the Chronicler's list. The names of the various lines should cause no difficulty.

nected with the Aaronic priesthood. On this account we should expect that Saul was an adherent by residence and inheritance of the P code and its institutions. We have shown above that in regard to the witches and other matters it was the P code which he carried out.

There came a breach between Saul and David, and the latter fled. It is probable that, if there were any other priestly line than that of P, it would, not being in the favor of the court, ally itself with those opposing the reigning king. It is only natural, then, that we should find among David's adherents, while yet he was a freebooter and pretender to the throne, the priesthood which was headed by Zadok. This priesthood would probably have become the sole favorite of David, had it not been for an event which complicated matters. Saul, in rage against the Eli line, which had aided the fleeing David with some shew-breads, caused Abimelech, the high-priest in that line, to be killed. His son Abiathar saved his own life only by precipitate flight to David, with whom he proceeded to make common cause. Thus David had two priesthoods on his hands.

When at length Saul was overthrown and David had been king for seven years, the latter succeeded in capturing Jerusalem, and thus in pacifying his entire kingdom. In order that this peaceful state of things might be made more secure it was necessary that he conciliate the various factions of his people. With all ancient peoples religious union or faction has had a large influence upon political union or faction. David, recognizing this, proceeded to unify the religious life of the people. To do this it was necessary to recognize in some fashion all the different lines of Levitical priests that there were. He found the

Eliezer lme, from Moses, and two Aaronic lines, that of Ithamar and that of Eli. He found, moreover, that the last named had always advanced the claim of being sole high-priests. He acknowledged the integrity of each of the three lines, and persuaded the Eliezer line and the Ithamar line to acknowledge a nominal precedence to the Eli or Eleazar line. In the light of our records of those times, this seems plainly to have been the course of events.

The amalgamation of the priesthoods was made still more close in the time of Solomon by the deposition of Abiathar and his, the Eli line, and the advancement of the Zadokite line to the high-priestly position, a move far more easy than it would have been in the time of David because of the greatly increased strength of the monarchy.

All of this, of course, had become confused in the time of the Chronicler, and he remained under the impression that the line raised to high-priesthood in Solomon's day was the original Aaronic line of high-priests. Consequently he took it that Eliezer, the ancestor of the high-priests of his day, was the same as the Eleazar, who was son of Aaron and really the ancestor of the line deposed by Solomon. The mistake seems natural and easy.

The Priesthoods in Judah and Israel

Let us now consider the history of the priesthood after the death of Solomon. In this consideration it is important that there be borne in mind the distinction that exists between "the priests the Levites," which is the D way of designating its priests, and "the priests and the Levites," which is the P way of pointing out those in charge of the services. It is further to be considered that these terms were simultaneous, and that the one did not succeed the other.

At the disruption of the kingdom Jeroboam I, in the north, established religion on the basis of the E code, as we have noticed, adding thereto certain innovations. The fact that any man could become a priest in the north left the Aaronic priesthood there in a very gloomy state. Consequently we find that "the priests and the Levites," i. e., the P or Aaronic priests, left there and settled in Judah, under King Rehoboam.[1]

But Rehoboam and his kingdom fell practically into idolatry.[2] His son, Abijah, followed in his footsteps. The priesthoods naturally suffered.

In the time of Asa we perceive a religious awakening in Judah, and we find that Asa made a covenant with the people on the basis of the P code.[3] His son, Jehoshaphat, continued his policy with even greater zeal for Yahweh and for the P code.[4] The Aaronic priesthood was thus at this time entirely in the ascendancy in Judah, and it is to be assumed that the high-priests, being politic, supported this trend of things, even though they themselves were not of Aaronic descent. Anyone who carefully compares the P and D codes realizes how much the former is the inferior in spirituality. It is largely ceremonial in character. Consequently, when we consider how weak in spiritual vigor a religion based solely on ceremonial is, it is not to be wondered at that the religion of these times in Judah was a demoralizing and deteriorating one. No wonder,

---

[1] II Chron. 11:13, 14; 13:9.
[2] II Chron. 12:1; I Kings 14:21–24.
[3] II Chron. 15:12–15; I Kings 15:11–15.
[4] II Chron. 17:6–10; 19:4, 8.

then, that soon after this we find King Jehoram, and the people with him, turning away from Yahweh, as is related in II Chron. 21:6.

This apostasy continued down to the reign of Athalia and Joash. The overthrow of Athalia was entirely planned by a priest, Jehoiada. It would seem that this man was not a high-priest, for his name is lacking in the high-priestly lists, nor is he so called in our records. His royal funeral may point, though, to his having been a high-priest, and if so, then in this place, too, the Chronicler's lists are incomplete. At any rate, his reforms were based on the Law of Moses, or D, and not on P.[1]

And now begins a period of spiritual awakening which extends down to the time of Amaziah, during which we can trace continually the influence of the D code. After the death of Amaziah, the Aaronic priesthood with its P code again resumed the ascendency, and irregularities became noticeable. King Uzziah undertook to enter the temple himself to offer incense. He was withstood and defied by the high-priest Azariah (III), who appealed to the law, which, in this case, could have been only the P code.[2]

In the time of Ahaz, grandson of Uzziah, the religion of Judah was at such a low ebb that Ahaz even closed the temple and built a heathen altar, copied after one in Damascus, where he sacrificed. The Chronicler himself attributes this to the low state of the priests. He means the Aaronic priests, for immediately afterward he calls them "the priests and Levites."[3]

[1] II Kings 11:4 ff., 16; II Chron. 23:1 ff., 17.
[2] II Chron. 26:16-20.
[3] II Chron. 29:34; 30:15.

Seeing the dangers besetting his kingdom, and attribut-
ing the same to the religious lethargy on the part of his
people, and guided by such men as Isaiah, King Hezekiah,
Ahaz' successor, started a religious reform. He repaired
and reopened the temple, and invited the people both from
the north and from his own kingdom to celebrate the
Passover in Jerusalem in the second month. His zeal for
D institutions is evident everywhere. At this opening
celebration the P priests were considered so far inferior
and so degraded that they were not permitted even to take
part in it until they had sanctified themselves, for they
"were ashamed."[1]   These Levites must, then, have been
a portion of the D priesthood. The reason why "the
priests and the Levites" were thus humiliated can only
have been because they had been serving at the heathen
altars which Hezekiah had just caused to be overthrown.[2]
At this celebration, then, the priesthoods were again
temporarily united, and the Aaronic priests, who had
become apostates, were forgiven. This we know, for
we read that, during the service, "the priests and the
Levites" rejoiced that they had been healed, while at the
same time "the priests the Levites" took their part too,
rising and blessing the people in a manner acceptable to
Yahweh.[3]

The next important reign is that of Josiah, Hezekiah's
great-grandson. The impulse of his reform was the
rediscovery of the D code in the temple, although some
of the reforms were, it is true, based on P. This was
in 621.

[1] II Chron. 30:15–17.
[2] II Chron. 30:14.
[3] II Chron. 30:18–20, 22, 25, 27.

Ezekiel's Proposed Reform

In 598, Ezekiel was carried away into captivity in Babylonia, and in 585 he began to write his book of prophecies. In this book there are four passages which have a bearing on the question of the priesthood.

1. "Thou shalt give to the priests the Levites that be of the seed of Zadok, which are near unto me, to minister unto me, says the Lord God, a young bullock for a sin-offering."[1]

2. "But the priests the Levites, the sons of Zadok, that kept the charge of my sanctuary when the children of Israel went astray from me, they shall come near unto me to minister unto me; and they shall stand before me to offer unto me the fat and the blood, says the Lord God: they shall enter into my sanctuary, and they shall come in unto my table, to minister unto me, and they shall keep my charge."[2]

3. "But the Levites that went far from me when Israel went astray, which went astray from me after their idols they shall bear their iniquity. Yet they shall be ministers in my sanctuary, having oversight at the gates of the house, and ministering in the house. They shall slay the burnt-offering and the sacrifice for the people, and they shall stand before them to minister unto them. . . . . But they shall not come near unto me, to exercise the office of priest unto me, nor to come near to any of my holy things, unto the things that are most holy, but they shall bear their shame, and their abomination, which they have committed."[3]

4. "It shall be for the priests that are sanctified of the sons of Zadok, which have kept my charge, which

[1] Ezek. 43:19. [2] Ezek. 44:15.
[3] Ezek. 44:10, 11, 13.

went not astray when the children of Israel went astray as the Levites went astray."[1]

Modern criticism is wont to explain these passages by saying that Ezekiel here tells of the degradation of certain of the priests because they had been idolatrous. In this we are willing to concur, with the further statement that the priests who were to be degraded were probably of that line who had been so shamefully lax in their duties in Judah during the various apostasies of that people, namely the P priesthood. It will be remembered that when David divided the courses he had two sets of them, one headed by Zadok, the other by Ahimelech. The former, we saw, were of JED origin, the latter of P origin. And in the former, the line of Zadok, was vested the high-priesthood after Solomon's deposition of the line of Eli. Now all that Ezekiel desired was the continuance of this Zadokite line, which had proved faithful, and the rejection of the line of Ahimelech, which was Aaronic, and which had apostatized. It was the prophet's desire that what priests there were of that line should be degraded to the condition of the greater number of the Levitical tribe, i. e., that they should become what we call technically, "Levites," or temple servants.

One more thing it is necessary to note in regard to these words of Ezekiel, i. e., that whatever is written in his prophecies in this regard cannot be looked on as records of historical fact, but only as expression of his desires. We have nothing to show that the thing he advocated was ever carried out.

The Priesthood in the Time of Ezra

The next period to receive attention is that of the return from exile. In 537 B. C. there returned 42,000 people.

[1] Ezek. 48:11.

Of these 4,289 were priests, or, practically, one out of every ten. But there were in this band only 74 Levites who were not priests![1] These 4,289 priests belonged to only 4 of the Levitical families. The number of these families was increased in the high-priesthoods of Jeshua and Joiakim to 22 families. Ezra brought 2 more families with him, one of the line of Eleazar (?), the other of the line of Ithamar.[2] He succeeded by direct entreaty in persuading 38 other Levites to accompany him.[3] We have then 112 Levites not priests in Jerusalem. In the time of Nehemiah there sojourned in the city 1,192 priests, but only 284 Levites and singers. The rest of the priests who had come from Babylon, of course, were resident outside the city proper. The Levites, though, had, all of them, to live in the city in order to care for the temple.

How are we to account for this large number of priests and this small number of non-priestly Levites? To our knowledge no one has advanced any adequate explanation of this remarkable situation. We venture, therefore, to advance ours, that the greater number of priests in Jerusalem and vicinity at this time were not P priests at all, i. e., were not of the Aaronic line, but were descendants of "the priests the Levites" of the Zadokite line, i. e., were priests of the JED code, which had no provisions for non-priestly Levites. During this whole chapter we have seen that there never was any reason to suppose that the Aaronic priests and the Aaronic "Levites" were existent in any great numbers.

Summary

In this chapter we first of all examined the accounts in the Hexateuch of the institution of the priesthood, as

---

[1] Ezra 2:40; Neh. 7:43.   [2] Ezra 8:2.   [3] Ezra 8:15–19.

contained in the various documents. We found that there are apparent two distinct priesthoods, one, called "the priests the Levites," in the E and D documents, the other, called "the priests and the Levites," in the P document. We then concluded that possibly there may have been two institutions of the priesthood, and not one. We then took this hypothesis and tested it in the light of the later history of the Hebrew people. We examined the history of the priesthood from the end of the Exodus to the return from Babylon. We considered the records of: (a) the time of the Judges; (b) the period of Eli and Samuel; (c) the reigns of David and Solomon; (d) the period of the later monarchy from Solomon to Josiah; (e) the period of the Exile, as illustrated by the prophecies of Ezekiel; and finally (f) the return from Babylon. In every one of these periods we found that the evidence was in favor of the hypothesis of the double priesthood, and that the distinction seemed to be plainly recognizable between "the priests the Levites" and "the priests and the Levites."[1] In view of all these facts, we venture to

---

[1] In connection with the question of the priesthoods should be mentioned the question of the ephods.

In Exod. 28:4 f., a P passage, God commanded Moses to make holy garments for Aaron and his sons. Among these was the ephod, a distinctive mark of the high-priesthood, or at least of the chief officer of a temple. This ephod was to be made of gold, blue, purple, scarlet, and fine twined linen (Exod. 28:6). From Exod., chap. 39, we learn that Moses carried out this command, and from Lev. 8:7 we find that when Aaron was consecrated high-priest he was clothed with this ephod. At a later time we find this ephod worn by the high-priesthood, and referred to simply as "the ephod." Thus Ahimelech had such an ephod, and so did Abiathar (I Sam. 21:9; 23:6–9).

Besides this ephod we find another mentioned, called "the linen ephod." Samuel, for instance, was girded in such an ephod (I Sam. 2:18). When the Ark of the Covenant was brought up from the house of Obed-Edom to Jerusalem, David was robed in one of these linen ephods (II Sam. 6:14; cf. I Chron. 15:27). This latter circumstance connects the linen ephod directly with the worship of

present as our conclusion that the hypothesis of a double exodus, elsewhere so strongly suggested, gains an emphatic indorsement from the history of the development of the priesthoods.

the Ark of the Covenant, which belongs to JED.   The seventy-five priests of Nob, slain by Saul, were also robed in linen ephods, if we are to trust the Hebrew text.   The Greek reads simply "ephods" (I Sam. 22:18).

A third kind of ephod seems to have been made by Gideon and Micah (Judg. 8:27; 17:5; 18:14–20).   These were of gold, and seemingly differed from the other two kinds of ephods.   Were these the ephods of the missing "statutes" of E?

With the ephod went the Urim and Thummim stones.   These determined by lot what was the divine will, and they seem to have been used by the chief priest in each temple (Num. 27:21; Deut. 33:8; I Sam. 28:6; Ezra 2:63; Neh. 7:65).   It is probable, too, that the Urim and Thummim were used in Judg. 1:1.

The breastplate described in Exod. 28:29 seems to have belonged exclusively to the Aaronic priesthood (cf. Lev. 8:8).

CHAPTER XXI

The Dates of the Exodi

In treating of the dates of the exodi, we need great care in dividing the text. We have already called attention to the fact that J and E cover the same history, and that D, written forty years after them, treats of the same series of events. To this same period undoubtedly belong those early P records which we call the **Toledoth** Book. The testimony of all of these documents enables us to determine the date of the Exodus according to JED.

The P document proper stands by itself. Those sections commonly ascribed to J and E which agree with P in everything except the use of the divine name, which critics are growing more and more inclined to regard as an uncertain criterion, will be treated together with P in determining the date according to that document.

We will take up, first of all, the P document and its chronological testimony.

A. The Date According to P

We have already seen that the people in this document could not have come into Egypt until there was a land of Raamses. We have seen that the city-land known by this name is not known before the time of Ramses II, who reclaimed it from the swamps and gained it for cultivation. He reigned from 1310 to 1244 B. C.[1] We know that the city of Raamses was in existence in his twenty-first year, because he then received the Hittite

[1] See Appendix II for the chronology of the Nineteenth Dynasty

ambassadors there.   We have, then, in his reign a definite
terminus a quo for the settlement of the Hebrews in Egypt.

Even if the settlement was in the reign of Ramses II,
the Oppression, too, could not have been in his reign, for
it is intrinsically improbable that a Pharaoh should, without apparent reason, change his attitude from extreme
favor toward the Hebrews to extreme opposition and
oppression.   The common critical opinion that Ramses
II was the Pharaoh of the Oppression is one that seems
impossible to hold.

Although we may admit that Joseph came to Egypt
in the reign of Ramses II, it is our belief that probability
points to the reign of his successor, Merneptah, as the
time when the settlement proper was made.   There are
several lines of circumstantial evidence which seem to
point that way.

We have in Egyptian a story, known as "The Tale of
the Two Brothers."   It is written on the Papyrus Orbiney,
which belongs to the time of Seti II, last king of the Nineteenth Dynasty, when he was still crown-prince.   It has
often been observed that this story of Anpu and Bata
shows remarkable similarity to the story of Joseph, when
he was tempted by his master's wife.   What could have
been more natural, if, indeed, the elevation of Joseph
had taken place only some thirty years before the story
was written ?

Now we know that in the time of Merneptah there
were settlements from southern Palestine made in Egypt,
and that these were being made because of lack of food
in the land whence the people came.   *Papyrus Anastasi*
VI, pl. IV, l. 13, to pl. V, l. 4, is a letter or report from a
frontier official at the fortress of Merneptah-Hotephirma

REPORT OF A FRONTIER OFFICIAL TO KING MERNEPTAH

Papyrus Anastasi VI P. IV, ll. 13–16)

REPORT OF A FRONTIER OFFICIAL TO KING MERNEPTA—Continued

Papyrus Anastasi VI P V, ll. 1–4)

in Succoth, and reads as follows: "Another matter for the satisfaction of my lord's heart: We have finished passing the tribes of the Shasu of Edom through the fortress of Merneptah-Hotephirma in Succoth, to the pools of Pithom, of Merneptah-Hotephirma in Succoth, in order to sustain them and their herds in the domain of Pharaoh, the good Sun of every land.   I have caused them to be brought. . . . . Other names of days when the fortress of Merneptah-Hotephirma was passed. . . . ." In the P document Jacob and his sons come from Hebron, a land on the border of Edom, from which these people in the inscription are said to have come. The Egyptian name "Shasu" refers to the people of southern Palestine, including Edom. The word "to sustain" indicates that they were suffering from famine. There was then a famine in Palestine in Merneptah's reign,[1] and a people from southern Palestine settling because of it in Egypt.

After Merneptah there were three short reigns, totaling twenty-three years, or thereabouts, and then a period of what Ramses III calls "anarchy." Probably this "anarchy" began before the twenty-three years mentioned were over. According to the Osarsiph story, as given by Josephus, who quotes from Manetho, the disturbance started in the reign of Amenophis (Amenmeses), under the leadership of one Osarsiph. This latter became the ruler of a "polluted people," called "lepers" by Manetho, and he got assistance from people who were his kindred and who lived in or about Jerusalem. If this revolt were put down by the Pharaohs who succeeded the period,

---

[1] For the evidence of a famine in Palestine, yea in Israel, at this very time in the beginning of the reign of Merneptah, see illustration on next page.

THE ISRAEL STELA OF MERNEPTAH, ll. 26–28

From W. M. Flinders Petrie, Six Temples at Thebes, Pl. XIV)

This nscrip ion reads: *The kings are overthrown, saying "Salâm." No one among the Nine Bows holds up his head. Wasted is Tehenu; he Hittite is pacified; plundered is the Canaanite land with every evil; carried off is Askalon; seized upon is Gezer; Yenoam is made as a thing not existing; Israel—its inhabitants are destroyed, it has no grain; he Horite land has become a widow for Egyp All lands are united, hey are pacified. Every one hat is urbulent is bound by King Mernep ah, giving life like Re, every day.*

namely Nakht-set, who reigned one year, and his son Ramses III, there would be every excuse for treating the revolters as a subdued people and inaugurating an oppression.

This anarchy, and his putting it down, are attested by Ramses III himself, in his great Papyrus Harris.[1] The quotation follows:

"Said King Usermare-Meriamon (Ramses III), the great God, to the princes and leaders of the land, the infantry and chariotry, the Sardinians, the numerous archers, and all those living in the land of Egypt:

"Let us hear, when I am informing you of my benefaction, which I did while I was king of the people. The land of Egypt was overthrown from without, and everyone was deprived of his rights; formerly they had no superior for many years, until other times (came). The land of Egypt was in the hands of chiefs and town rulers; one slew the other, both great and small. Other times came after it, with empty years, and Osir-siw[2] (Osarsiph), a certain man from Kharu,[3] was chief among them. He placed the whole land under tribute to him; he united together his companions, and plundered their (the Egyptians') possessions. *They made the gods like men*, and no offerings were presented in the temple.

"Then the gods inclined themselves to peace, and gave the land its right, according to its accustomed manner; they established their son, who came forth from their limbs, to be ruler of all the land, upon their great throne:

[1] *Papyrus Harris*, Pl. LXXV, l. 1 to Pl. LXXVI, l. 6.

[2] Breasted, *ARE*, Vol. IV, p. 199, reads *yarsu;* but see Toffteen, *Ancient Chronology*, Part I, p. 208.

[3] The Horite land.

(namely) Userkare-Setepnere-Meriamon, son of Re, Nakht-set-Mererre-Meriamon.   He was Khepri-Set, when he is enraged.   He set in order the entire land, which had been rebellious; he slew the rebels who were in the land of Egypt; he cleansed the great throne of Egypt; he was ruler of the Two Lands on the throne of Atum.   He restored those ready of face, which had been turned away. Everyone recognized again his brother, after having been walled in.   He re-established the temples to receive divine offerings, for sacrificing to the Ennead, according to their customary stipulations.

"He appointed me to be hereditary prince in the place of Keb.   I became superior prince of the lands of Egypt, and commander of the whole land united in one.   He (Nakht-set) went to rest in his horizon like the gods.   The same rites that were performed for Osiris were performed for him: he was rowed in his royal barge upon the river and laid to rest in his eternal house in western Thebes.

"Then my father, Ammon-Re, lord of gods, Re-Atum, and Ptah, beautiful of face, crowned me as lord of the Two Lands, on the throne of him who begat me.   I received the office of my father with joy.   The land rested and rejoiced, in the possession of peace, being joyful over seeing me as ruler of the Two Lands, like Horus when he was called to rule the Two Lands on the throne of Osiris. I was crowned with the Etef crown, bearing the Uraeus. I assumed the double-plumed diadem, like Tatenen.   I sat upon the throne of Harakhte.   I was clad in the regalia like Atum.

"I organized Egypt into many classes, consisting of butlers of the palace, great princes, numerous infantry, chariotry by the hundred-thousand, Sardinians, innum-

PAPYRUS_HARRIS, PL. 7

erable *qeheqs*, attendants by the ten-thousands, and serf laborers of Egypt."

Putting the letter to Merneptah, the Osarsiph story according to Manetho,[1] and Papyrus Harris together, we feel that there is every reason for the following historical reconstruction:

A people from southern Palestine settled in Egypt, in the most eastern Delta, while Merneptah was king, being driven there by a famine. Under Merneptah's weak successors, this people arose in rebellion, under the leadership of Osarsiph, thus precipitating a condition of general anarchy in the kingdom. This anarchy lasted for about a generation, when it was put down by Ramses III and his short-lived predecessor. The leaders in the anarchy were naturally the ones most severely punished. And this people who rebelled and were punished, we believe, may well have been those Hebrews who, according to P, sojourned in Egypt at this time. And the beginning of the reign of Ramses III, we are convinced, was the beginning of the Oppression according to the P account. This was in 1181 B. C.

Ramses III reigned thirty-one years, or until 1150 B. C. In his inscriptions there are numerous passages which state that he used serf labor for the rebuilding of temples and cities, among which latter were Raamses, Pithom, and Northern Heliopolis. Very often we are told that these serf laborers were Palestinian captives. Ramses III was succeeded by Ramses IV, who reigned for six years. Then the records cease very abruptly, and for a long time, up to the reign of Ramses IX, we know hardly anything about affairs in Egypt.

[1] Toffteen, *Ancient Chronology*, Part I, pp. 159–64.

It is a remarkable fact that a people called *Apwriw*, or *Apriw*, which a large number of Egyptologists identify with the Hebrews, is mentioned frequently on the monuments in the reigns of Ramses III and Ramses IV; and then utterly disappears.

We believe that the reign of Ramses IV marks the end of the Oppression, and that the Exodus took place at the end of his reign. We date the going-forth from Egypt, therefore as *ca.* 1144 B. C.

We then allow three years for the wandering in the wilderness, for reasons stated above. This brings us to 1141 B. C., which is the beginning of the judgeship of Samson. And here we call attention to the remarkable fact that in the Book of Judges the first clear evidence of the existence of the P code and its institutions is to be found in the judgeship of this very man.[1]

The Date According to JED

This date which we have seen made necessary by the internal evidence of P, absolutely disagrees both with the statement in I Kings 6: 1 that the temple of Solomon was founded 480 years after the Exodus, and with the internal evidence furnished by the JED documents.

We know that the temple of Solomon was founded in the year 968 B. C.[2] According to Kings the Exodus was 480 years before this.[3] This would carry us to 1447 B. C.

[1] E. g., Samson is the first Nazarite known in the Bible; but the law on Nazaritism is found only in P (Num. 6: 1–21).

[2] See evidence for this in Toffteen, *Ancient Chronology*, Part I, pp. 7, 8.

[3] The Greek (both A and B) states that it was 440 years. All other versions, however, say 480, except, of course, those based on the Greek. This difference, at first glance, is very annoying, but can, it seems, be satisfactorily explained. In the time of Josephus, and, indeed, in the whole Hellenistic

We must note here, that this date is found in an admittedly early document, written most probably in the reign of Solomon, and based on the Canaanitic calendar system then in use.[1]

The JED Settlement in Egypt

According to Exod. 12:40 the entrance into Egypt was 430 years before the Exodus. This statement belongs to the JE document, which uses the Egyptian calendar system, which has a year of 365 days. The text emphasizes the fact that the Exodus took place on the very same day of the month and year that the entrance had taken place. This would indicate that the text had taken account of the 107 days that would be the difference between Julian and Egyptian years in this space of time. But even if this be not conceded, the difference amounts to hardly a third of a year, and need therefore not be taken account of. If the Exodus took place,then, in 1447, the settlement in Egypt took place in 1877 B. C.

The going into Egypt took place in the third year of a famine, which began, therefore, in 1880–1879 B. C. Before this famine there were seven good years, at the beginning of which Joseph had become governor of Egypt. This event must have been, then, in 1887–1886 B. C. If we could establish the historicity of Joseph at this time, which we

---

period, the Jews assumed that the Exodus was identical with the expulsion of the Hyksos. (See Toffteen, *Ancient Chronology*, Part I, pp. 155 ff.) If we now add together the reigns of the kings of Judah from Rehoboam to Zedekiah inclusive, as given in the Book of Kings, we find that in the Massoretic Hebrew text the period is 394½ years, but in Greek B (Codex Vaticanus) 429½ years, and in Greek A (Codex Alexandrinus) 449½ years. According to the latter text the Exodus took place in 1513 which falls within the reign of Thutmose I.

[1] This is shown by the use of the Canaanitic month-names, and the word *yarakh* for month.

have deduced from the Bible, the statement in Kings would then become historically very probable.

a) If Joseph became governor in 1887–1886, he must have been born in 1917–1916 B. C., for he was raised to power in his thirtieth year.[1] As he was sold in his seventeenth

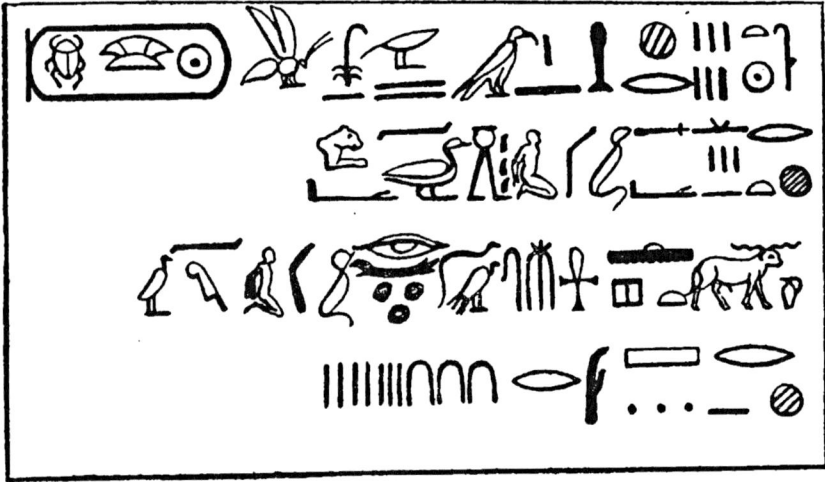

THE REPORT OF THE SECRETARY OF KHNUMHOTEP II

Dated in the sixth year of Sesostris II, and announcing the arrival of "37 Asiatics of the desert, who are bringing eye-cosmetics."

(From Rosellini, *Monumenti Storici*, Pl. XXVI)

year,[2] his going into Egypt must have been in 1902–1901 B. C. This would be in the reign of Sesostris II (1906–1887). The monuments acquaint us with the fact that in the sixth year of this king, i. e., 1901 B. C., there was a caravan of thirty-seven Palestinian people, under the leadership of one Abishah, which visited Khnumhotep II, a prince or under-king of the nome of Oryx (Benihassan). They brought with them eye-cosmetics and other beautiful presents, which they presented to the prince. A slave boy was also in their company. The representations on

[1] Gen. 41:46.   [2] Gen. 37:2.

the monuments show that these Asiatics possessed a
very highly developed culture. This is shown by their
gorgeous costumes, their musical instruments, their
boomerangs and spears. The culture seems equal, if
not superior, to that of Egypt itself.

Now, according to the Bible, the Ishmaelites of the
J story also carried cosmetics down to Egypt.[1] And
even if it was not in this very caravan that Joseph
was carried as a slave, it is of great value to know
that caravans at this time, even in this very year of 1901
B. C., were passing from Palestine to Egypt, bearing
down spices and cosmetics and slaves, even as the J
account states. Further, Joseph is said to have been the
possessor of a coat of many colors, i. e., a variegated
coat, and the monument shows that such coats were
the usual wear of these people, at least of the rich
merchantmen.[2]

b) We have a stela of Sebek-khu, discovered at Abydos,
and published by Mr. John Garstang in *El-Arabah*, plate
IV, which throws important light upon the history of this
very time. This stela was erected beside the staircase
of the temple of Osiris at Abydos as a memorial of Sebek-
khu and six of his nearest relatives. His figure appears
on the stela with the superscription "son of Jaqp."[3]
Before him is an altar with offerings. Then, in two rows,
are the figures of his relatives, three figures to a row.
The name of the last figure in the second row is that of

---

[1] Gen., chap. 37.

[2] All in the monument have them on, except, of course, the slave boy.

[3] According to the photograph, this is the reading, and not *Yata*, as Newberry reads it. Furthermore, the determinative is evidently *kp* (or *ḳp*), not
Tawy.

his "wife" or "lady," and reads "Is-nt "[1]   The inscription then reads as follows:[2]

"His majesty proceeded northward to overthrow the Mentiu-Sati.   His majesty led the good way in proceeding to the palace.   Sekmem, it had fallen, together with the wretched Retenu.   I was forming the rear guard when the Ankhu of the army joined in combat with the Aamu (Palestinians).   I captured an Aam, and I caused his weapons to be seized by two Ankhu of the army, for one did not turn back from the fight, but my face was to the front, and I did not give my back to the Aam.   As Sesostris lives I speak the truth.   Then he gave me a staff of electrum into my hand, a bow, and a dagger wrought with electrum, together with his weapons.

"The hereditary prince, count, firm of sandal, satisfied in going, treading the path of him that favors him, whose plenty the lord of the Two Lands has furnished, whose seat his love has exalted, the great commandant of the city, Zaa, he says, I have made for myself this splendid tomb, and established its place at the staircase of the Great God, Lord of Life, Presider over Abydos, at the bend, Lord of Offerings, and at the bend, Mistress of Life, that I may smell the incense that comes forth from this . . . . as divine dew.

"The great commander of the city, Zaa, he says, I was born in the year twenty-seven, under the majesty of the king of Upper and Lower Egypt, Nub-kau-Re (Amenemhet II), triumphant.   The majesty of the king of Upper

---

[1] Newberry reads *Nebt-An-nt*.   But the *in*-sign appears below in the inscription, and is quite different.   The sign here comes nearest to the *is*-sign. *Nebt* need not be a part of the name, and from the analogy of the other names on the stela it is a title, signifying "wife" or "lady."

[2] *El-Arabah*, Pl. IV, a reproduction of which is given in Pl. I.

PLATE I

STELA OF SEBEK-KHU
(From GARSTANG, *El- Arabah*, *Pl.* IV)

and Lower Egypt, Khe-kau-Re (Sesostris III), triumphant, appeared with a double diadem upon the horus-throne of the living. His majesty caused that I should render service as a warrior, behind and beside his majesty, with five men of the court.

"I was ever ready at his side, and his majesty promoted me to be a follower of the ruler. I furnished sixty men, when his majesty proceeded southward to overthrow the Troglodytes of Nubia. I captured a negro . . . . alongside my city. Then I proceeded northward, following with six of the court; then he appointed me commander of the attendants, and gave to me one hundred men as a reward."

In this inscription we have an Egyptian official who was born in the year twenty-seven of Amenemhet II, i. e., 1917 B. C. This, it will be noted, was the same year in which Joseph was born, according to the JED account. In the inscription he passes by entirely the reign of Sesostris II. According to the biblical account, Joseph was at the time of his reign in prison. This officer, Sebek-khu, got his great promotion at the accession of Sesostris III, i. e., 1887 B. C. According to JED, this is the same year in which Joseph was made governor.

In Gen. 41:41–43 we are told that at this time, immediately after this elevation, the people started to say before Joseph, "Abrek." The proper translation of this is not yet certain, but it probably means "Bend the knee," or "Bow the knee," as it is translated in our English versions. It is worth noticing that the chief title of Sebek-khu, when he was raised to office, was in Egyptian *Wertu* which probably means "commandant," the sign for which, in Egyptian, is *the sign of a bended knee.*

The name of the father of this Sebek-khu we render Jaqep. The resemblance between this and Jacob, which in Hebrew is spelled Jaqob, is so remarkable as to need no comment.

In Gen. 41:45 we are told that Joseph received a second name, "Zaphenath-Paneah." Egyptologists are as yet unable to agree just what could have been the original from which this name could have come. But Sebek-khu also received a second or "beautiful" name, Zaa, which is an exact equivalent of the first part of this second name of Joseph's.

Joseph's wife in the JED account is called Asenath.[1] The wife of Sebek-khu had the name Is-nt, which, vocalized, is Asenat.

The most remarkable fact recorded on this tablet of Sebek-khu's is the expedition to Palestine against the Retenu and the Aamu of Sekmem. This is the first certain account in the monuments of the Middle Kingdom of an expedition to this land. The text indicates that there had been a rebellion in Sekmem, and that the Retenu had fallen away. Still, from the monuments, we do not know that Egypt had any possessions in Palestine at this time. And this absence of mention of such territory is the more remarkable when we remember that the monumental records of this period are exceedingly full. At any rate, we know that at this time a great military expedition was sent out to Sekmem. Some scholars have sought to identify this place with Shechem. But this is probably incorrect. In the Greek versions there are two words both of which are rendered in the Hebrew text Shechem, two words so different as to presuppose different originals.

[1] Gen. 41:45,50.

One of these is Sychem; the other is Sikima (a neuter plural). The Hebrew equivalent of the former is *Shechem;* of the latter, *Shikmim.* The Egyptian *Sekmem* is an exact rendering of this latter. A study of the Greek text shows that Sikima (Shikmim) is a name of the territory around Mount Gerizim, or possibly south thereof, while Sychem (Shechem) was originally a personal name, given to the son of Hamor (the Amorite), who settled in middle Palestine in the region afterward called Shechem. The Hebrew text has confounded and identified the two names.

Sebek-khu went down, then, to this Shikmim or Sekmem and conquered a people called the Aamu, who had rebelled. Now these Aamu correspond to the biblical Amorites. When we remember this, Gen. 48:22 becomes significant: "Moreover I have given to thee Sikima (Shikmim) as a portion above thy brothers, which I took out of the hand of the Amorite with my sword and with my bow." These are the words of the dying Israel to Joseph. Now, since Joseph had become a subject of the Egyptian king, his lands had become subject territory to that king. Further, these Aamu are mentioned as having fallen in connection with the Retenu, whose land, at this early time, was the land east of the Jordan, that land which in the Bible is called the possession of Lot.

Just before Israel died, he requested that he be buried in the land of Canaan; and after his death Joseph set out with an expedition to fulfil this dying request. But he took with him a great army. "With him went up all the servants of Pharaoh, the elders of his house, and all the elders of the land of Egypt, and all the house of Joseph, and his brethren, and his father's house. . . . . And there went up with him both chariots and horsemen: and it was a very great army.[1]" Why all this force for a mere funeral expedition? Evidently there were battles to be fought before that land could be used for burying in which Israel had asked to be interred.

The funeral expedition proceeded to "the threshing floor of Atad, beyond Jordan," and there Israel was buried.[2] Now we know that when Israel had settled in Canaan, years before, he had fixed his habitation in Succoth, south of the Jabbok, and east of the Jordan.[3] A little later he removed to "beyond the tower of Eder."[4] This Eder is identical with the city known elsewhere as Edrei, a city of Bashan east of the Jordan. It seems probable, then, that the name of the threshing-floor of Atad is a corruption of the name of the threshing-floor of Eder, d and r being exceedingly much alike in Hebrew. This place, and indeed all this land east of the Jordan, is located in the land which the Egyptians called the land of the Retenu.

Nothing is more possible, in view of all these facts, than that the expedition against the Aamu in Sekmem and the Retenu is identical with that great warlike expedition on which Israel was buried. It is true that the Bible speaks of no great battles fought by this military expedition. But it must be remembered that the biblical writer is interested here merely with the patriarchal bearing of the expedition, and not at all with its importance from the point of view of Egyptian history.

Was this Sebek-khu the man whom we know as Joseph? Of course we are not able absolutely to affirm it. But it is rare indeed that so remarkable a parallel is found

[1] Gen. 50:7-9.
[2] Gen. 50:10, 11.
[3] Gen. 33:17.
[4] Gen. 35:21.

between biblical narratives and those of the monuments. Both men are born in the same year, of fathers of the same name. Both marry wives of the same name. Both are raised in the same year to an office the title of which in both cases is the same, at which time both are given "beautiful" names that are very similar. And they both lead expeditions against the same peoples in the same lands in the reign of the same king.[1] This remarkable coincidence demands explanation from those who claim that an Exodus at this early date, which we have deduced from Kings and the evidence of JED itself, is impossible.

c) Among the scarabs of the Twelfth Dynasty which have been discovered there are several which bear the name of Yakeb,[2] and several others with the name Yakeb-her, which means "the God Yakeb," which corresponds to the title "King Yakeb." And that this is to be the meaning attached is plain from the fact that the title "Son of Re" is on these scarabs, a title which is reserved for royal personages. Petrie has suggested[3] that the name of this king, who was admittedly not an Egyptian, is derived from that of "the Syrian God Yakeb" (or Jacob). This might be plausible if there were any evidence of the existence of such a God. But unfortunately there is no such evidence, and his existence is merely hypothetical. Who then is this king, Yakeb or Yaqeb? He cannot be one of the Twelfth Dynasty, for we know who all of them were. And moreover, as we have said,

---

[1] According to the Bible, Jacob died and was buried *ca.* 1860 B.C. This is within the reign of Sesostris III (1887–1854 B. C.).

[2] Some read *Yakeb*, others *Yaqeb*(*p*). At this early time there was little if any distinct difference between *k* and *q*. The same thing is true in the early Babylonian inscriptions.

[3] Petrie, *History of Egypt*, Part. I, p. xxi (4th ed.).

SCARABS OF JACOB
"Son of Re, Yakeb"

SCARABS OF JAQOB-EL
"User-Re, the beloved Son of Re, Yaᶜqeb-el, giving life."

(From Newberry, *Scarabs*, Pl. XXII, Nos. 7–12, 27–30; Pl. XXIII, Nos. 1–3)

the name is non-Egyptian. Still, he lived in Egypt at this very time. May he not have been the sheik Jacob of the Bible story?

Yet one more circumstance remains to be noted concerning these scarabs. In the J and E documents Jacob has two names, Jacob and Israel, corresponding to the birth name and the throne name of the Egyptian kings. Now there is a scarab published by Professor Petrie in which the birth name is given as Yakeb-her (King Jacob), and the throne name is Wser-Re. Any Egyptian or non-Hebrew name beginning in *w* by the phonetic laws of Hebrew must be changed to *y*. In Hebrew, then, this throne name would be Yser-Re. Now the Egptian Re, while properly the name of the Sun-God of Heliopolis, was often used for denoting god. This Re then is equivalent to the Hebrew El. Thus we get the name Yser-El, which, of course, is an exact equivalent for Israel. We have then the record of a non-Egyptian king (of course an under-king), resident in Egypt in the Twelfth Dynasty, whose birth name was King Jacob, and whose throne name was Israel. This is either evidence of the truth of the Biblical story, or else it is a most remarkable coincidence.

d) Let us refer back for a moment to Sebek-khu. The stela that we have discussed was erected in the reign of Sesostris III, and does not pretend to give his later career. We know, however, from another monument,[1] that he was still living in the ninth year of Amenemhet III, i.e., 1846 B. C. At that time he must have been seventy-one years old. We find him engaged in superintending the king's observations of the height of the inundation, with

[1] Lepsius, *Denkmäler*, II, 139*b*.

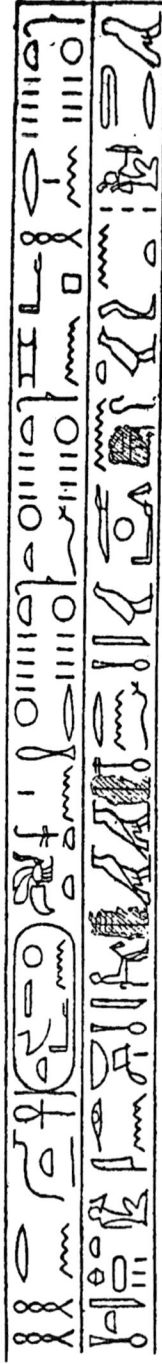

INSCRIPTION MENTIONING SEBEK-KHU

Dated in the 9th Year of Amenemhet III.

From Lepsius *Denkmäler*, II. 139b).

the title "Commander to the Ruler." Of the end of his career, or of anything other than this in his later career, the monuments tell us nothing. There is, then, nothing in the monuments to contradict any later history of Joseph which we may find in the Bible, if indeed he and Sebek-khu are the same man.

The Reign of the Hyksos Kings

The Bible tells us that Joseph died at the age of one hundred and ten years,[1] i. e., in the year 1807 B. C. Strangely enough, this is the date of the death of the first of the Hyksos or Shepherd Kings.

Manetho, as quoted by Josephus, asserts that the Hyk sos ruled two hundred and fifty-nine years and ten months. From the monuments and from Josephus both we draw the date for the expulsion of these Hyksos from Egypt, and find that it is *ca.* 1566 B. C.[2] The beginning of the Hyksos rule is, then, about 260 years before this date, or *ca.* 1826 B. C. This falls within the reign of Amenemhet III, the successor of Sesostris III. And Josephus indeed states that he was the ruler at the time.[3] This, it will be seen, places the beginning of the Hyksos rule in the nineteen last years of the life of Joseph as given by the JED documents in the Bible.

The name of the first Hyksos king was Salitis or Salatis. This name is a perfectly good Semitic word, and means "ruler." Our "sultan" is derived from it. The Hyksos were certainly a Semitic people from the beginning.[4]

[1] Gen. 50:26.

[2] Toffteen, *Ancient Chronology*, Part I, p. 192.

[3] Toffteen, *Ancient Chronology*, Part I, p. 153, n. 2.

[4] It may be only a coincidence, but it is perhaps worth noting, that Joseph received the title "governor" in Egypt (Gen. 42:6), which is rendered in Hebrew with *salet*, of course, an exact equivalent of *Salitis*, the first Hyksos king.

The second king of this Hyksos Dynasty was called Bnôn. He ruled for forty-four years after the death of the first king, Salitis. And Eusebius tells us that these two kings were brothers, and adds the interesting note that it was in these times that Joseph was in Egypt and began to rule there. The name of this second king is surprisingly similar to Benoni, the name given by Rachel to her youngest child, a name which was changed, by the father, according to the tribal idea, to Benjamin.[1] Not only was Benoni, or Benjamin, Joseph's brother, but he was his younger brother, and his favorite brother. The question comes naturally, "Was Salitis (the ruler) Joseph, and was Bnôn his younger brother Benoni?"

The latter part of the reign of Amenemhet III was, as the monuments show, one of perceptibly decreasing power. And after him one weak king and one weak queen brought the Twelfth Dynasty to an inglorious close. Meanwhile the Hyksos, starting, as we have seen, in the middle of Amenemhet III's reign, grew stronger and stronger, until at the close of the Twelfth Dynasty they were the supreme overlords of Egypt. Is it too much to suppose that Joseph, as Amenemhet III's great minister, in the latter part of his life grew so strong that he was able to throw off his allegiance to his weakening lord and to found a dynasty of his own, that which we call the Hyksos?[2]

There is a blank in the records of the Bible from the death of Joseph to the birth of Moses. Meanwhile until Ahmose I's reign, the monuments tell us that Semitic kings, these Hyksos, ruled in Egypt.

[1] Gen. 35:18.

[2] For the relations of the Hyksos to the Twelfth Dynasty, cf. Toffteen, "Ancient Chronology, Part I, pp. 150, 219.

The Exodus of JED

e) Finally, under Ahmose I, *ca.* 1566 B. C., these Hyksos were overthrown. They may have been expelled in part from Egypt. The monuments, contrary to general belief, do not give explicit evidence of this expulsion, but in view of the statements in Josephus it seems probable. The monuments *do* imply that many of them were captured and made slaves. And from this time on Semitic slaves are not uncommon in the inscriptions. That among these Semitic slaves there were Hebrew slaves is not hard to believe. May this, then, the overthrow of the Hyksos, not be the beginning of the enslavement of the people of which the J and E documents give evidence?

It is not hard to calculate the date of the birth of Moses. He died at the end of the forty years' wandering, forty years, that is, after the date of the Exodus. This was, of course, 1407 B. C. He was then one hundred and twenty years old.[1] Consequently, he was born about 1526 B. C. At that time Thutmose I was king of Egypt.

This king had a daughter named Hatshepsut, one of the truly remarkable women of all time. She was born about 1540–45 B. C. She must, then, have been between fifteen and twenty years of age when Moses is said to have been born. The events of Moses' early life and the history of this Hatshepsut fit together most remarkably. She became co-regent with her father in 1522 B. C., and, after his death, became sole ruler of Egypt in 1508 B. C. She would indeed make a powerful patroness for a humble Hebrew. She died in 1486 B. C., and was succeeded by her half-brother, Thutmose III, who hated her so that he

[1] Deut. 34:7.

erased her name from all the monuments which he could lay his hands on. Her partisans, doubtless, all fled. If they had not done so, their deaths must soon have resulted. Now, if the biblical dates are to be trusted, this must have been in Moses' fortieth year, seeing that he was born in 1526 B. C., and this death took place in 1486 B. C. And Josephus, indeed, states that Moses did flee from Egypt in his fortieth year.

We know of Thutmose III that he used Asiatic serf labor for brick-making and for building his numerous temples. So states explicitly his vizier Rekhmire.[1] We know also that he had Hebrews in his army.[2] The cruel, grim Thutmose III fits beautifully with the Pharaoh of the Oppression, according to JED.

Thutmose III died in 1450 B. C. If the Exodus took place in 1447 B. C., then it must have happened in the reign of Amenhotep II, three years after Thutmose III's death. And indeed the Bible says that Pharaoh the Oppressor died, and that then it was that God appeared to Moses and sent him back to lead out the people. Now Amenhotep's constant title on the monuments is "Ruler of Heliopolis," which indicates that that was his residence city. And Heliopolis is only a few miles distant from Goshen, where, according to JED, the people were centered. Thus the frequent visits of Moses to Pharaoh were neither inconvenient nor improbable. And perhaps the utter absence of all record of a Hebrew exodus at this time is due to the fact that most of the inscriptions and monuments of Heliopolis have been forever lost from the face of the earth.

[1] *ARE* II, 758, 759.
[2] Papyrus Harris 500.

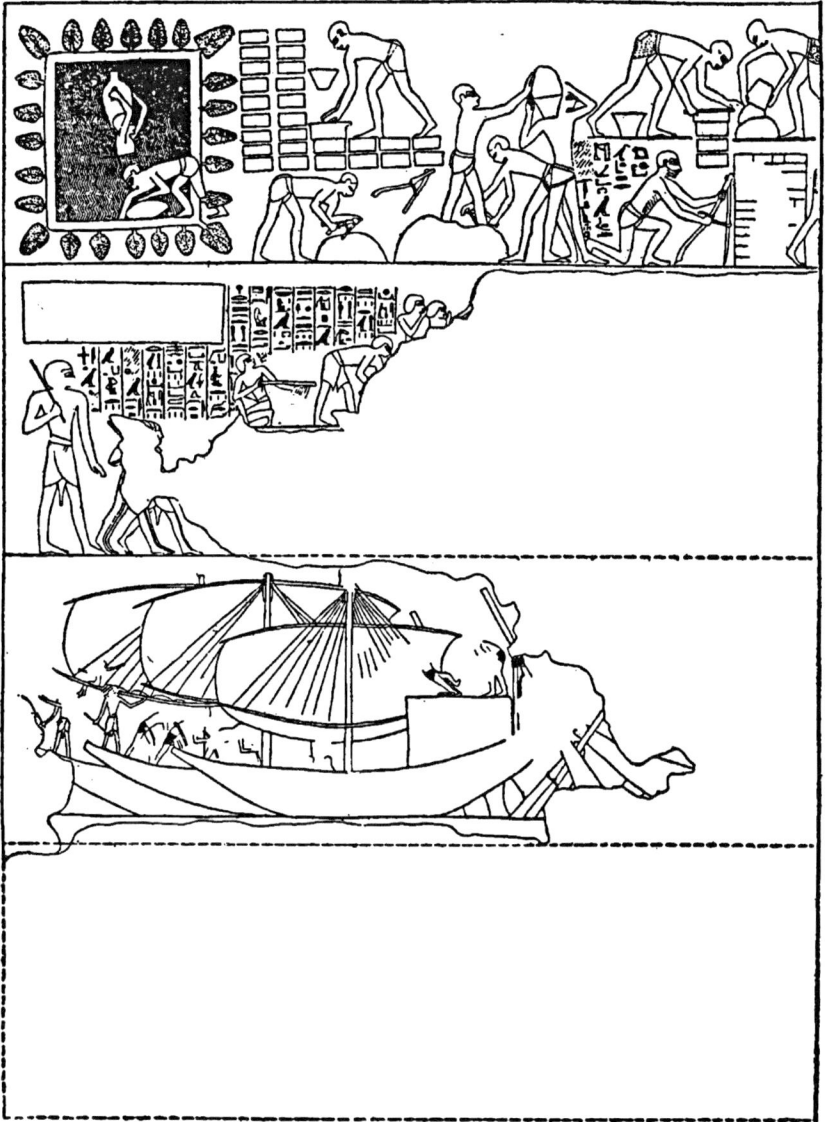

PART I

REKHMARE, VIZIER OF THUTMOSE III, INSPECTS THE
BRICKMAKERS

(From Newberry, *The Life of Rekhmara*, Pl. XXI)

PART II

REKHMARE, VIZIER OF THUTMOSE III, INSPECTS THE
BRICKMAKERS

(From Newberry, *The Life of Rekhmara*, Pl. XXI)

The Conquest and the Amarna Period

ƒ) Following the Exodus, according to JED, there was a forty-years' wandering in the wilderness. The absence of all monumental evidence of this is not surprising, for monuments do not as a rule mark the path of nomadic tribes. Some forty years after leaving Egypt, they entered Palestine, i. e., *ca.* 1407 B. C.

Now at this time Amenhotep III was king of Egypt. He reigned from 1438 to 1402, and was succeeded by his son, Amenhotep IV, who ruled from 1407 to 1370. During these two reigns falls the so-called Amarna period, for during it the Amarna letters were written.

Most of these letters were unearthed in 1888, in the modern city of Tel el-Amarna. Three hundred and ten were found at this time. Now there have been discovered about 350 in all. They are despatches and reports. A few are written by kings of Babylonia, Assyria, Mitâni, the Hittites, and Arzawa, to the kings of Egypt, Amenhotep III and Amenhotep IV. By far the larger number, however, are reports to the Egyptian kings, ladies of the court, and high officials, from Canaanitic princes and governors. These letters are very important to us in this our survey, for they expose to view the conditions in all parts of Canaan at the very time, when, if the biblical dates are correct, the Hebrew people were entering that land.

At the beginning of the period of these letters it is plain that Egypt is sovereign over all Canaan. But it becomes increasingly apparent that the Egyptian power is in this region a gradually declining one. This decline is seen to be due to two causes, one internal, the other external. The internal cause is that several of the tributary princes are apparently determined to revolt, while others are equally determined to remain faithful to Egypt. Thus intrigues are astonishingly frequent and complex, while the most remarkable lies are being continually passed around in a most unscrupulous diplomacy. While this internal disruption is weakening their defensive power, the Egyptian provinces in Canaan are being harassed by three external trouble-makers.

In the north the Hittites are making conquests, and moving southward. All over the land are roving bands, called *sa-gaz*, which seems to mean "the robbers," a people whose origin is unknown, but who may have some connection with that portion of the Hyksos which had been driven out of Egypt, if Josephus be correct, some century and a half before. In the south, in the vicinity of Jerusalem, there are two peoples entering from a south-easterly direction, one called *Ha-bi-re*, the other called *Sutu*.

Who were these invaders called *Ha-bi-re?* By Winckler, and still more by Knudtzon,[1] they are thought to have been either precursors of the biblical Hebrews, or else the biblical Hebrews themselves. It is our firm conviction that Knudtzon's supposition is correct, that these are none else than the biblical Hebrews. Those who express doubts concerning this seem to do so because of unwillingness to accept the biblical dates, and for little other reason. The names are exactly the same, and the chronologies fit perfectly.

And even the acts which these *Ha-bi-re* are represented as doing are the same, in many instances, as those of the biblical records. For instance, they attack the city of

[1] *Die El-Amarna-Tafeln*, pp. 45–63.

Jerusalem.[1] The Bible, in both Judges[2] and Joshua,[3] says the same thing.

Again there is a letter[4] from a certain Mut-Baal to Yanhamu, Egyptain captain-general in Palestine. In it he reports that a certain Aiab has fled; that the king of Bi-ti-lim[5] has also fled; that there are three men, Bi-en-e ni-(ma), (Ī)-ud-du-a,[6] and Ja-shu-ia, whom he thinks Yanhamu ought to call to account for the defection of these kings; that some sub-king has been driven out of the city of Astarte; that U-du-mu, A-du-re, A-ra-ru, Me-ish-tu, Ma-ag-da-lim, Hi-ni-a-na-bi, and Za-ar-(ki), all cities of the land of Ga-re, are in revolt, and that two cities, Ḥa-pi-ni[7] and Ja-bi-shi, have been captured.

How does this fit in with the biblical records of the time of the conquest? Aiab, who had fled, may be identified with the biblical Hobab (which in the Greek is written

[1] Knudtzon, *VB*, II, Nos. 285-91.   [3] Josh. 10:1-11.

[2] Judg. 1:21.   [4] Winckler, No. 237.

[5] The name is generally read Bi-hi-si. Such a local name is otherwise unknown in Palestine, both in the Bible and in the monuments. But the signs can also be read Bi-ti-lim. Except for the use of ṭ (Hebrew *teth*) the name is an exact equivalent of the biblical Bethel. Nor can this be regarded as an insuperable obstacle, in view of the fact that at this time we not infrequently find emphatics used where we expect spirants, and vice-versa.

, Later. While reading proof of this section, the present writer received Böhl's *Die Sprache der Amarnabriefe* (Leipzig, 1909), in pages 18 and 19 of which are numerous examples of the indiscriminate interchange of *d*, *ṭ*, and *t* in these letters. Of special interest to us is the use of *ṭi* (sign *ḫi*) for *ti*. The identification of this name *Bi-ti-lim*, with the biblical Bethel is thus absolutely certain.

[6] Only the two last signs are plain in the photograph of this letter. Both Knudtzon and Winckler read it *Ta*. The latter part of the sign is, however, clearly *ud*, and there are traces of a preceding *Ī*-sign.

[7] The name Ḥa-pi-ni, which can also be read Ḥa-wa-ni, is a geographical name unknown in eastern Palestine, or in all Palestine, for that matter. I assume, therefore, that the scribe has left out the *aš*-sign, which consists of a single horizontal wedge, and that the name should be read *Ḥa-aš-pi-ni*. This is an exact equivalent of the biblical Heshbon.

REVERSE.

LETTER OF MUT-BAAL

Bu. 88-10-13, 15

(From the Tell El-Amarna Tablets, No. 64)

Obverse

Reverse

LETTER OF MUT–BAAL

(From the *Tell El-Amarna Tablets*)

Aiab), who had been living near Jericho, but who left there and went up to settle in the highlands of Judah.[1] The king of Bi-ti-lim, who also fled, is probably to be identified with the ruler of the people of Bethel, the house of Joseph which Joshua persuaded to join his army.[2] The letter places the blame for these defections upon three men. One of these is (Ī)-ud-du-a, who may be identified with Ehud, the judge who lived in Jericho at this very time.[3] Another of them is Ja-shu-ia, which is so similar to the biblical Joshua as to make identification almost instinctive. The third of the men, Bi-en-e-ni-(ma) may be Beon (or Meon) of Num. 32:3, 38, and the name is identical with the common Hebrew name Benôni. Seven cities of the land of Ga-re the letter declares to be in rebellion. This is the same as the Biblical land of Gerah,[4] (which name, save for the late Massoretic pointing, can just as well be read Gareh), a land in the southern portion of the older land of Benjamin. Of the seven cities six can be identified without much difficulty with six biblical cities, all in this land, namely Admah, Eder, Aroer, (Meshah?), Migdal, Anab, and Zoar. The sub-king, so says the letter, has been driven out of the city of Astarte, which, of course, is the biblical Ashtaroth, captured by Moses.[5] Finally, Ḥa-pi-ni and Ja-bi-shi are said to have been captured. These cities are to be identified with Heshbon captured by Moses,[6]

[1] Judg. 4:11, with which cf. Judg. 1:16 and Num. 10:29.

[2] Cf. p. 128.   [3] Cf. Appendix II, p. 300.

[4] Gera is a "son" of Benjamin. But, as both Ehud and Saul are descendants of this Gerah, or Gareh, it is evident that "son" stands here for people or land.

[5] Deut. 1:4; Josh. 9:10; 12:4; 13:12, 31.

[6] Num. 21:25–34; 32:3, 37; Deut. 1:4; 2:24, 26, 30; 3:2, 6; 4:46; 29:7; Josh. 9:10, etc.

and Jabesh, a city near-by,[1] which must also have been captured by Moses, since he took the whole country round about.[2]

According to this letter, then, cities east of the Jordan have been captured, the land around the Dead Sea and the lower Jordan is in anarchic revolt, the governor has fled from Astarte, and, influenced by certain men, several of the governors have deserted the Egyptian cause. Nothing could harmonize better with the events of the last year of Moses and the first of Joshua, as given us in the JED accounts in the Bible.

One of the names in Mut-Baal's letter we have read (Ì)-ud-du-a. If the reading may be accepted, the iden tification with the biblical Ehud lies close at hand. It would seem that this man was quite important, if a num ber of the letters ascribed to a certain judge Addi belong to him. The name in these letters is written Ši-ip-tu(ti)-Addi. The first part of the name thus read, Ši-ip-tu, is an equivalent of the Hebrew Šophet,[3] meaning "judge." This much, then, is not a part of the name, but is a title. This is made the more probable by some other letters from, we are convinced, the same man, where the name is written Addi-dân or Addi-šiptu. Here the second part of the name is expressed ideographically with the sign for "judge."[4] The important fact is that in these letters siptu follows after Addi, which in the other letters it precedes, thus showing that it is not an integral part of the

[1] Judg. 21:8–14.

[2] Deut. 2:36; 3:10–16; 4:43; 34:1–4.

[3] This is certain, because in one letter, Knudtzon, No. 333, ll. 5, 9, the name is written with the ideogram for "judge."

[4] As the letter comes from Canaan, this second part should evidently be read as the Hebrew Ši-ip-tu or Šophet, not the Babylonian daian.

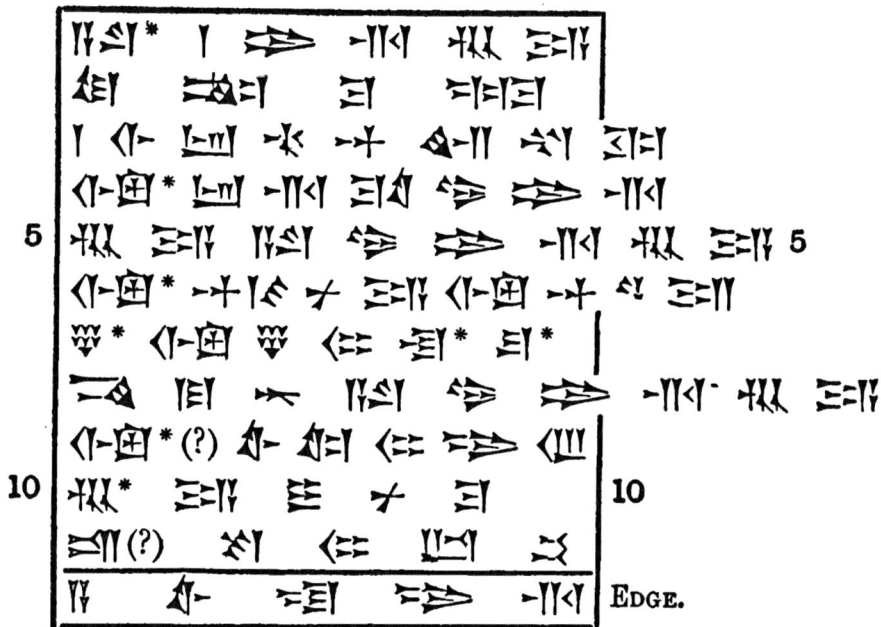

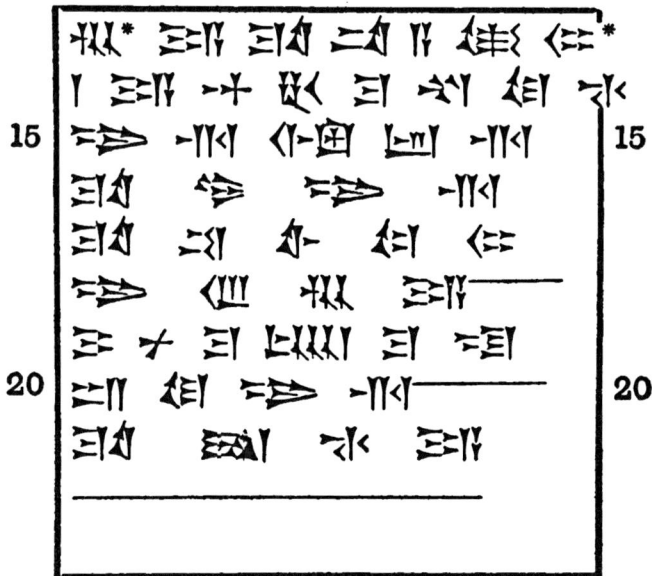

LETTER OF ŠIPTI-ADDI
Bu. 88–10–13, 36
(From the Tell El-Amarna Tablets, No. 65)

LETTER OF ŠIPTI-ADDI

(*MOSB*, I–IV, No. 200)

LETTER OF ADDI, THE JUDGE

Rostovicz 1900

(From Schiel, *MAFC*, Vol. VI, p. 298)

Reverse

LETTER OF ADDI, THE JUDGE

Rostovicz 1900

(From Scheil, *MAFC*, Vol. VI, p. 298)

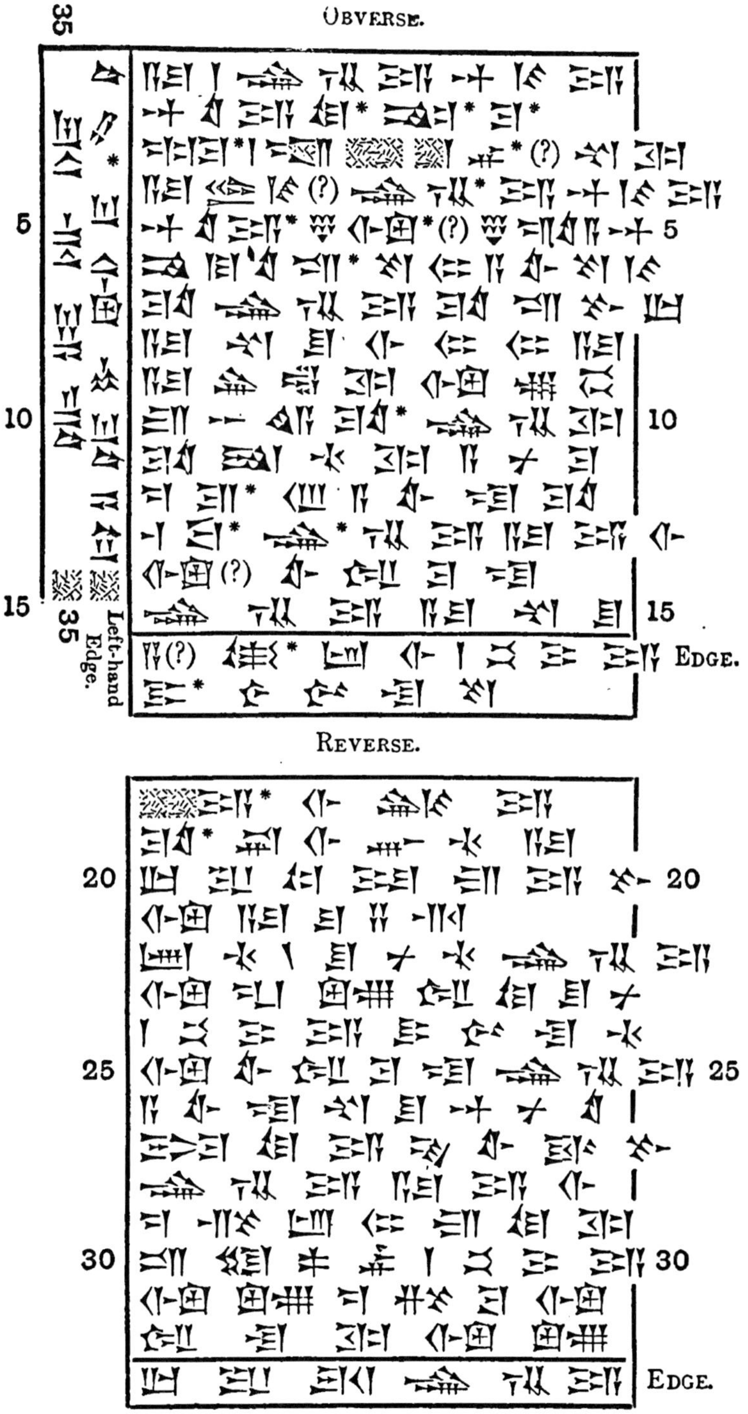

35

5   5

10   10

15   15

35

Left-hand Edge.

EDGE.

REVERSE.

20   20

25   25

30   30

EDGE.

LETTER OF ADDA(?) THE JUDGE

Bu. 88–10–13, 1

(From the Tell El-Amarna Tablets, No. 71)

name, but rather a title. We have thus the welcome
news that in the Amarna period there was a man,
bearing the title of judge in the same sense that the
word is used in the Book of Judges, at the time when,
according to biblical chronology, Ehud should have
been in that position.

The name of this judge has been read by Winckler
and most other Assyriologists as Addi or Adad. It is
written with the ideograph for Hadad or Adad, *An-Im*,
and the reading seems to be correct. Knudtzon's reading
of Baal seems to rest on insufficient grounds, for *An-Im*
most certainly is the ideograph for Adad.

At any rate, in one of these letters[1] Judge Addi writes
to Egypt that his city of Tu-mur(-ka)[2] has been taken away
from him, and that there is discontent—even rebellion—
in the city. Now *tumur* is the Arabic plural of *tamar*,
meaning "palm-tree," and corresponds to the Hebrew
plural *temarim*, meaning "palm-trees," which at this time
was the name of Jericho, Ehud's home. This judge, then,
writes that Jericho is in rebellion, and the governorship
has been taken away from him. But at this time, if we
may trust the Bible, Ehud is judge in Jericho, and at this
very time Joshua with his army is drawing near to take
the city.

Now there was a captain of the army of Yahweh who
visited Joshua a few days before the siege of Jericho began.[3]
May not this captain have been the captain of a people
who worship Yahweh, instead of the supernatural, super-

[1] See inscription on p. 262, l. 4.

[2] Knudtzon reads, "from the mountain." The signs are not absolutely
certain, but we prefer Winckler and Scheil's reading, as given.

[3] Josh. 5:13, 14.

human agent which people ordinarily suppose him to have been? May he not have been even Judge Ehud himself, who was a Yahweh worshiper and a Hebrew, who, after his deposition from the governorship of Jericho had decided to make common cause with Joshua's forces against the city? And if this be so we can easily understand how the walls of Jericho fell to the invaders at a shout, a shout which was merely the prearranged signal for co-operating revolt by a party within the city.

Two letters are written by a certain woman, whose name has been read in various ways but is not certainly to be determined.[1] Her position is so unique that a number of Assyriologists have compared her with the biblical Deborah. Possibly the name in this letter should be read Deborah. But more probably Deborah is a mere title held by a woman who held the office of prophetess,[2] whose name has been lost from the biblical records. At any rate, we have seen above[3] that Deborah belongs to this very Amarna period, that she was a contemporary of Joshua, and that she was one of the commanders in the war with Jabin of Hazor and one of those who thus enabled the Hebrew peoples to unite permanently.

These examples serve very well to illustrate the bearing these Amarna letters have on the historicity of the JED account. The historical situation which they present as existing in Palestine at this time is exactly that which the biblical account, from its point of view, presents.

[1] Kundtzon, *Die El-Amarna Tafeln*, No. 273, reads the name *amêltu Belit-Ur-Mah-Mes*, and interprets it "lady of lions."

[2] Deborah may be connected with Hebrew *dabar*, "to speak," and *debir*, "oracle-place."

[3] P. 131; cf. Appendix II, p. 300.

LETTER FROM A LADY IN PALESTINE (*Belit-Ur-Maḫ-Meš*).

V.A.Th, No. 1686

(From *MOSB*, I–IV, No. 137)

LETTER FROM A LADY IN PALESTINE
(From *MOSB*, I–IV, No. 138)

The Midianites in JED

g) The Bible says that, when Moses and his army drew nigh to Moab, Balak, king of Moab, asked "the elders of Midian" for aid.[1] The context indicates that these Midianites were neighbors of Moab. It is impossible to assume that Moab was here dealing with the Midianites of the northern Sinaitic peninsula, or with the Midianites proper of the land of Mitâni in Mesopotamia. Apparently on the advice of these elders of Midian, Balak sent for Balaam, a Midian priest. He sent for him clear up to the city of Pethor, which is on the upper Euphrates, in the land of Mitâni. This passage has greatly puzzled commentators, for a land of Midian in the immediate vicinity of Moab has been felt to be impossible. The accuracy of the biblical story has therefore been impugned.

In the summer of 1907, however, Winckler excavated the ruins of the modern Boghaz-köi, located in Cappodocia, which proved to be the old capital of the Hittites. Not only Hittite inscriptions were found, but also some in Babylonian cuneiform script and language. The history of the Hittites from the time of Amenhotep III of Egypt down to the end of the Nineteenth Egyptian Dynasty has by these excavations been considerably cleared up. It was in this period that the Hittites began to expand and to go south to conquer Palestine. There are, consequently, a number of references to kings and events in Syria and Palestine.

In particular, a good deal of light has been thrown upon the land of Mitâni in Mesopotamia. We knew before, from the Amarna letters, the names of a few of their great kings, e. g., Artatama (I), Suttarna, and Dushratta. The

[1] Num. 22:4.

last was contemporary with Amenhotep III, and lived a few years into the reign of Amenhotep IV. From these new inscriptions we learn that there was a branch of the kingly line, headed by Artatama (II), contemporary with Dushratta, and surviving him, i. e., in the time of the Amarna letters, and, if the Bible be correct, the time of the Hebrew conquest. This Artatama (II) was not king of the land of Mitâni on the upper Euphrates, but ruled over a people called the Harre, a people which the Hebrews knew as the Horites, and which we know, both from the Egyptian inscriptions and from the Bible, lived south and west from Edom toward the border of Egypt. The inference is that this Artatama (II) had come down with some Mitâni followers from the land on the Euphrates, and had conquered some Horite clan in southern Palestine. There was, then, a Mitâni people, a Midian people, who lived as neighbors to Moab at the time when, according to JED, Balak of Moab wished to consult them. And the con nection between these Midianites and those of the parent land of Mitâni is plain in the Bible itself, when we remem ber that after consulting the elders Balak sent to the home land, to Midian, or to Mitâni, up in the north, for a priest to curse his enemies.[1]

---

[1] *MDOG*, No. 35, pp. 32 and 37. Another part of the biblical history of this time receives confirmation and elucidation from these newly discovered monuments. In Judg. 3:7-11 we are told that "the anger of Yahweh was kindled against Israel, and he sold them into the hand of Cushan-Rishathaim, king of Mesopotamia." The children of Israel then served this king for eight years, until Othniel delivered them from him. Who was this Cushan-Rishathaim, king of Mesopotamia? The Hebrew name here for Mesopotamia is Aram-Naharaim, which is the equivalent of the Egyptian Naharina, a part of which at this time was known by the name of Mitâni. The name of the king himself, Cushan-Rishathaim, is rendered in the Greek, which, as we have now often said, is usually more accurate than our mutilated Hebrew, with Cus-Arsathaim. The latter half of this name is an exact equivalent of

III. Conclusions

We find, then, that the P account of the Exodus, when taken by itself, is perfectly authenticated by the monuments of the Nineteenth and Twentieth dynasties. We find, also, that the JED account, when considered apart from P, and in connection with the statement in I Kings 6: 1 in regard to the Exodus, is authenticated, too, by: (1) the monuments regarding the Israelites who visited Egypt at the time of Joseph's being sold; (2) the Sebek-khu stela; (3) the Jacob and Jacob-Israel scarabs; (4) the records of the Hyksos; (5) the monuments of Hatshepsut and Thutmose III; (6) the Amarna letters; and (7) the newly discovered Hittite inscriptions.

The evidence is so strong that it is without hesitation that the hypothesis of two exodi is advanced, and the following dates assigned to them:

JED

The settlement in Egypt . .	. 1877 B. C
The beginning of the Oppression .	ca. 1566 B. C.
The Exodus	. 1447 B. C.
The beginning of the conquest	1407 B. C.

P

The settlement in Egypt	ca. 1340–24 B. C.
The beginning of the Oppression .	. 1183 B. C.
The Exodus	. ca. 1144 B. C.
The arrival in Palestine	ca. 1141 B. C.

the name Artatama. (When Hebrew *sh* is a palatal sibilant it is invariably rendered in Aramaic with a *t*.) Now, in the inscriptions found at Boghaz-köi, there is mentioned a city in Mitâni called Ku-us-sar, which seems the same as the first half of the biblical name, i. e., Cus(ar). The name of this king, then, long so mysterious, means simply Artatama of Ku-us-(sar). There is no doubt that this "Cushan-Rishathaim" was Artatama, the Midianite king who ruled over the Horites of southern Palestine (*MDOG*, No. 35, p. 17).

CHAPTER XXII

Similarities in the Two Stories

The only valid ground of objection to the hypothesis of the two exodi seems to be that the stories are too similar to be anything more than different versions of the same history. Even allowing for the confusion which was current in the minds of those who in later times combined the accounts, a fact which must not be underestimated, it may well be asked, "How can these remarkable similarities be explained on this new double-exodus basis?"

For instance, is it intrinsically probable that there should have been two exodi of nearly related Semitic peoples, or even two distinct sojournings in Egypt? How does it happen that the two routes are so similar, and that they have, practically, the same starting-point and the same point of arrival? How can the two very similar law-givings, the one at Horeb and the other at a different mountain, Sinai, be explained? Why are the two sets of plagues so similar? Finally, and most of all, how does it happen that both exodi were led by a trio of men of the same names, Moses, Aaron, and Joshua?

Of course all these objections are natural, and do demand an answer. And we must admit that they seem to us very real and important. On account of them there was for a long time great hesitancy on our own part about accepting the suggested hypothesis. We recognize the feeling that is doubtless in the minds of many readers, the impression that the theory is preposterous, the unwillingness to consider it as even possible. The plausibility and value of the theory remain to be considered in the last chapter. Let us now take up these more prominent similarities which have occurred to us, and doubtless to many, if not most, of our readers, and see if their admitted difficulties are so great as to be insurmountable.

I. The Intrinsic Possibility of Two Exodi

It must be remembered that each of the migrations into Egypt, if there were two, is accounted for by a famine in Palestine. It is not to be forgotten that Egypt, especially the Nile Valley, was the natural storehouse or granary of western Asia. It seems probable, then, that there should have been continual migrations from western Asia into and out of Egypt, according as the food supplies in these neighboring countries waned or increased.

And from examination of the monuments we see that there were many migrations from time to time both into and out of Egypt from the lands to its east. For example: (1) in the XIth Dynasty a Mentuhotep fights with Asiatics in the neighborhood of Thebes;[1] (2) the very large number of Semitic names found in the monuments of the XIIth Dynasty show that there must have been numerous Asiatic settlements in Egypt at that time; (3) the Hyksos people, from the XIIIth to the XVIIth dynasties, are admittedly Asiatic; (4) in the XVIIIth Dynasty we have an express statement by Haremhab that he gave pasture lands to famine-striken Asiatics; (5) in the XIXth Dynasty we have another statement, to the effect that Merneptah also gave pasture lands to other Asiatics, and especially to Edomites from Mount Seir: (6) in the time of the XXVIth Dynasty both Greeks and Semites settled in large numbers in Egypt; and (7) in the Persian period, from Cambyses

[1] Cf. Toffteen, *Ancient Chronology*, Part I, p. 234.

onward, Semites were mustered into the Persian armies in Egypt, and, as the Asuan-Elephantine papyri attest, the Jews were numerous in the region of the first cataract. Prior to this time, the prophecies of Jeremiah testify that large numbers of Jews settled in Egypt at the Fall of Jerusalem.

Further, the distance from Jerusalem to the border of Egypt, by way of the Philistines, was only about two hundred miles, and by way of Shur, through the wilderness, even shorter. Why, in those seminomadic times, should we deem it improbable that Jewish bands, impelled by hunger or other causes, wandered down to Egypt and back again, not two only, but half a dozen times? The objection, which may seem at first glance so insurmountable, really has little force.

II. The Similarity of the Routes

We have shown that the two routes are anything but identical. Nevertheless it may be urged that their general outline is suspiciously the same. This may be granted. The geographical conditions made it possible to go by land from Egypt to Judaea in only two ways, by way of the Philistines or by way of Shur. If a man wishes to take an eighteen-hour train from Chicago to New York, he has the choice of only two routes. If a traveler takes two trips on one of these lines, say the Pennsylvania, are we necessarily to assume that they are not really two trips, but only one? The routes taken out of Egypt could not have been anything else than similar.

III. The Similarity of the Law-Givings

It is urged that both law-givings were on mountains. But among ancients the mountain was often regarded as peculiarly the abode of divinity, and this is especially true among the Semites. Moreover, Yahweh, the Hebrew God, was regarded as essentially a mountain-god.

In both cases tables of stone, written with the finger of God, were delivered. Stone and clay, though, were only the common writing materials of that time, as the monuments of the Hittites, the Egyptians, the Assyrians, the Babylonians, and the Amarna letters, all testify. That in both cases God should be said to have written the laws is not remarkable or peculiar to these law-givings. All laws in those times were supposed to have been given directly by God. And is it not true that, in the Hammurabi code, Shamash, the great judge of Heaven, holds the stylus in his hand as the code is delivered?

IV. The Similarities in the Plagues

It may be thought that certainly the plagues are too much the same for there to have been two sets of them. But let us see what the plagues are in each of the accounts. In JED we have: (1) water turned to blood,[1] (2) frogs,[2] (3) flies,[3] (4) Murrain,[4] (5) hail,[5] (6) locusts,[6] (7) darkness,[7] and (8) death of the first-born.[8] In P we find; (1) water turned to blood,[9] (2) frogs,[10] (3) lice,[11] and (4) boils and blains.[12] It may be considered that the presence of the Passover presupposes the death of the firstborn in P. But if our theory be correct this does not necessarily

[1] Exod. 7:14–18, 20b–21ab, 22b–25.

[2] Exod. 8:1–4, 8–15ab.　　　　　　[5] Exod. 9:13–35.

[3] Exod. 8:20–32.　　　　　　　　　[6] Exod. 10:1–20.

[4] Exod. 9:1–7.　　　　　　　　　　[7] Exod. 10:21–29.

[8] Exod. 11:1–10; 12:11–13, 21–23, 25–27, 29–42.

[9] Exod. 7:19, 20a, 21c–22a.　　　　[11] Exod. 8:16–19.

[10] Exod. 8:5–7, 15c.　　　　　　　　[12] Exod. 9:8–12.

follow, for at the time of the P exodus the Israelites might have already the custom of celebrating the Passover introduced at the time of the JED exodus long before. The P account shows only a slight modification in the mode of celebrating the feast.

There are but two plagues, then, which are the same, and a third case where they are similar, namely, the flies and the lice. The two identical plagues are frequent in Egypt, even to this day. The reddening of the water is not unusual, often being due to the decay of vegetable matter. This rotting assists the rapid production of frogs. As for the flies or lice, these are natural where there is superabundance of animal and vegetable decomposition. The similarity of the plagues, then, is by no means an insurmountable difficulty.

V. The Similarity in the Names of the Leaders

It is true that our Massoretic text calls the leaders of both exodi by the same names, Moses, Aaron, and Joshua.

But the more ancient and reliable LXX throws some further light. In that text the name of Moses is generally written *Mouses*, but not less than 107 times we find it written *Moses*. Upon this, we cannot, of course, build too much. But the presence of these two spellings in the Greek presupposes an ancient Hebrew in which there were also two spellings. Is it impossible to assume that these were originally two distinct though similar names, that they were present in the different documents which were in the final redactor's hands, that he had forgotten, as we must admit that he had, the distinction between the two exodi, and that he hopelessly confused the spellings?

This hypothesis might be sufficient to solve the diffi-

culty, but there is still another possible. We learn, in
Exod. 6:9; Num. 3:20; I Chron. 6:19, 47; 23:21, 23;
24:26, 30, that there was a Levitical clan called *Mushi*,
which is a gentilic of the name *Mouses*. This was a whole
Levitical clan, any one of which might be called *Mouses*.
There may have been a thousand Levites, or almost any
number one chooses to name of Levites, called by this
name. In view of all these facts the explanation advanced
seems to us anything but impossible.

In regard to Aaron the problem is a little more difficult.
In all the Old Testament the name appears only in connection with the man who figured in the Exodus. But
we venture to suggest there is no positive proof that the
name was not frequent in the older time. Mere silence
does not make a valid argument. Moreover, the name,
as Redslob suggests, may mean nothing more than "the
one who is concerned with the Ark," in which case it was
not a personal name at all, and might have been applied
to many different people.

The name of Joshua remains to be considered. In
Num. 13:8, 16, and in Deuteronomy 32:44, we read
that the name of the Joshua of these documents was
not originally *Joshua, son of Nun*, but *Hoshea*. In Numbers 13:16 we are told that "Moses called *Hoshea the
son of Nun Joshua*."

The names of the leaders, it must be admitted, do present difficulties, but perhaps not such great ones as might
at first be supposed.

CHAPTER XXIII

Conclusion

This study of the historicity of the Exodus has now been completed. What the value of the theory of the double exodus may be, of course the author cannot determine. At all events he is certain that it will only prove valuable as it may prove to be true. It is the result of a great many years of study and of consideration of the evidences furnished both by the Hebrew documents and by the monuments and inscriptions of the period. It is not at all from a desire to obtain notoriety that he has here presented his beliefs. It is not from a desire to oppose or overthrow the valuable critical endeavors of the past. Least of all is it from a desire to destroy the traditional interpretations which for ages have prevailed. It is merely from a wish possibly to throw some light on what is admittedly one of the most difficult problems connected with Holy Writ. The author believes that the theory explains satisfactorily the great majority of the difficulties and apparent contra dictions, geographical, historical, chronological, biographical, as well as most of the variations in religious conceptions and religious institutions, which are so apparent in the Hexateuch when interpreted in any other way.

Dates of the Documents

At the beginning of our inquiry we stated two sets of principles which serve as bases of the Evolutionary Hypothesis of modern higher criticism. The first set dealt with the evidences for the existence of several complete docu-

ments in the Hexateuch. The second dealt with the
hypothesis according to which these documents are to
be dated. In chaps. ii, vi, vii, and xi, we have given
reasons why we cannot accept these usually advanced
dates. We have found that these documents seem to have
been composed at the time, or nearly subsequent to the
time, when the events they record took place. The arguments for this, we feel, are of such a nature that a mere
categorical denial of them will not suffice. Even though
in all cases our evidence may not be direct testimony, even
though it may seem to some readers to be in places merely
circumstantial, still the evidence is such that it must be
regarded, it must be proved to be in many cases irrelevant,
before it can be conclusively shown that our dates for the
documents are too early. Nor do we feel that this line
of evidences has been exhausted. A large part of it,
dealing with the problems of Genesis, has been reserved
for the volume on the patriarchs, which, it is hoped, may
in the future be issued. But however much this evidence
in Genesis confirms our early dates, the arguments derived
from the exodus stories alone seem to us ample to demand
a reconsideration of the dates of the documents.

The Number of Documents

Chaps. iii, ix, and xi deal with the number of documents
in the Hexateuch. We came to the conclusion that the
Hexateuch contains not four, but at least seven different
documents, and that none of them, except the original D,
is contained complete in our Hexateuch. Though the
integral existence of these documents at some past time
may be conceded, we concluded that they appear now as
fragmentary. And we further ventured to doubt whether

many of the parts now designated as portions of J, E, and P, were ever parts of those documents at all. The evidence seemed to show that often they were rather to be regarded as still other originally independent documents or fragments.

But we found that these numerous documents or fragments seemed to group themselves naturally into two sections, each centering and clustering about an exodus from Egypt. The first set, the Toledoth Book, and JED, told the story of the Exodus from Goshen, and the legislation at Horeb and in Moab. The second set, P proper and small sections which we have called J^2, E^2, and D^2, told of the Exodus from Raamses and the legislation at Sinai. In each set the documents differed from one another in viewpoint and mode of expression; but, aside from this, the documents within a set offered no contradiction, no real discrepancy, not even a divergent tradition.

We venture, therefore to believe that the Hexateuchal stories of the Exodus are reliable even to the most minute details, except where the later compiler of the documents has misunderstood and changed his material, and where the copyists of later ages have miscopied the text or annotated it with their own explanations. The Bible, we are convinced, in dealing with the Exodus, is *absolutely* historical, in the best sense of that word, and trustworthy in its evidence, even to details, contrary to the usual modern hypothesis.

It will be seen that the theory we advance requires no upheaval of the fundamental principles of higher criticism. But the historical viewpoint which we have attained offers us new and valuable criteria for a proper division of the documents and a new dating of them.

We venture, then, to take up in turn each of the methods of dividing the text, and examine them in the light of this new viewpoint.

I. Differences in Language and Style

The differences in language and style in the different documents are by no means to be under-rated or denied. They are most certainly present and deserve attention and study. As we have seen in chaps. iv, x, and xi, they do not help in the dating of the documents. But they assume the greatest importance in the study of the Hebrew language in that they show us the presence in that language of several dialects, each of which was developing and decaying through the centuries. By means of this new method of observing the differences in language and style, this discovery, if we may venture so to term it, it is possible to study all Hebrew literature and resolve it into its constituent dialects and literary epochs.

II. Doublets and Triplets of Texts

There is no evidence of triplets in the story of the Exodus. Still the presence of these need not be categorically denied. In the nature of things we should rather expect it. But the available data seem to indicate that in the compilation of the documents, when the Toledoth Book and the older J and E documents offered three accounts of the same event, only one was selected, or else two stories were worked together into one in such a way that only one story remains.

But in the stories of this period there are a large number of doublets, doublets so absolutely divergent as to be genuine contradictions. But these doublets, in the new way of looking at the records, do not undermine in the least the historicity of either of the conflicting records.

For the doublets are not genuine doublets. They do not refer to the same event or series of events, but to different, though similar, ones.

III. Similarity or Divergence in Laws and Law-Codes

From the new viewpoint, all the history of Israel advances its evidence that the three or four law-codes are not by any means contradictory. They are the products of the times and surroundings which they seem to reflect, they originated at an early epoch in the life of the people, and they had a profound influence upon the development of Israel from the exodi down to exilic and post-exilic times.

IV. Different Historical, Geographical, and Biographical Statements

The numerous historical, geographical, and biographical statements with which the Hexateuch abounds, especially in the stories of the Exodus, are to us no longer contradictory, nor do they demand as explanation the theory of a faulty oral tradition. The "contradictions" quietly disappear as soon as they are fitted into that series of events which each of the documents purports to describe. We deal no more with contradictions but with varying historical verities. And not only in the Hexateuch itself do the difficulties vanish in the light of this theory of ours. The Book of Judges, too, long considered as contradicting the evidence of the books of Numbers and Joshua, emerges as historical and reliable. Even its long-despised chronology is found not only not to contradict, but even to support the documents of the Hexateuch.

V. Differences in Religion, Morals, and Ceremonies

Finally, the contradictions in the realm of religion which these early historical books have been thought to contain, also disappear, and with them all the insuperable objections to the unity of the Hexateuchal records and the early date of the documents which they have been thought to prove. We have tried to show that Israel was not a harmonious unity in religious belief and practice until a very late date, and that side by side varying priesthoods and institutions existed in a state of mingled toleration and rivalry. We have further endeavored to show that there was not one of the religious beliefs or institutions of the Hebrews which was not accounted for either by ânte-cedent history or by the legislations of Horeb, Moab, and Sinai; that they were not mushroom growths springing up apparently out of nothing in a night; but that none of them came into existence without a law to shape and define it. A large number of questions, dealing with divine names and religious institutions, belong to Genesis and have therefore not been treated here, or, if they have, have only been touched upon. But, so far as we can now see, there is not one of these but can be explained con-sonantly with our present hypothesis.

The author recognizes that this theory may, and prob-ably will, have to be modified on future investigation. He hopes, however, that he has suggested a line of investiga-tion which scholars may deem worthy of their careful attention, a line of investigation which may, perhaps, aid them in clearing up problems which are puzzles to us all, and, most of all, a line of investigation which may serve to more firmly establish the historicity of at least this por-tion of God's revelation. May He who gave that revela-tion prosper all in this book which is in accord with His will, and pardon all things which are against it.

APPENDICES

APPENDIX I

The Jews and Their Temple at Elephantine

Bibliography

J. Barth. "Zu den Papyrusurkunden von Elephantine," *ZA*, XXI, pp. 188–94.

Clermont-Ganneau. *EAO*, VIII, fasc. 6–9.

S. R. Driver. *Guardian*, November 6, 1907.

Fraenkel. *Theologische Literaturzeitung*, November 23, 1907.

G. Hoffmann. "Bemerkungen zu den Papyrusurkunden aus Elephantine." *WZKM*, XXI, pp. 413–15.

J. A. Kelso. "The Unity of the Sanctuary in the Light of the Elephantine Papyri," *JBL*, XXVIII, pp. 71–81.

Lagrange. "Les nouveaux papyrus d'Elephantine," *RB*, XV, pp. 325–49.

D. H. Müller. "Die Korrespondenz zwischen der Gemeinde von Elephantine und den Söhnen Sanabalats," *WZKM*, XXI, pp. 416–19.

Th. Nöldeke. "Neue Jüdische Papyri," *ZA*, XXI, pp. 195–205.

E. Sachau. *Drei Aramäische Papyrusurkunden aus Elephantine.* Berlin, 1907.

Sayce and Cowley. *Aramaic Papyri Discovered at Assuan.* London, 1906.

Staerk. *Die Jüdisch-Aramäischen Papyri von Assuan.* Bonn, 1907.

In the year 1901 a strip of papyrus was offered for sale in Luxor, Egypt. It was written on both sides, but the text was badly damaged. Shortly afterward the Imperial Library of Strassburg came into possession of it, and it was found to be written in the Old Aramaic script and language of the Persian period. Professor Euting undertook, in 1903, the difficult task of editing and translating it, and succeeded in extracting a generally correct meaning of the same. He found that it dealt with a complaint about a revolt or some mischief, instigated by a certain Wi . . . g. He failed, how-

ever, in identifying the locality, with which it dealt, and in appreci-
ating the real character of the document.

Professor Clermont-Ganneau then took up the questions, left
unsolved by Dr. Euting. He perceived that the locality was here
called JB, which could be nothing else but the Egyptian Jeb, the
Greek Elephantine. Still more remarkable was his penetrating
insight into the character of the document. He reasoned that it
could not have been written by a native Egyptian because it was a
complaint against Egyptian officials and priests. Neither could it
be of Persian or Babylonian origin, because it failed to designate
Khnub, god of Elephantine, as a god. He argued, therefore, that the
man who made complaints against the priests of the god Khnub,
without calling Khnub a god, must be a Jew. His hypothesis seemed
daring, but it was built on sound principles, and later discoveries
have confirmed it in every detail.

About the same time a new find of Aramaic papyri was placed on
sale in Assuan, a city on the eastern bank of the Nile, opposite the
island of Elephantine, and just below the First Cataract. Professor
Sayce acquired one of them for the Bodleian Library, two went to
the British Museum, a large number to the Cairo Museum, and still
others have been acquired by other museums, while there is reason
to believe that some of these papyri are now in private ownership.

Professors Sayce and Cowley published, in 1906, not less than
sixteen of these papyri. Almost all of them were in perfect preserva-
tion, undisturbed and uninjured since the day they were laid aside
some 2,350 years ago. The strings were still tied around them, and
the old clay-seals were still fastened to the string-knots. Their script
and language is also that of the old Aramaic. They deal with business transactions in the city or fortress Elephantine, and there seems
to be good reason for assuming that all the Assuan papyri as well as
the Euting papyrus have come originally from that city.

The chief interest in these papyri centers about the fact, that they
present us with a vivid picture of a prosperous Jewish community
in that city in the fifth century B. C. And the picture is so vivid that
we can not only follow these Jews in some details of the daily routine
of their life but we know even how they built their homes and where
their houses were located. The Jews of Elephantine had quarters

of their own in the northwestern part of the city; they had their own court, besides a Hebrew tribunal in Assuan, making their oaths in the name of Yahu (Yahweh), an oath which was as valid in Egyptian

MAP OF THE JEWISH QUARTER IN ELEPHANTINE, SHOWING THE LOCATION OF JEWISH PROPERTY AND THE TEMPLE OF JAHU

	Street	3. Mahseiah, son of Yedôniah		Street		Street
1. Peftônît, saylor		4. Qôniah son of Zadok	7. Zechariah, son of Nathan		10. Temple of Yahu	
2. Espemet, son of Peftônît, saylor	Street 15.	5. Mibh- tayah	8. Yezaniah, son of Uriah	King's Street 14.		Street 16.
		6. Dargman, son of Harshin	9. Hoshea, son of Uriah		11. Mibh- tahyah 12. Yecôr son of Penuliah	13. Gadol, son of Hoshea

law as an oath made in the name of Khnub and Sati, the ancient gods of Elephantine.

But even a minute description of ancient property would not be particularly novel at the present time, since several monuments have lately been discovered in Egypt and Babylonia, acquainting us with similar documents of a far higher age. Not even the fact that the agents are Jews in this case, is extraordinarily novel, for we have found from the Babylonian documents that Jews possessed property and conducted large business transactions in several cities of Babylonia at this very time. The all-absorbing interest in these Assuan deeds is the fact that two of them locate properties as adjoining the "chapel" of Yahu. Now the Aramaic word used here for "chapel" is *Êgûra'*, which otherwise denotes "temple" in the Assyrian, Babylonian, and Aramaic languages. But it seemed improbable to Professors Sayce and Cowley, that there could be a Jewish temple in Elephantine, and, therefore, they translated it with "chapel," "synagogue." For who could dream that there existed a Jewish temple in Egypt in the fifth century B. C. ? Happily, all this is now changed.

The assured fact, however, that a "chapel," or a "synagogue," consecrated to the worship of Yahweh, existed in Egypt at that time, awoke the keenest interest among scholars all over the world. Within a few months, a considerable literature of learned treatises had sprung up around this splendid publication of Professors Sayce and Cowley.

While this was going on Dr. Rubensohn was busy with excavations on the island of Elephantine, and in the spring of 1907 he discovered three Aramaic papyri, found in a house that probably had belonged to the original owner of them, the chief priest Yedôniah. All three papyri were well preserved and they were written in the Aramaic script and language. They were immediately brought to Germany and turned over to Professor Sachau. He undertook to read them, and at the session of the Philosophical-Historical Department of the Royal Prussian Academy of Sciences in Berlin on the 25th of July, 1907, he presented an able and scholarly translation of these documents, together with notes and explanations of the more important points. This was immediately ordered to be printed, and was published on the 10th of October, 1907.

Of the three Elephantine papyri, two are concepts, drawn up for a petition to the governor of Jerusalem. The third is a memorandum of an order, issued by the governor of Jerusalem and sent to the Jews of Elephantine in answer to their petition. The two concepts cover essentially the same ground, but as only one of these is published in facsimile, we shall confine our translation to the same. It contains thirty lines and reads as follows:

1. *To our Lord Bagohi, Governor of Judah, thy servants, Yedôniah and his companions, the priests in the Yortress Ele‹ phantine, (send)*

Greeting !

2. *May our Lord, the God of heaven, grant abundance at all time,*
3. *and place thee in favor before King Darius and the sons of the palace. Prosperity, one thousand-fold more than now, and long life may he give thee, and may there be joy and gladness at all time!*
4. *Now, thy servant Yedôniah and his companions, we speak thus:*

   In the month of Tammuz, in the fourteenth year of King
5. *Darius, at the time when Arsham had departed and gone to the King, the priests of god Khnub, which were in the fortress Elephantine, made a league with Waidrang, who was chief commander here, saying:*
6. *"The temple of God Yahu, which is in the fortress Elephantine, let them take (it) away from thence!"*
7. *Thereupon that accursed Waidrang sent a letter to Naphâyân, his son, who was commander of the garrison in the fortress Assuan, saying:*

   "Let them destroy the temple, which is in the fortress Elephantine!"
8. *Thereupon Naphâyân ordered the Egyptians together with the other forces; they came to the fortress Elephantine with their*
9. *weapons of destruction, entered into this temple, destroyed it to the ground, and the pillars which were there they brake asunder, they discomfited.*
10. *Furthermore, there were five stone-gates, built of hewn stone, which were in this temple; them they destroyed, and their doors*
11. *they removed, and their copper-hinges, which (were fastened) in marble-blocks, and the covering (made) of cedar-beams, all of*
12. *which, together with the rest of the equipment and other things which were there, all they burnt with fire; and all the golden*
13. *basons, and the silver, and whatsoever there was in this temple, all they took, and appropriated for themselves.*

    Now, in the days of the King(s) of Egypt our fathers had
14. *built this temple in the fortress Elephantine. And when Cambyses entered Egypt, he found this temple built. Although they overthrew all the temples of the gods of Egypt, no one injured anything in this temple.*

15.   *But since they did thus, we with our wives and our children have put on sackcloth, and we have fasted and prayed to Yahu,*

16.   *the Lord of heaven, who has vindicated us on Waidrang, that dog—they have laid[1] his feet in fetter(s), and all the property*

17.   *which he acquired has perished, and all the men who had wished evil against this temple are slain, and we have seen our desire upon them.*

18.   *Furthermore, before this, at the time when this evil was done to us, we sent a letter (to) our lord, and to Jehohanan, the high-priest, and to his companions, the priests which are in Jerusalem,*

19.   *and to his brother Ostan, i. e., Anani, and to the nobles of the Jews, (but) not a single letter did they send to us.*

         Furthermore, from the Tammuz-day of the fourteenth year

20.   *of King Darius and until this day we have put on sackcloth and*

21.   *fasted; our wives have become like widow(s); we have not anointed ourselves with oil, nor drunk wine.*

         Furthermore, from that time until this day of the fourteenth year of King Darius they have not offered in this temple a meal-offering, or frankincense, or a holocaust.

22.   *Now, thy servants Yedôniah and his companions, and the Jews, all the citizens of Elephantine, say thus:*

23.   *If it seem good to our lord, think upon this temple, that it may*

24.   *be rebuilt! Look upon the recipients of thy bounty and goodness, who are here in Egypt! May a letter be sent from thee unto them*

25.   *concerning the temple of God Yahu, that it may be rebuilt in the fortress Elephantine, as it was built in former times. Then they*

26.   *shall present meal-offerings, and incense-offerings, and holocausts upon the altar of God Yahu in thy name; yea, we will pray for*

27.   *thee at all times, we and our wives and our children and the Jews, all who are here, if they do thus, until this temple is rebuilt; yea, a legitimate portion shall belong to thee, before Yahu, the God of*

28.   *heaven, from any one who shall present to Him a holocaust and sacrifices, in value equivalent to a sum of 1,000 talents. And in*

29.   *regard to the gold—concerning that we have (already) sent information.*

---

[1] Orig. "established," used also of a decree, that "went forth," i. e., "was established."

> *Furthermore, we have sent concerning all the(se) matters in a letter to Delayah and Shelemayah, sons of Sanballat, Governor of Samaria.*

30. *Furthermore, Arsham has no knowledge of all that which has been done to us.*

> *On the [twentieth] day of Marcheswan, in the seventeenth year of King Darius.*

NOTE

I. Bagohi

This governor of Jerusalem and Judah is known from Josephus (*Antiquities*, xi, 7:1). Josephus calls him Bagoas, and mentions him as serving in the time of Artaxerxes II (404–359 B. C). The high-priest of Jerusalem at this time was Jehonan, called Jehohanan in this document.[1] Joshua, a brother of Johanan, was an intimate friend of Bagoas, and had been promised by the latter the high-priestly office at his brother's death. This seems to have made him so aggressive, and his conduct so offensive, that his brother Johanan, the high-priest, one day killed him in the temple. This crime was so outrageous and so heinous, that it gave Bagoas an excellent opportunity for entering the temple and punishing the offender, in spite of the protests of the Jews. Bagoas vindicated the death of his friend by imposing a heavy fine on Johanan, consisting of a large share of all the sacrifices offered in the temple for the following seven years. This punishment affected the high-priest and the people alike.

It is evident from these documents that Bagoas or Bagohi was appointed governor of Judah by Darius II, and not by Artaxerxes II. Since the first letter of the Jews of Elephantine was addressed to him in 411 B. C., it follows that he was governor of Judah at that time, and that his appointment, therefore, could not have been made by Artaxerxes II, as some scholars have inferred from Josephus. It is, of course, possible that he was succeeded by another Bagoas, appointed by Artaxerxes II, but it is more natural to interpret Josephus as saying that Bagoas got his appointment as general in the reign of Artaxerxes II, but that he became governor of Judah in the time of Darius II.

It is possible, indeed, that the murder of Joshua took place in the interval of 411–408 B. C. When the Jews appealed to Jerusalem for

[1] Cf. above, l. 18.

help in the year 411 B. C., their petition was addressed both to the governor and the high-priest. Now, in 408 the high-priest is ignored and the governor of Samaria, whom we should expect to have been abhorred by every Jew, takes his place. It is possible, therefore, that the murder of Joshua had taken place in the meantime. The Jews of Elephantine were evidently well posted on affairs in Jerusalem, and knowing the disgrace into which the high-priest had fallen, were well aware that they would only weaken their cause by mentioning him in this second petition. Consequently they passed him by entirely. This stratagem may even have been one of the reasons that inclined the governor to grant them the favor they asked for.

The name Bagoas seems to have been common among the Persians. Thus we find a Persian nobleman bearing this name in the service of Darius I.[1] The eunuch general Bagoas served under the sixth Persian king.[2] Even among the Jews this name became common in the Persian period. A certain Bigvai sealed the covenant of Nehemiah,[3] but Bigvai should undoubtedly be pronounced Bagoy or Bagoas. One of the princes of the returning exiles was called Bigvai,[4] and another Bigvai appears in Ezra's caravan.[5]

II. The Temple at Elephantine

The Jewish temple at Elephantine was not simply a synagogue or an altar-house, but a real temple, because our papyrus designates it as a temple by the same word that it uses for the Egyptian temples. This temple had a naos with columns in front of it, and an altar of incense and a seven-branched candlestick[6] within it. It was surrounded by a court which contained the holocaust-altar, and which was girdled by a wall with five gates.

There is nothing in this papyrus to show that the naos contained more than one room—the Holy Place. It had no Holy of Holies. Nor did the Jewish community of Elephantine have a high-priest. Jedôniah was their chief-priest, equal with his "companions," but he was

[1] Herodotus, iii:128.

[2] About 342 B. C.

[3] Neh. 10:16.

[4] Ezra 2:2, also mentioned in Neh. 7:7.

[5] Ezra 8:14.

[6] A Jewish ostracon, found by Professor Maspero at Elephantine, shows a seven-branched candlestick.

not a high-priest. The high-priest of Jerusalem was high-priest of the Jews in Elephantine, and all other Jews as well. The Holy of Holies in the temple at Jerusalem was the oracle-place of all Jews, both in Elephantine and elsewhere.

Thus we see that the temple at Elephantine was in strict accord with Deuteronomy, which restricted the "dwelling-place of Yahweh's name" to one central sanctuary, now established at Jerusalem, but permitted sacrifices everywhere. The Jews of Elephantine were, then, worshiping in entire accord with Deuteronomy, and the utterances of Isaiah.[1]

Further, this papyrus shows us that the Jews of Elephantine conducted their worship according to the strict regulations of the whole P code—the holocausts, peace-sacrifices, meal-offerings, incense, fasting, prayers, all point to the laws of the P code, which thus must have been in operation in Egypt not later than 525 B. C., and probably from the beginning of the seventh century.

[1] Isa. 19:19.

APPENDIX II

Ancient Chronology[1]

Bibliography[2]

E. Amélineau. "Chronologie des rois de l'époque archaique," *RE*, XII, pp. 185–204.

W. E. Beecher. *The Dated Events of the Old Testament*. Philadelphia, 1907.

A. Bosse. "Die chronologische System im Alten Testamente und bei Josephus," *MVG*, 1908, pp. 101–76.

J. H. Breasted. *A History of the Ancient Egyptians*. New York, 1908.

A. T. Clay. "The Assyrian, Neo-Babylonian, and Persian Periods," *BE*, Ser. A, Vol. VIII, Part I, pp. 3–5.

S. A. Cook. "Babylonian Chronology," *PEFQS*, 1907, pp. 318 ff.

———— "Notes on the Dynasties of Omri and Jehu," *JQR*, Vol. XX, pp. 597–631.

G. Cormack. *Egypt in Asia*. London, 1908.

H. Dhorme. "Sargon, Père de Narâm-Sin," *OLZ*, 1909, pp. 53–63.

F. C. Eiselen. *Sidon, a Study in Oriental History*. New York, 1907.

W. Erbt. "Das Jobeljahr," *OLZ*, 1907, pp. 636–38.

Folkeringham. *The Chronology of the Old Testament*, Cambridge, 1906.

I. A. Galvão. "Note sur la IVe et la Ve dynasties," *RE*, XII, pp. 120–22.

A. B. Gardiner. "Mesore as First Month of the Egyptian Year," *ZÄ*, XLII, pp, 136–44.

F. K. Ginzel. *Handbuch der Mathematischen und Technischen Chronologie*. I Band. Leipzig, 1906.

F. Ll. Griffith. "The Length of the Reign of Amenhotep II," *PSBA*, XXXI, pp. 42, 43.

---

[1] Supplement to the author's *Ancient Chronology*, Part I, Chicago, 1907.

[2] This bibliography represents merely the books and articles that have come to the notice of the author since the publication of his *Ancient Chronology*, Part I.

H. R. Hall. "The Discoveries in Crete and Their Relation to the History of Egypt and Palestine," *PSBA*, XXXI, pp. 135–48.

——— "Mursil and Myrtilos," *JHS*, XXIX, pp. 19–22.

H. V. Hilprecht. "Der Zwölfte König der ersten Dynastie von Isin," *OLZ*, 1907, pp. 385–87.

C. Hirschenzohn. *Yamim Miqqeden*. Hoboken.

E. W. Hollingworth. "The Hyksos and the Twelfth Dynasty," *PSBA*, XXX, pp. 155–58.

F. Hommel. "Die Genealogie des Kassitenkönigs Agum des Zweittens," *OLZ*, 1909, pp. 108, 109.

M. Jastrow, Jr. "Urumuš," *ZA*, XXI, pp. 177–82.

C. H. W. Johns. "On the Length of the Month in Babylonia," *PSBA*, XXX, pp. 221–30.

———. "The First Year of Samsu-Iluna. *PSBA*, XXX, pp. 70, 71.

———. "The Babylonian Chronicle of the First Dynasty of Babylon," *PSBA*, XXIX, pp. 107–11.

———. "Note on the Chronicle of the First Dynasty of Babylon," *PSBA*, XXIX, pp. 108–10.

———. "Some Further Notes on the Babylonian Chronicle of the First Dynasty," *PSBA*, XXXI, pp. 14–19.

———. "The Chronology of Ashurbanipal's Reign," B. C 668–626, *PSBA*, XXIX, pp. 74–84.

F. A. Jones. "The ancient Year and the Sothic Cycle," *PSBA*, XXX, pp. 95–106.

L. W. King. "Sargon I, King of Kish, and Shar-gani-sharri, King of Akkad," *PSBA*, XXX, pp. 238–42.

J. A. Knudtzon. "Die El-Amarna Tafeln," *VAB*, II, pp. 25–42.

F. X. Kugler. "Darlegung und Thesen über altbabylonische Chronologie," *ZA*, XXII, pp. 63–78.

St. Langdon. "Sumerians and Semites in Babylonia." *Babyloniaca*, II, pp. 137–62.

F. Legge. "Was Khasekhmui called Mena?" *PSBA*, XXXI, pp. 128–32.

C. F. Lehmann-Haupt. "Die Sothis-Periode und der Kalender des Papyrus Ebers," *Klio*, VIII, pp. 213–26.

———. "Berossos' Chronologie und die keilinschriftliche Neufunde," *Klio*, VIII, pp. 227–51.

C. F. Lehmann-Haupt. "Zur Aufnahme der Israeliten in Gosen," *Klio*, IX, pp. 260 ff.

J. Lieblein. "The Exodus of the Hebrews," *PSBA*, XXIX, pp. 214–18.

———. "Le nom royal et la date du Papyrus Ebers," *Sphinx*, XII, pp. 155 ff.

E. Lindl. "Ein Datum Libit-Istars, Königs von Isin," *OLZ*, 1907, pp. 387, 388.

G. Maspero. *Ancient Egypt*, Eng. transl. by E. Lee. New York, 1909.

B. Meissner. "Lipit-Ištar," *OLZ*, 1907, pp. 113–15.

L. Messerschmidt. "Zur altbabylonischen Chronologie," *OLZ*, 1907, pp. 169–75.

Ed. Meyer. *Nachträge zur Ägyptischen Chronologie*. Berlin, 1908.

———. "Neue Nachträge zur ägyptischen Chronologie," *ZÄ*, XLIV, p. 115.

M. A. Meyer. *History of the City of Gaza*. New York, 1907.

Miketta. *Der Pharaoh des Auszuges*. Freiburg i. B., 1903.

E. Newberry and J. Garstang. *A Short History of Ancient Egypt*. London, 1907.

E. E. Peiser. "Synchronistische Geschichte und Chronik P," *OLZ*, 1908, pp. 7–10.

——— "Die Dynastie von Paše," *OLZ*, 1907, pp. 615–18.

W. M. Flinders Petrie. "The Structure of Herodotus, Book II," *JHS*, XXVII, pp. 275 ff.

A. Poebel. "Der Zehnte König der Dynastie von Isin," *OLZ*, 1907, pp. 461–64.

———. "Das zeitliche Verhältniss der ersten Dynastie von Babylon zur zweiten Dynastie," *ZA*, XX, pp. 229–45.

———. "Das zeitliche Verhältniss der zweiten Dynastie der grosseren Königsliste zur dritten Dynastie," *ZA*, XXI, pp. 162–75.

H. Ranke. "Immerum von Sippar," *OLZ*, 1907, pp. 207–10.

——— "Zur altbabylonischen Datierungsweise," *OLZ*, 1907, pp. 231–34.

——— "Zur Königsliste aus Nippur," *OLZ*, 1907, pp. 109–13.

H. Radau. "The Genealogy of the Kassite Kings," *BE*, Ser. A, Vol. XVII, Part I, pp. 59–71

A. H. Sayce. "Notes on Assyrian and Egyptian History," *PSBA*, XXX, pp. 13–19.

P. Schnabel. "Erba-Adad und Karaindaš." *OLZ*, 1909, pp. 54–58.

———. "Studien zur babylonisch-assyrischen Chronologie," *MVG*, 1908, pp. 1–100.

Fr. Thureau-Dangin. "Un nouveau roi de Hana," *OLZ*, 1908, p. 93.

———. "La généalogie d'Agum-kakrime," *OLZ*, 1908, pp. 31–33.

———. "Damiq-ilišu contemporain de Sin-muballit," *OLZ*, 1907, pp. 256, 257.

———. "L'emplacement de Kiš," *OLZ*, 1909, pp. 204–7.

———. "Notes pour servir à la chronologie de la dynastie kassite," *JA*, dix. ser., Tome XI, pp. 117–34.

———. "La deuxième dynastie du canon royal et la dáte de la fondation du royaume babylonien," *ZA*, XXI, pp. 176–87.

———. "Les synchronismes de l'époque d'El-Amarna," *OLZ*, 1908, pp. 445–47.

———. "Kuri-galzu et Burna-buriaš," *OLZ*, 1908, pp. 275, 276.

———. "Sargon l'Ancien," *OLZ*, 1908, pp. 313–15.

A. Ungnad. "Sumerer und Akkader," *OLZ*, 1908, pp. 62–67.

———. "Zur Chronologie der Kassiten-Dynastie, *OLZ*, 1908, pp. 11–17.

———. "Bêl-šimanni, ein neuer König Babylons und der Länder," *OLZ*, 1907, pp. 464–68.

———. "Die Chronologie der Regierung Ammiditana's und Ammisaduga's," *BA*, VI, 3, pp. 1–53.

———. "Ḫallušu," *OLZ*, 1907, pp. 621, 622.

R. Weill. "Le séjour des Israelites au désert et le Sinai dans la relation primitive," *REV*, LVII, pp. 19–54, 194–238.

E. H. Weissbach. "Zur Chronologie der Bisutun-Inschrift " *OLZ*, 1908, pp. 485–91.

H. Winckler. "Ausgrabungen in Boghaz-Köi im Sommer 1907," *MDOG*, No. 35.

———————

In the two years that have passed since the manuscript for *Ancient Chronology*, Part I, was sent to the press, a surprisingly large number of articles and books have been written on the subject. About seventy-five such articles have been observed by the author. And during these two years some really important discoveries bearing on this subject have been made. All these, together with reviews on *Ancient Chronology*, Part I, and several private letters from eminent Assyriologists and Egyptologists, have been carefully considered and weighed by the author; and it is a pleasure to state that in no case has he deemed it necessary to change or deviate from the principles laid down in that work as those used in building up the chronology. It is equally pleasant to record that the results reached, the dates given, in that volume, although often only approximate, still remain within the limits of high probability. That some modifications are necessary after this lapse of time is, of course, to be expected. The author is quite willing here to record them, wherever the evidence seems to require.

Many of the new hypotheses offered in this field are such that he finds himself unable to accept them. Space forbids him even to discuss most of them. It is with regret that he cannot accept the scheme of ancient chronology which Professor Petrie, the brilliant Egyptologist, advocates, inserting, as he does, a whole Sothic cycle, (1,460 years) between the XIIth and XVIIIth Egyptian dynasties. Not only is this against biblical evidence, but the scarcity of monuments of this period in Egypt precludes the elapsing of so long a period. The parallel and simultaneous development of culture in Egypt and Crete is so important and of such a nature that the 250 years which the author postulated for this period fulfil all the requirements of archaeology for this important age. The contention advanced in the former book that we deal here with a number of contemporary dynasties is too important to be overlooked or ignored by any scholar wishing to grasp the significance of the Hyksos rule.

With equal regret is recorded the inability to accept the brilliant hypothesis advanced by Professor Lieblein for the interpretation of the Sothic dates in Egypt, and the chronology which he endeavors to build thereupon. With Professor Knudtzon the present author agrees that considerations of contemporary Babylonian chronology, especially that of the Amarna period, make it necessary to set it aside. Nor is Professor Lieblein convincing in his reading of the name on the *verso* of Papyrus Ebers. The writing is peculiar, it must be admitted. But why may it not represent the throne-name of Amenhotep I ?

Here and there, however, it has become apparent that some modification of the dates assigned to reigns and events in the earlier book are necessary. This was anticipated and emphasized several times both in preface and text too, when periods were being treated where material was as yet too scanty for dogmatic certainty. It is, therefore, surprising to find how correct or how nearly correct most of these approximations were. Of course, even as yet there are no final and certain results on these points. Let us, however, examine and enumerate the principal items of what in these two years has been added to our store of knowledge and incidentally treat some of the questions that in the former book were openly and purposely passed by.

A. Biblical Chronology

In *Ancient Chronology*, Part I, it was definitely stated that in treating of the biblical chronology of the period there was to be no discussion of the dates nor of the veracity and historicity of the documents. The data and dates were merely recorded and it was shown where such dates landed us if applied to some certain historical date like the founding of Solomon's temple. In regard to this date there has as yet arisen no necessity for changing it. The present volume may indicate somewhat why there could not there be a discussion of previous biblical dates. Nor is it as yet the author's wish to express any opinion upon the historicity of any Biblical dates therein given, except those which have been treated in this volume. Neither a categorical affirmation nor a categorical denial of their historicity is sufficient. Each date, and each document, must be treated separately and treated with the utmost care and consideration.

The Chronology of the Book of Judges

In regard to the Book of Judges it is hoped that the present volume has shown that the contention made in regard to its dates was correct. It needs qualification, however, in the following ways:

1. The even numbers of 20, 40, and 80, may in some cases, possibly in all, be round numbers merely. Still, the summary of dates up to Deborah shows that they are approximately correct, for the

victory of Deborah and Barak over Jabin belongs to the time of
Joshua, just subsequent to the Amarna period, and this is just where
the chronology of Judges places it. If, then, one of these round
numbers be found to exceed the actual number of years by one, two,
or more, we may assume that the reverse prevails in others of them,
and that their sum is correct or approximately so.

2. We have found in this present volume[1] that it was only after
the conquest of Jabin by the co-operating forces of Joshua and
Deborah that the Hebrews of Canaan were united into one people,
into one political unit, if such a term may be used in dealing with
those times. The conquest recorded in Judges was carried on by
each tribe separately. It would seem, then, that the judges living
before Deborah, i. e., Othniel and Ehud, were not judges of all Israel,
but only of their respective tribes. And if this be so, these two men
may have been contemporary. Othniel was judge of that Israel
which lived in the land of Judah, with Kiriath-Sepher as his
capital. Ehud was judge in Benjamin, with Jericho as his place
of abode.

3. The Book of Judges affirms that Cushar-Arshataim ruled the
sons of Israel for eight years, and that then Othniel became judge
for forty years. This makes a period of about forty-eight years. But
we have already identified Cushar-Arshataim with Artatama II of
Mitâni, who was, therefore, of Aram-Naharaim. The identity of
Mitâni and Midian can scarcely be questioned. Now these Midianites were settled in the south in the Horite land, before the death of
Moses, because Balak, king of Moab called in their elders for assistance, when Moses and his army camped on the border of Moab.
Artatama and the Midianites, we must assume, would have been
there for some time prior to this event, at least two or three years,
because they seem to be firmly settled, when Balak calls upon them.
It lies near at hand to assume that it was this Artatama and his
Mitâni people in Mount Hor that deprived Caleb of Hebron and made
Judah tributary to him. This would then be the eight years' oppres-
sion under Cushar-Arshataim. Now Caleb came to Joshua at
Gilgal, *ca.* 1402, asking his assistance to repossess Hebron, which
Joshua agreed to, and shortly after we find Joshua marching south-,

[1] Cf. p. 131.

ward to conquer Judah and the Negeb. He was successful in this campaign, and this means, then, that the Mitânians or Midianites in Mount Hor were overpowered. The Bible says indeed that Joshua conquered a king of Arad, or a King Arad, and it is possible that this name may be an abbreviation of Artatama. Anyhow, the oppression of Cushar-Arshataim lasted, then, from about 1410 to 1402, which, viewed in this light, seems extremely probable. After the conquest of the south, it would be quite natural that Othniel, the renowned nephew of Caleb, should be appointed governor or "judge" over this territory. As he was judge for forty years, his judgeship would then extend from *ca.* 1402 to *ca.* 1363 B. C. This is only a few years after Deborah's victory over Jabin, 1366, and it was shortly after this victory that the tribes gathered at Shiloh, when Joshua established with them the well-known covenant, and the tribes were reunited. Soon after this Joshua died at the age of 110 years. If he died in 1363, he would have been born in 1473, and would have been about twenty-five years old, when he was with Moses at Horeb. And indeed the Bible says that Joshua was then a young man. Othniel's judgeship would thus partly cover the period of Jabin's oppression. Even this is probable. Of all the tribesmen that gathered about Deborah and Barak in the battle against Sisera, none came from Judah. Evidently because Jabin's dominion did not extend that far south. For the same reason none came from the trans-jordanic tribes, except Machir who was at this time settled in Western Manasseh. Othniel continued, therefore, as governor of the south until the reunion covenant at Shiloh was established.

, 4. Eglon, king of Moab, ruled Israel for eighteen years, until Ehud killed him, when the land had rest for eighty years.[1] It is not stated that Ehud was judge for eighty years, nor should we assume it. The eighty years of peace merely indicate eighty years of Hebrew supremacy around Jericho. This period must have preceded Jabin's oppression, because Benjamin took part in the war against him. Ehud's murder of Eglon would then come about 1465 B. C., and Eglon's conquest about 1483 B. C. Both these dates come before the Exodus. The Annals of Thutmose III assert that he conquered the lands of Jacob-el and Joseph-el, both situated in Canaan. If these

---

[1] Judg. 3:30.

names mean anything, they affirm the fact that there were Hebrew
tribes and Hebrew possessions in the land of Canaan not only in pre-
Joshuanic, but even in pre-Mosaic times.   These people may have
been among the Hyksos who had been expelled from Egypt, or they
may have been descendants of the Hebrews of the days of Jacob-
Israel, Hebrews who had not gone down to Egypt at all.

YAᶜQEB-EL   YAŠAP-EL
(Jacob)   (Joseph)

(From W. Max Müller, *Die Palästinaliste Thutmosis III*).

In any case the Rahab story shows that the people of Jericho
when Joshua besieged it were acquainted with the Yahweh worship,
while her name shows affinity with Egyptian culture as we would
expect at this time when Canaan was made up of dependencies of
Egypt.[1]

[1] Shamgar, son of Anath, was also a judge at this time.   Several scholars
identify him with Gershom, son of Moses.   This is possible, especially if the
record was taken from a cuneiform tablet, on which the name was written with
two signs *Gir-Šam*.   If this be so, "Son of Anath" denotes "inhabitant of
Anath."   This Anath we would identify with Anathoth, a city a few miles north
of Jerusalem.   Nearby lived the seventy-five priests that were murdered by Saul.
These priests wore linen ephods and were therefore under the Deuteronomic
Code.   The establishment of this code in this vicinity would be quite natural,
if Gershom (=Shamgar), son of Moses, had been judge there.   Jeremiah
was born in Anathoth and had his home there.   Would not this account

B. Babylonian Chronology

a) Thureau-Dangin has shown that the Kassite name *Bi-til-ia-shu* should be read *Kas-til-ia-shu*.

b) Clay has shown that the divine name *En-lil* was pronounced *En-lil*, and not *Bêl*. Proper names compounded therewith should be read so.

c) Hommel has reached the conclusion advanced for the first time in *Ancient Chronology*, Part I, that the name *Su-li-li* is a later abbreviation or reading of *Sumu-la-ilu*.

d) Eduard Meyer has agreed with the date the present author advanced for Sargon of Akkad, placing him *ca.* 2550 B. C.

e) Thureau-Dangin has confirmed our argument that there was a lacuna between Dynasties A (of Babylon) and C (Kassite), and he has placed Dynasty B (of Sea-land) contemporary with both the dynasties A and C, and independent in the interval between these two dynasties.

f) Winckler has discovered at Boghaz-köi a Hittite tablet, written in Babylonian, in which Hattusil, king of the Hittites, informs a Babylonian king who is the successor of Kadashman-Turgu that he (Ḫattusil) has concluded a treaty with the king of Egypt. This Babylonian king is evidently Kudur-Enlil, although his name does not appear in this letter,[1] and the letter was evidently written in his second or third year. Now we know, from the Egyptian monuments, that this treaty between Egypt and the Hittites was closed in the twenty-first year of Ramses II. We have here, then, a most welcome synchronism. The twenty-first year of Ramses II is the second or third year of Kudur-Enlil. This makes necessary the placing of the Kassite dynasty a few years later, some ten to twenty years, than was done in *Ancient Chronology*, Part I. When that book was written there was no evidence whatever to show that Dynasty C (Kassite) did not wholly precede Dynasty D (of Pashe). The date of the latter

---

for the many similarities in language between Jeremiah and Deuteronomy, even in such parts of Jeremiah (e. g., chap. 7) that were delivered before Deuteronomy was discovered? The peculiarities in language and thought of Jeremiah reflect the dialect and traditions of Anathoth and Nob.

[1] The beginning of the letter, where we would naturally expect to find the name, has been broken away.

is certain, but judging from the Kudurru inscriptions of the dynasty, dealing, as they do so frequently, with property in southern Babylonia, it is safe to conclude that this dynasty began to rule at first only in southern Babylonia, or, more definitely, over Isin. It may therefore have been easily contemporary with the last twenty years of Dynasty C, when we know the Kassite kings to have been very weak. From considerations which we shall take up in a moment it seems probable that Ramses II should be placed some years later than was done in *Ancient Chronology*, Part I, and this fact, together with the synchronism just discussed, makes it necessary to place the Kassite dynasty of Babylon some twenty years later than was before proposed.

g) Thureau-Dangin has proposed the same date as was given in *Ancient Chronology*, Part I, for the beginning of Dynasty A of Babylon, i. e., 2233 B. C. There could be no better affirmation than that of this eminent Assyriologist, especially as his conclusions were reached by entirely independent research, only a few months after *Ancient Chronology*, Part I, was published.

h) Thureau-Dangin and King have shown that the kings known as *Sharru-gi* and *Shar-gani-sha*rri were not identical. The former was King of Kish. The latter was father of Narâm-Sin, and king in Agade. In later times the two names were confused, and the two kings identified, precisely as we have suggested was the case with Mouses and Moses or with Horeb and Sinai.

Furthermore, Thureau-Dangin has shown that Kish was located west of the Euphrates, and we believe that it was the predecessor of the *Kash-di* or *Kal-di* land.

C. Egyptian Chronology

a) Eduard Meyer has accepted Sethe's reading of the Turin Papyrus in regard to the last king of the XIth Dynasty. Breasted has later accepted the same interpretation. These scholars have thus changed their views and reached the same result in regard to the close of that dynasty as was presented in *Ancient Chronology*, Part I. Naville had assumed that Neb-hepet-Re-Mentuhotep and Neb-hru-Re-Mentuhotep were identical. This seemed reasonable. But Naville has later changed his view, and Hall and Meyer regard them as two different kings. This is possible, of course. But the Turin Papyrus asserts that there were only six Theban kings of

Dynasty XI. There is, as yet, no reason to doubt this. Of course Manetho says there were sixteen kings of this dynasty, and Eduard Meyer enumeraties five Intefs and six Mentuhoteps. But it is not certain that all of them lived in Thebes, and the Turin Papyrus may be quite correct in its statement that there were but six *who ruled in Thebes*. May not some of them have lived in Gebelen? The Turin Papyrus says that the XIth Dynasty lasted 160 years, while Manetho accords it only forty-three years. Breasted insists upon the 160 years, and dates the Xth Dynasty of Heracleopolis back of these 160 years of the XIth Dynasty. This cannot be correct. There is no question that the Turin Papyrus is correct in giving 160 years to the dynasty *in Thebes*, but it is yet to be shown that the dynasty reigned *over all Egypt* for any such period. On the contrary, as was pointed out, it is practically certain that it was the next to the last king of the dynasty, Neb-hru-Re-Mentuhotep, who overthrew Dynasty X of Heracleopolis. The forty-three years of Manetho are ample time for the period from the fall of the Xth Dynasty to that of the XIIth. Meyer's and Breasted's chronologies should therefore be lowered 117 years for dates back of the XIth Dynasty. This can hardly be disputed, and it is important enough to demand consideration.

b) A. Gardiner has shown that the Egyptian month-names are derived from the names of the chief festivals occurring in those months. He has further shown that Mesore, formed from *Meswt-Re*, "Birth of Re," was in the Middle and New empires, the first month, not the last month of the year. There was, therefore, a calendar reform in Egypt sometime between the beginning of the XIXth Dynasty and the Ptolemaic period.

In the Middle and New empires the civil new-year began, then, with Mesore.

c) Professor Petrie has suggested that the 36 years which Man etho and Josephus ascribe to Oros, may designate the duration of the Aton-faith, and not the length of reign of Amenhotep IV. This seems possible, especially as his seventeenth year is yet the highest on the monuments. It may, therefore, be that he did not reign longer than 17 years, and of that period the 6 years at the beginning of his reign was a coregency with his father Amenhotep III. The

36 years which Josephus ascribes to Oros would then begin with the accession of Amenhotep IV (Ikhnaton) in 1407, and extended to 1371. The latter date comes two years before the death of Tutanekh-amon, and we know that this king changed from the Aton to the Amon-religion shortly before his death. The reign of Haremhab, extending over all Egypt would, on this account, have lasted for twenty-four years, 1345–21 B. C.

d) In *Ancient Chronology*, Part I, we assumed, following Jose-phus, that the reign of Seti I was included in that of Ramses II. We called attention also to some indications of this on the monu-ments of Ramses II. It is, however, possible, that this means only that Ramses II was appointed crown-prince in early childhood. The monuments of Seti seem to show that his reign was entirely independent of that of Ramses II. Still he could not have reigned for any considerable length of time. His ninth year occurs on the monuments, and nine years were probably the duration of his reign, 1319–1310 B. C. This makes it necessary to lower the succeeding dates of the Nineteenth Dynasty with nine years.

For more minute details of this reconstruction, reference is made to the synchronistic table, hereto appended.[1]

---

[1] Professor Erman, in a private correspondence, has called the author's attention to the statement on p. 259 of the *Ancient Chronology*, Part I, in regard to the two ancient Egyptian legends. Of course it was not meant that these legends appear on the Egyptian monuments, but merely that they dealt with the early history of Egypt. However, the expression is liable to misunderstanding and the opportunity is here taken to call attention to it.

SYNCHRONISTIC TABLE

SYNCHRONISTIC TABLE

	SEA-LAND	BABYLONIA	
2	*Sharru-gi*	**Dynasty of Ki-en-gi**	
3		*Enshagkushanna*	
	Dynasty of Kish		
4	*Ma-an-ish-tu-su ca.* 3050	**Dynasty of Telloh**	
5	*Utug*	*Engilsa*	
6	*Sharru-gi*	*Urukagina I, ca.* 3050	
7	*Mesilim*	*Lugal-shag-engur*	
8	*Lugal-tar-zi*		
9			
10	*Ur-zag-e*		
11	*Lugal - - -*	*Ur-Ninâ*	
12	*Uru-mu-ush*	*Akurgal*	Assyria settl
			Semites
13	**Dynasty of Gishkhu**	*Eannadu*	
14	*E-abzu*		
	Ush	*Enannadu I, ca.* 2800	
15	*Enakalli*	*Entemena*	
16	*Ur-lumma*	*Enannadu II*	
17	*Ukush*	*Enliltarzi*	
18	**Dynasty of Erech**	*Lugalanda*	
19	*Lugalzaggisi, ca.* 2675	*Urukagina II, ca.* 2675	
20			
21	*Lugalkigubnidudu*		
22	*Lugalkisalsi*		
23			
24	**Dynasty of Agade**		
25	*Shar-gani-Sharri, ca.* 2550	*Lugalushumgal*	*Kikia*
26			
27	*Narâm-Sin, ca.* 2525	*Ur-ba-u*	
28		*Ur-gar*	
29	*Bingani-Sharri, ca.* 2485	*Nam-makh-mi*	
30	*Ubil-Ishtar*	*Urninsun*	
31	**Dynasty of Ur**	*Gudea*	*Aushpia*
32	*Ur-Engur,* 2477–59	*Urningirsu*	
33	*Dungi,* 2459–01	*Ur-ab-ba*	

SYNCHRONISTIC TABLE

	EGYPT	MISCELLANEOUS	
pachshad,	Predynastic Kings		
nan, ca. 3191	**Dynasties I–IV** *ca.* 3285–2729		2 3
lah, ca. 3062			4 5 6
er, ca. 2933			7 8 9 10 11 12
eg, ca. 2800		Beginning of Sothic Cycle, 2781–4	13 14 15
	Dynasty V *Userkaf,* 2729–2701		16 17
, ca. 2671	*Sahure,* 2791–2688 *Nefererkare,* 2688–2668	Temple of Baal at Tyre, *ca.* 2730	18 19
	Shepseskare, 2668–2661 *Akauhor,* 2661–2641 *Nuserre,* 2641–2597 *Menkauhor,* 2597–88 *Dedkare,* 2588–44		20 21 22 23 24
ug, ca. 2540	*Unas,* 2544–11	*Lasirab* of Gutium	25
	Dynasty VI *Teti,* 2511–2497 *Userkaf,* 2497–81 *Pepi I,* 2497–44	*Anu-Banini* of Lulubu	26 27 28 29 30
			31 32
	Mernere I, 2444–37		33

SYNCHRONISTIC TABLE—*Continued*

	SEA-LAND	BABYLONIA	
34	*Bur-Sin I*, 2401–2392		
35	*Gimil-Sin*, 2392–85	*Galu-ka-zal*	
36	*Ibi-Sin*, 2385–60	*Ur-lama*	
37	**Dynasty of Isin**	*Al-la*	
38	*Ishbi-Ura*, 2360–28		
39	*Gimil-ilishu*, 2328–18	*Arad-Nannar*	
40	*Idin-Dagan*, 2318–2297		
41	*Ishme-Dagan*, 2297–77		
42	*Libit-Ishtar*, 2277–66		
43	*Ur-Ninib*, 2266–38	**Dynasty A of Babylon**	
44	*Bur-Sin*, 2238–17	*Sumu-abi*, 2233–18	*Ilu-shuma, ca*
45	*Itêr-ka-sha*, 2217–12	*Sumu-la-ilu*, 2218–2183	*Erishum, ca.*
46	- - - , 2212–05		*Ikunum, ca.*
47	*Sin(?)* - - -, 2205–04		
48	*Bêl-bâni*, 2204–2180		**Dynasty of Be**
49	*Zambia*, 2180–77	*Zabu*, 2183–69	*Shar-kên-kâte*
50	- - - - - , 2177–72		
51	*Ae* - - -, 2172–68		
52	*Sin-mâgir*, 2168–57	*Apil-Sin*, 2169–51	
53	*Dâmiq-ilushu*, 2157–35	*Sin-muballit*, 2151–31	*Bêl-tâbi, ca. 2*
54	*Sin-muballit*, 2135–31	*Sin-muballit*, vassal, 2131–21	*Bêl-kabi ca.*
55	*Eri-Aku*, 2131–2079	*Hammurabi*, vassal, 2121–09	
56	**Dynasty B of Sea-Land**	*Hammurabi*, king, 2109–2066	*Shamshi-Ada* 2100
57	*Ilu-ma-ilu*, 2079–2019	*Samsu-iluna*, 2066–31	
58			

SYNCHRONISTIC TABLE.—*Continued*

	EGYPT	MISCELLANEOUS	
or, ca. 2411	*Pepi II,* 2437–2343		34 35 36
	Mernere II, 2343–42 *Nitokris,* 2342–30		37 38
	Dynasty VII, 2330		39
	Dynasty VIII of Memphis, 2330–2230	*Kudur-Nankhundi* of Elam	40 41
	Dynasty IX of Heracleopolis, 2330–2230	*Ninus* and *Semiramis*	42 43
h, ca. 2233	**Dynasty X** of Heracleopolis, 2230–2043		44 45
			46 47
		Belus conquers Assyria	48 49 50
am 2165	**Dynasty XI** *Wahanekh-Intef,* 2162–2112		51 52
		Kudur-Mabug, ca. 2140	53
	Nakhtneb-Tepnofer-Intef, 2112–2086		54
		Chedor-Laomer of Elam	55
	Sanekh-ib-tawi-Mentu-hotep, ca. 2100–2086		56
aan, 2090		First Hyksos settlement, *ca.* 2084	57
ypt, ca.	*Nebhapetre-Mentuhotep,* *ca.* 2086–77	Kassites in Babylonia, *ca.* 2058	58

SYNCHRONISTIC TABLE—*Continued*

	SEA-LAND	BABYLONIA	
59			
60			
61			
62		*Abeshu,* 2031–06	
63	*Ki-an-ni-bi* 2019–1963		
64			
65		*Ammi-ditana,* 2006–1981	
66		*Ammi-zadugga,* 1981–60	
67			
68	*Damqi-ilishu,* 1963–37		
69	*Qadushshi,* 1937–22	*Samsu-ditana,* 1960–29	
70	*Milkipal,* 1922-1898		*Ishme-Daga*
71			
72			
73	*Gulkishar,* 1898–43		
74			
75			
76			
77	*Kir-gal-dara-bar* 1843–		*Ishme-Daga* 1850
	1793		
78			
79			*Shamshi-Ad* 1830
80			
81		**Dynasty C of Kassites**	
82	*Adara-kalama,* 1793–65	*Gandish,* 1762–45	
83	*Ê-kur-ul-anna,* 1765–39	*Agum,* 1745–25	
84	*Melamma,* 1739–31	*Kashtiliash* I, 1724–02	

SYNCHRONISTIC TABLE.—*Continued*

BIBLE	EGYPT	
Battle of Dan, *ca.* 2080		**Dynasty XVI** Shepherds, *ca.* 2084
Birth of *Ishmael,* 2078	*Nebtawire-Mentuhotep,* *ca.* 2077–62	
Birth of *Isaac,* 2065		
Marriage of *Isaac,* 2046	*Neb-hrure-Mentuhotep,* *ca* 2062–12	Fall of Dynasty X,
Death of *Sarah,* 2022	*Sanekhkare-Mentuhotep,* *ca.* 2012–02	
	Dynasty XII	
Birth of *Jacob,* 2006	*Amenemhet I,* 2006–1986	
Death of *Abraham,* 1990	*Sesostris I,* 1986–40	**Dynasty XIII**
Marriage of *Esau,* 1967		of Diospolis, 1986–
Death of *Ishmael,* 1943	*Amenemhet II,* 1944–02	D
Jacob in Haran, *ca.* 1931		Hittites in Babyloni
Marriage of *Jacob, ca.* 1924		
Birth of *Joseph,* 1917		Birth of *Sebek-khu,*
Jacob in Canaan, *ca.* 1911	*Sesostris II,* 1906–1887	Asiatics visit *Khn* *hotep II,* 1901
Joseph sold to Egypt, 1901		
Joseph governor in Egypt 1887	*Sesostris III,* 1887–54	
Jacob in Egypt, 1877		
Death of *Jacob,* 1860		**Hyksos Kings**
Death of *Joseph,* 1807	*Amenemhet III,* 1854–06	*Salatis,* 1826–07
	Amenemhet IV, 1806– 1797 *Sebeknefrure,* 1797–93	Bnôn, 1807–1763
	Dynasty XIV of Sebennitos, 1793–1569	*Apakhnan,* 1763–2
	Dynasty XVI of Iliopolis, 1793–1579	

SYNCHRONISTIC TABLE.—*Continued*

	SEA-LAND	BABYLONIA	
85	*Ae-gâmil*, 1731–11	*Du(?)-shi*, 1709–1693	
86		*Abi-rattash*, 1694–	
87		*Tashshigurumash*	
88		*Agum-kakrime*	
89		- - ·	
90		- - ·	
91		- - ·	
92		- - - - -	
93		- - - - -	
94		*Kadashman-kharbe*	
95		*Kuri-galzu I*	
96		*Meli-shipak I*	*Ashur-bêl-nisi*
97		*Kara-indash I*	*Ashur-nâdin-*
98		*Kadashman-Enlil I*	
99		[- -]- *buriash*	
100		*Kuri-galzu II*	*Puzur-Ashur*
101		*Burna-buriash*, *ca.* 1386– 61	*Erba-Adad*
102		*Kara-indash II*, *ca.* 1361– 58	*Ashur-uballit*
103		(*Nazibugaš*, usurper, *ca.* 1358)	
104		*Kuri-galzu III*, 1358–34	*Bêl-nirari*
105		*Nazi-maruttash*, 1334–08	*Arik-dîn-ili*
106		*Kadashman-turgu*, 1308–1291	*Adad-nirari*
197		*Kadashman-Enlil II*, 1291–85	*Shalmaneser*
108		*Kudur-Enlil*, 1285–77	
109		*Shagarakti-Shuriash*, 1277–64	*Tukulti-Ninî*

BIBLE	EGYPT	
		Apophis, 1726–166
	Dynasty XVII of Hermopolis, 1793–1533	*Iannas,* 1665–15
	Dynasty XVIII *Ahmose,* 1579–1554	*Aseth,* 1615–1566 Expulsion of Hyksos 1566
Birth of *Moses, ca.* 1526	*Amenhotep I,* 1554–33 *Thutmose I,* 1533–08	War in Syria
Flight of *Moses, ca.* 1486	*Thutmose II,* 1522–09 *Hatshepsut,* 1509–1486	
Eglon of Moab, 1483–65	*Thutmose III,* 1486–1473	War in Syria
Ehud, 1465–1385	*Thutmose III,* whole reign, 1504–1450	**Kings of Mitâni**
Exodus, 1447	*Amenhotep II,* 1473–47	*Artatama I*
Cushar-Arshathaim, 1410–02	*Thutmose IV,* 1447–38	*Shutarna*
Death of *Moses,* 1407	*Amenhotep III,* 1438–02	*Dushratta: Mattiu*
Conquest begins, 1407	Amenhotep, IV (Ikhnaton) 1407–1390	**Hittite Kings**
Meeting of Joshua and Caleb, 1402	*Sakare,* 1390–78	*Supliliuma*
Othniel, ca. 1402–1363	*Tutanekhamon,* 1378–69	*Mursil: Arandas*
Jabin, 1385–65	*Ai,* 1369–57	
Deborah, 1365	*Akerkheres,* 1357–45	
Covenant at Shiloh, *ca.* 1364	**Dynasty XIX**	
Death of Joshua, *ca.* 1363	*Haremhab,* 1345–21	*Mutallu*
	Ramses I, 1321–19 *Seti I,* 1319–10	

SYNCHRONISTIC TABLE.—*Continued*

	SEA-LAND	BABYLONIA	
110		*Kashtiliash II*, 1264–56	
111		*Enlil-nâdin-shum*, 1256–54	*Ashur-nâzir-*
112		*Kadashman-kharbe II*, 1254–53	*Tukulti-Ashı*
113		*Adad-shum-iddin*, 1253–47	*Bêl-kudur-uz*
114		Adad-shum-uzur, 1247–17	*Ninib-apil-E*
115	**Dynasty D of Pashe**	*Meli-shipak II*, 1217–02	
116	*Marduk - - - -*, 1205–1187	Marduk-apil-iddin, 1202–1189	
117		*Zamama-shum-iddin*, 1189–88	
118		*Enlil-shum-[iddin]*, 1188–85	*Ashur-dân*
119			
120			
121	- - - -, 1187–81		*Mutakkil-Nı*
122	- - - - ⎱		
123	- - - - ⎰ 1181–*ca.* 1146		*Ashur-rêsh-iš*
124	- - - -		
125	*Nebuchadrezzar I, ca.* 1146–30		
126	*Enlil-nâdin-aplu*, 1130–16		*Tiglath-piles*
127	*Marduk-nâdin-akhê*, 1116–1094		*ca.* 1125–1
128	*Marduk-akhê-erba*, 1094–93		
129	*Marduk-shapik-zêr-mâti*, 1093–81		*Ashur-bêl-kal*
130	(*Adad-apil-iddin*, 1081)		
131	*Nabû-nâdin*, 1081–73		
132	**Dynasty E of Sea–Land**		
133	*Simmash-shipak*, 1073–55		
134	*Bêl-mu-kin*, 1055–54		
135	*Kashshû-nâdin-akhê*, 1054–51.		*Shamshi-Adaa*

SYNCHRONISTIC TABLE.—*Continued*

	EGYPT	MISCELLANEOUS	
5–18	*Ramses II*, 1310–1244	*Hattusil:* Hittite treaty, 1290	110
278		*Dudchalia*	111
75		*Armanta*	112
	Merneptah, 1244–25	Hebrew settlement in Egypt	113
	Amenmeses, ca. 1225–08		114
–12	*Siptah, ca.* 1208–02	*Kidinkhutrash* of Elam	115
–06	*Seti II, ca.* 1202–1200		116
9			117
	Thouris, 1200–1183	Asiatic rule in Egypt	118
		Fall of Troy, 1183	119
	Dynasty XX		120
	Nakhtset, 1183–81	Heraclides in Lydia, *ca.* 1190	121
	Ramses III, 1181–50	Heb. oppression in Egypt	122
81–41		Philistine migration	123
	Ramses IV, 1150–44		124
	Ramses V, 1144–*ca.* 1134	Exodus of Hebrews from Egypt, *ca.* 1144.	125
	Ramses VI ⎫	Heb. conquest of Canaan	126
	Ramses VII ⎬ *ca.* 1134–1113	*Shadi-Teshup, ca.* 1125	127
	Ramses VIII ⎭		128
	Ramses IX, ca. 1113–1092		129
			130
	Ramses X ⎫ *ca.* 1092–77		131
	Ramses XI ⎭		132
81–61			133
			134
9	*Ramses XII, ca.* 1077–50		135

INDICES

INDICES

A. BIBLICAL REFERENCES

B. INDEX OF NAMES AND SUBJECTS

CPSIA information can be obtained
at www.ICGtesting.com
Printed in the USA
FSOW02n2111040916
24623FS

9 781330 212080